D1339408

THREE PLAYS ROBERT BOLT

THREE PLAYS

Robert Bolt

HEINEMANN

LONDON

Heinemann Educational Books Ltd

LONDON EDINBURGH MELBOURNE AUCKLAND TORONTO
SINGAPORE HONG KONG KUALA LUMPUR
IBADAN NAIROBI JOHANNESBURG
LUSAKA NEW DELHI

ISBN 0 435 23102 2

First published in one volume in Mercury Books 1963
First published in one volume in HEB Paperbacks 1967
Reprinted 1971, 1974

Published by
HEINEMANN EDUCATIONAL BOOKS LTD
48 Charles Street, London W1X 8AH
Printed Offset Litho and bound in Great Britain by
Cox & Wyman Ltd, London, Fakenham and Reading

CONTENTS

Flowering Cherry

FLOWERING CHERRY *was first produced in London on 21 November* 1957 *at the Theatre Royal, Haymarket. The play was presented by Messrs H. M. Tennent Ltd and Frith Banbury Ltd with the following cast:*

ISOBEL CHERRY	Celia Johnson
TOM	Andrew Ray
GILBERT GRASS	Frederick Piper
CHERRY	Ralph Richardson
JUDY	Dudy Nimmo
DAVID BOWMAN	Brewster Mason
CAROL	Susan Burnet

The play directed by
FRITH BANBURY
with settings by
REECE PEMBERTON

PEOPLE IN THE PLAY

ISOBEL CHERRY	Wife to Cherry
TOM	Her son
GILBERT GRASS	An office worker
CHERRY	
JUDY	His daughter
DAVID BOWMAN	A seedsman
CAROL	An art student

THE SET. It is the kitchen-living-room of an old semi-detached house and, at one side, a strip of garden. The 'wall' between to be indicated as the designer wishes but to be transparent – scrim, for example. There are two exits, one from the garden and one from the room. There is also a communicating door (the side entrance of the house) between the two acting areas.

ACT ONE

The kitchen and garden of MR CHERRY'*s house in the suburbs. The year is the present one, the season early spring, the hour about 6 p.m.*

ISOBEL *is washing up at the sink, while* TOM *reads a book by the stove.*

ISOBEL *is a slender woman of forty to forty-five. She is graceful and lively but the fundamental pattern of her features is one of melancholy. The liveliness is purchased with a certain amount of strain; it is applied, though now habitual. Her dress is neat and becoming. She wears slippers and a clean, bright apron.*

TOM *is approaching nineteen or twenty, lean, sensitive, much occupied with styles of behaviour, but warm, and young enough to show it.*

As TOM *reads, he mindlessly clinks back and forth the draught control of the stove. There is a rattle and slap, off.* ISOBEL *raises her head.*

ISOBEL: Tom . . . Tom.

TOM: M-hm?

ISOBEL: I think that's the post.

No response. She wipes her hands and goes.

TOM (*rising and timing it so as to be just too late*): I'll get it.

He sits down again without taking his attention from the book. ISOBEL *returns.*

ISOBEL: *Farmer's Weekly . . . Smallholder . . . Mm . . .*

Places other magazines on table unscrutinized. Picks up letters. Is arrested. Takes one to TOM, *who does not notice. Irritated:* Tom!

TOM (*attending*): Oh, Lord!

7

He opens it while ISOBEL *returns to the sink.*

ISOBEL (*tense; not looking round but watching him through the mirror*): Well, tell me, you ass.

TOM: Same again. Deferred.

ISOBEL (*relaxing*): Oh.

TOM: Is that a relief?

ISOBEL: You've got to go some time; the sooner the better, I suppose.

TOM (*with playful indignation*): Is that so?

ISOBEL: Certainly. Don't be so conceited.

TOM: I bet you make a scene when I do go.

ISOBEL: My goodness, you *are* conceited. I'll be glad to see the back of you.

TOM (*grunts, returns to his book but can't, and looks up*): Why?

ISOBEL: To bring you to your present state of perfection, Thomas Cherry, has taken nineteen years of my life.

TOM: So?

ISOBEL: So I'll be glad to see the back of you.

TOM: Hey! Is that the truth?

ISOBEL (*conceding, with a smile*): It's not the whole truth.

TOM (*fishing*): What's the rest of it like?

ISOBEL: Complicated, sonny. Very, very complicated.

TOM (*indifferent*): Yeah. (*Nodding.*) Yeah. (*Returns to book.*)

ISOBEL: Tom?

TOM: Yes?

ISOBEL: I wonder where they'll send you.

TOM: Aldershot.

ISOBEL: That'd be nice, you could get home for week-ends.

TOM: I might not want to.

ISOBEL (*dryly*): You would.

TOM (*surprised*): Wouldn't you want me to?

ISOBEL: We'll keep a light burning in the window.

TOM (*angry*): What's the matter with you, anyway?

ISOBEL: Nothing. I'm talking over your head, that's all. I can still talk over your head, you know.

TOM: Well, I'm glad it gives you so much pleasure . . .
(*Returns to book.*) You've been alive twice as long . . . it'd be
a poor look-out if you couldn't.

   ISOBEL *turns her head, smiles at his sulking back and goes to
   him.*

ISOBEL: Look, Tom, when the post comes and I'm washing
up, don't say, 'I'll get it,' and sit there reading T. S. Eliot.
Either stay where you are and tell me to get it, or say, 'I'll get
it' – and get it.

TOM: Sorry. You're making a lot of it, aren't you?

ISOBEL: No, Tom, it's an attitude. Either do things or don't do
them, but whichever it is, know it. Otherwise, as sure as fate,
you'll end up like—— (*Breaks off.*) It's a terrible habit, that
'I'll get it' and sitting where you are. It's shifty.

TOM: Yes. Like 'D'you want a drink, old chap?' when you
want one yourself.

ISOBEL (*coldly*): We're talking about you now, nobody else;
and it's shifty! (*Urgent, appealing.*) I'm a little bit worried
about you, Tom, because you're going away soon and you
know we have had this trouble in the past about not speaking
the truth and – not being quite careful about money – and
you're going away and I don't want you to – I don't want
you to be . . .

TOM (*rejecting her warmth with injured pride*): Shifty.

ISOBEL: Yes.

TOM (*calmly*): Well, don't worry; I dare say I'll end up in the
dog-house – (*shaking his head rhythmically*) – but not like the
old man.

ISOBEL (*going, defeated*): I've asked you not to call him that.

   They return to their occupations.

CHERRY (*unseen, behind the trellis*): Come in and have a drink,
Gilbert.

   The lattice gate opens. CHERRY *and* GRASS *enter the garden.*
   CHERRY *is a burly man of about fifty with a round red face and
   thinning grey hair. His carriage is confident, his expression heavy,*

but there is about the eyes and mouth the sadness and confusion of the immature. His clothes are good and timidly sportif, of earth colours, and include a trilby turned down back and front and a fawn waistcoat with leather buttons. GRASS *is more correctly dressed in a city suit, but in the subtle gradations of cut and buttoning his clothes express that he is a junior figure to* CHERRY. *He is an undersized, bespectacled man with a face boldly designed to express fear, but wearing the covert confidence of those not hampered by self-respect. Either he was formed by Nature for office life or office life has formed his nature; either way he is a condemnation of it.*

GRASS: Oh well, mm – ha ha——

CHERRY: This way. Tiptoe through the tulips.

GRASS: Very pretty.

CHERRY: Dutch bulbs.

GRASS: Are they? Pretty. (*Eagerly.*) Go on.

CHERRY: Oh well, then I said: 'If people don't want to buy insurance, good luck to them. I'm not insured myself!'

GRASS (*admiring*): Are you not?

CHERRY (*sturdy*): No, that's not the way to live. Look at it this way: you can't insure happiness, can you? You can't insure that you'll get on with your wife . . . for example. You take it from me, Gilbert, if a thing can be insured – it's not worth insuring.

GRASS: Oh, dear.

CHERRY: It isn't.

GRASS: I shall have to think about that.

CHERRY: Well, that's what I told him.

GRASS (*prompting*): Yes?

CHERRY: 'That's not the way to live,' I said. 'I *despise* people who buy insurance.'

GRASS: Good heavens! What did he say?

CHERRY: Och, you know what he's like.

GRASS: He wasn't rude, I hope.

CHERRY: Rude? No, he wasn't rude. 'That's a very peculiar attitude for our sales manager to have,' he said.

GRASS: Oh, dear.

CHERRY: I wasn't going to let him get away with that——

GRASS: No——

CHERRY: So I said, quietly – I didn't want a row – 'Are you dissatisfied with my work? Because if you are,' I said – (*Here he forgets that he is recounting a tale and begins to lose and listen to himself*) – 'you can give the job to someone else; I don't want it. As a matter of fact,' I said, 'this entire establishment makes me vomit. And you can keep the job!'

GRASS: Gracious heavens, do you mean you've given notice?

CHERRY: What does it sound like?

GRASS: But——

CHERRY (*turning at door to kitchen*): Er – Keep it under your hat, old man.

GRASS: Oh, yes, yes. But——

CHERRY opens door and enters kitchen.

CHERRY: Hullo, darling.

ISOBEL: Hullo, darling.

GRASS: Good evening, Mrs Cherry; I'm here again.

ISOBEL (*still at the sink*): How are you, Mr Grass?

GRASS: Nicely, thank you.

CHERRY (*with satisfaction*): Ah!

He unwraps the magazines on the table and inspects them almost feverishly.

ISOBEL: Had a good day?

CHERRY: About usual.

GRASS: Oh, hardly that, I think!

ISOBEL: Oh?

CHERRY (*putting down magazines*): Have a chair, Gilbert, I'll draw you a drink.

GRASS (*sitting, but with a curious cringing eagerness for trouble*): No, indeed, a momentous day, I should have said.

He looks at CHERRY, drawing cider from the barrel; so does ISOBEL.

CHERRY: Glass for you, darling?

ISOBEL: Not now, darling. (*To* GRASS.) What happened?

GRASS (*ducking his head fussily*): No, no, no, it's your husband's news, not mine.

ISOBEL (*looking from* CHERRY *to* GRASS): What news?

GRASS: No, no, no, he should bear his own good tidings. I feel they are good tidings; I know Mr Cherry does.

He is a little breathless at his own temerity, but helpless.

ISOBEL: Well, Jim?

CHERRY (*handing a half-pint glass to* GRASS): You're being a bit tactless, old man.

GRASS (*promptly abasing himself*): I do beg your pardon. I'll say no more.

Hides behind his glass, from which he takes tiny sips.

CHERRY: Damage is done now.

ISOBEL: Do tell me. What happened, Mr Grass?

GRASS: I really don't think I ought——

TOM (*who has been sitting very still, but very attentive*): Come on, Mr Grass, you've got nicely started.

CHERRY (*furious*): Oh, you're there, are you? . . . I've given notice, that's all!

TOM: Given notice?

CHERRY: Do you mind?

TOM: On the contrary.

CHERRY (*happy to hide fear of his wife behind rage with his son*): That's a relief. I shouldn't like to do anything *you* disapproved of!

TOM *returns to his book.*

ISOBEL: How did it happen?

CHERRY (*at* TOM): It would upset me dreadfully to think I had lost *your* good opinion!

ISOBEL: When? Today? This afternoon?

CHERRY (*at* TOM): That has been my principal preoccupation, of course! My first thought, naturally, was to wonder if *you* would approve of it!

ISOBEL (*with sudden anger*): Jim!

CHERRY (*facing her with the aid of his temper*): Well?

ISOBEL: Have you?

CHERRY: I've just said so, haven't I?

ISOBEL: But definitely?

GRASS (*with an admiring chuckle*): More than definitely, emphatically!

ISOBEL: But, Jim——

CHERRY (*joining* GRASS *at the table*): What's the matter?

ISOBEL: Let me get used to it. You've actually done it?

CHERRY: Why not, dammit?

ISOBEL (*passing her hand over her head and laughing*): I dunno. There must be some reason why people don't.

CHERRY (*draining his pint glass*): Cowardice! . . . That's what stops 'em. Gilbert'd give notice, if he dared.

GRASS: Oh——

CHERRY (*turning with relief to his friend*): Yes, you would. You tell yourself you wouldn't, but you would. That's what this lousy life does for a man. It rots you. It's artificial.

GRASS (*to* ISOBEL): There's a lot in it, you know.

CHERRY (*rising, refilling glass*): Don't tell me, old man, I know. If you'd ever known a natural life – a life close to the earth, you'd understand all right. (*Sitting.*) Well, that's what I came from, and that's what I'm going back to.

GRASS: Ah, those orchards of yours.

CHERRY (*during first part of this speech, he unwraps magazines, scattering wrapping paper*): That's it. Apples, fifteen acres, bush trees – no picking difficulties; thorough pest control and – *proper grading*; there's a fortune in it. And allow me to tell you, old man, that fifteen acres of apple trees in blossom, with a few white hens on the grass, perhaps, and some high white clouds in a blue sky, like you get it in May and early June down there; it's a sight for the gods, it's Shangri-la.

GRASS (*solemnly, raises his glass*): And here's to your success.

CHERRY: I appreciate that, Gilbert.

    They drink.

Of course, it's going to be damned hard work. Nobody knows that better than me!

ISOBEL (*cool*): How did it happen, Jim?

CHERRY (*vague*): Oh, I had a bit of a row . . .

ISOBEL: Who with?

CHERRY (*waving his glass, unwillingly*): Ooh . . .

GRASS: Mr Burridge, wasn't it?

ISOBEL: You had a row with Mr Burridge?

CHERRY (*roaring*): D'you think I'm afraid of him?

ISOBEL: Well, no.

CHERRY: Afraid of Burridge!

ISOBEL: He *is* your boss.

CHERRY: Not any more he isn't! (*Laughs.*)

ISOBEL (*brightly*): Well, that's that, then.

> *Going.*

CHERRY (*immediately anxious*): Where are you going, Bel?

ISOBEL (*going*): Oh, I've got things to do.

CHERRY (*uneasy, stepping after her*): Well, what about it, Bel?

ISOBEL: Fine. I'm all for it. Excuse me, will you, Mr Grass?

> *Going.*

CHERRY: Aren't you going to stay? Where are you going?

ISOBEL (*at the door, right, but turning, with sudden strain*): Oh, Jim, I've got things to do!

> *Exit* ISOBEL *to hall.* TOM *watches her go.*

CHERRY: She can't take it in.

GRASS: It's natural. (*With conscious discretion.*) Would you like me to go?

CHERRY (*hastily*): No. She's better left to herself.

> TOM *looks at him.*

It's bound to be a shock at first, a thing like that. Women don't like change.

> TOM *turns determinedly to his book.* CHERRY *finishes his second glass and goes to the barrel.*

Drink up, old man.

GRASS: I'm afraid I've no capacity for this stuff.

CHERRY (*bluff*): What, scrumpy?

GRASS: I like a glass of ordinary cider——

CHERRY: This *is* ordinary cider. (*Takes a gulp to prove it.*)

GRASS (*shuddering genteelly*): I don't know how you can.

CHERRY: Mind you, I'm not a serious scrumpy drinker. (*Sitting at table with* GRASS.) Scrumpy, that's what we call it. Some of the labourers, you know, they'll drink a couple of gallons a day as a matter of course.

GRASS: Good heavens; it's a wonder it doesn't kill them.

CHERRY: That's a lot of rot. There was a chap on my father's farm, you never saw him without his jar of scrumpy, he slept with it on the washstand. He lived in a little cottage – oh, five hundred years old, maybe – dark as a cave, with a big clock ticking and, as I say, this jar of scrumpy by the bed. I used to be sent down in the morning to wake him up. Well, that man was fit like an animal, beautiful, an absolute Apollo, could have lifted a horse on his back. . . . And that was really rough scrumpy my father made. It's all made on the farms, you know.

GRASS: Yes, I remember you telling me. It's very interesting.

CHERRY (*mechanically*): Drink up, old man. She can't get used to the idea of my not having a settled income. It's frightening to a woman.

GRASS: Oh, yes. You must give her time.

TOM *covers his ears.*

CHERRY: Bit of luck for you, eh?

GRASS: I hadn't thought of it in that light.

CHERRY: I'll believe you, thousands wouldn't. You'll get it all right.

GRASS *laughs.*

Senior agent, aren't you?

GRASS (*complacent*): Yes. Twenty-seven years on the road this November.

CHERRY (*gloomy*): Well, then.

GRASS: Well, I won't deny that I should like to come inside the office now. In a senior capacity, of course.

CHERRY: That's only natural.

GRASS: I may say I shall have my work cut out to fill the post as well as the – er – previous incumbent.

CHERRY: You'll fill it a darn sight better, I've no illusions about that. If I hadn't turned it in, they'd have turned me out pretty shortly.

GRASS: Oh, come now, Mr Cherry!

CHERRY: By God, it's true. Old Burridge hates my guts. D'you never see him looking at me when I come in? Oh, the writing was on the wall. But I can't, I can't give myself to a job like that. Those green lampshades every morning and that blasted rubber carpet! D'you know what it makes me think of?

GRASS (*ready to take the joke*): No?

CHERRY: It's like walking on corpses.

GRASS: Oh ho – that's a hot one! . . . I know, you hate it.

CHERRY: 'Tisn't hate, exactly; it's like doom.

GRASS: Well.

CHERRY: Yes . . . 'You keep the job,' I said . . . (*Brightly.*) Drink up, now; there's beef in that. This chap I'm telling you about, he always put a piece of beef in the barrel; what was his name, now?

TOM (*dry, without looking up*): Jesse Bishop.

CHERRY (*looking at him stonily*): That's right.

GRASS: Well, I must be going.

CHERRY: No. Don't pay any attention to him.

GRASS: I only intended to pop in for a minute.

CHERRY: See that poker – the thick one?

GRASS: Er – yes?

CHERRY: I've seen Jesse Bishop bend a bar of iron thicker than that into a complete circle. I can bend the other one myself. (*Fetches the thinner poker.*) Here.

GRASS (*fingers it gingerly*): It's a stout piece of metal.

CHERRY: It's iron. D'you believe me? (*He takes it at either end and bends it into a loop.*)

GRASS: Good heavens!

    TOM *claps as though at a show.*

CHERRY (*offers him the hooped poker*): All right. You straighten it.

TOM: No, thanks.

CHERRY: Why not?

TOM (*attempting disdain*): It's dirty.

CHERRY (*excitedly produces a snowy white handkerchief and wipes the poker vigorously*): Now it isn't; go on; straighten it.

TOM: No.

CHERRY: Go on.

TOM: I can't!

CHERRY: Then keep quiet!

TOM (*attempts superior eloquence, achieves sixth form verbosity and stumbles, fatally*): I didn't know the ability to bend pokers constituted a sestival pepquit – a – an essential prerequisite of——

CHERRY: Aha! (*Points a finger at him.*) You want to stick to words of one syllable! (*Turns, still malignant, and seizes on a framed reproduction on the wall.*) How d'you like this, Mr Grass?

GRASS: Gracious me, what is it?

CHERRY (*taking it down*): Oh. This is Art.

TOM: Put it back!

CHERRY: There you are, Mr Grass, a work of genius. Someone paid five figures for the original of that.

GRASS (*tutting*): T-t-t-t.

CHERRY: Guess what that is.

GRASS (*giggling*): Could be anything.

CHERRY: That's her head. Unless it's her bottom. Very handy, you see; it's just as good either way up.

GRASS: Dear, dear, dear—— Well, it's certainly over *my* head.

TOM: It'd be surprising if it wasn't.

CHERRY: Here! That's enough! Mr Grass is a guest in this

house. They might have taught you a few manners along with your – (*contemptuous*) – higher mathematics. My word, boy, you've got a rude awakening coming; they'll teach you quick enough in the army. I only hope you get an R.S.M. like one or two I've known. There's no State Scholarships there.

TOM: All right. (*Standing.*) Now for Christ's sake, leave me alone!

CHERRY: Don't you use that language here!

TOM (*choking*): Dad, you – you make me ill! You make me sick in the guts! (*Going.*)

CHERRY: Thomas!

> *He goes and seizes him by the arm.* TOM *turns his face away.* CHERRY *peers at his son's face, still further averted. His anger deserts him.*

'Ey. Lad——! You'll grow to it. You've got a fine pair of shoulders there. You'll bend the big one some day – which is more than I can do. It's only a knack.

TOM: Let go of me.

> *Exit* TOM, *right.*

CHERRY (*subdued*): He's too sensitive.

GRASS: He's very like his mother, isn't he?

CHERRY (*robust*): Aye, that's where he gets it. Nothing sensitive about me, thank God!

GRASS (*preparing to go*): Well——

CHERRY: Now sit down, Gilbert. (*Goes to cupboard below sink.*) There's some beer in here. That's more in your line.

GRASS: No, I really must get along.

CHERRY (*holding up bottle*): Empty. All right, go on then. (*Sits.*)

GRASS: You see, my wife——

CHERRY: I know. She's expecting you.

GRASS (*at the door*): Well, the best of luck to you, Mr Cherry. I imagine we'll be seeing you at the office till the end of the month?

CHERRY: Yes. I expect they'll want me to stay on to the new Quarter.

GRASS: I shouldn't let them make a convenience of you.

CHERRY: Don't worry. I'll be gone by the end of the month.

   Enter ISOBEL.

ISOBEL: Are you going, Mr Grass?

GRASS: Well . . .

CHERRY (*rising*): Yes, we're just going to celebrate a bit.

ISOBEL: You haven't eaten.

CHERRY: I'll be back in a jiffy. Just a couple of shorts. Come on, Gilbert.

GRASS: Oh, well——

CHERRY (*hustling him*): Back in a jiffy, darling.

GRASS (*peevish*): Well, don't push me, Mr Cherry!

   Exit to exterior GRASS *and* CHERRY. ISOBEL *sits motionless and looks at the door through which they have gone.*

CHERRY: My God, you've got big feet. 'Don't push me.'

GRASS: You did push me.

CHERRY: I didn't push you.

GRASS: Yes, you did. (*Peevish.*) You're still pushing me.

CHERRY: All right. I'm sorry. You coming?

GRASS: No. I must get home. I'd like to.

CHERRY: Don't apologize. I've no objection to my own company.

   They go out through the trellis gate.

I expect some of the boys will be there.

   Enter JUDY, *from hall.* JUDY *is about the same age as her brother but has a manner which will be hers, barring accidents, to the end. Her glance is cold, her lips already pursed. Hygiene is her ideal, irritation her emotion, competence her haven – and it's no good; the something frantic behind it all is visible. Her appearance aims at smartness – fly-away spectacles, crisp white blouse, sensible shoes, box shouldered top coat, real hide handbag, neat red mouth – and accentuates the angularity of her movements and indeed of all the awkward tender surfaces she presents to life.*

JUDY (*regarding her mother's back*): What a terrible mess! What's the matter?

ISOBEL (*without looking round, but pleasantly*): Hullo, dear.

JUDY (*taking off her coat, still regarding* ISOBEL): Where's father?

ISOBEL: He's just gone out, Judy. Do you want him?

JUDY: No.

She surveys with complacent hatred the mess CHERRY *has made: the magazines and wrappings strewn about, the cider glasses, his hat, the chairs misplaced, the beer bottles, the poker, the once white handkerchief. She pours the cider remnants into the sink, curling her mouth contemptuously, and leaves the glasses there.*

Phew!

She replaces the chairs. She collects briskly the waste paper and drops it into the slop can. She smooths the magazines and secures them with a weight. She picks up the handkerchief.

This will have to be washed.

ISOBEL: I'll take it, dear. (*Does so.*)

JUDY *hangs up the hat, picks up the hooped poker, pulls at it viciously and replaces it on table with an impatient exclamation, is about to replace beer bottles beneath the sink and changes her mind.*

JUDY (*meanly*): I think these can go in the dustbin! (*Going to door.*)

ISOBEL: There's some money back on those.

JUDY takes no notice but goes out to garden and throws them hard into the dustbin and returns, closing door.

(*Gently reproving.*) Judy . . .

JUDY: Well?

ISOBEL (*mildly*): Don't speak to me like that, Judy . . . I thought you were bringing Carol home today?

JUDY: She's coming on the bus. She didn't come into the studio.

ISOBEL: She doesn't seem to take her work very seriously, Judy.

JUDY (*with a private, indulgent smile*): Oh, Carol . . .

ISOBEL: I wish you'd tell us something about her.

JUDY (*stilted, defending* CAROL *with a previously formulated conclusion*): Actually she's a very worthwhile person. She's extremely attractive – one of the most popular girls at college actually. But she has a deep inner morality that most people don't see. It's unusual. Good-looking girls are usually so shallow.

ISOBEL: Mmm.

JUDY: I think we *shall* be able to have the flat, mother.

ISOBEL: Oh?

JUDY: Well, I've got the prize——

ISOBEL (*interrupting*): Yes, I know, darling. Fifty pounds is a lot of pocket money, dear, but it's *nothing* as rent.

JUDY: . . . There's something else. (*She makes her voice quite flat.*) They're going to give me the student award for this year.

ISOBEL: No! Darling, when?

JUDY: Mr Herring told me this morning. The Industrial Design Prof. And they'll pay me. So I'll be able to afford the flat.

ISOBEL: Oh . . . Well, it's splendid, anyway. D'you know how much?

JUDY: Well, it depends. The studentship's worth seventy-five pounds.

ISOBEL: Oh, very good.

JUDY: And if the manufacturers take up my designs——

ISOBEL: Yes——?

JUDY: Well, they pay commission on the sales.

ISOBEL: D'you mean they'll pay you——?

JUDY: A percentage, yes.

ISOBEL But that's wonderful! Judy, why – (*kisses her*) – that's very good; a commission's rather different——

JUDY: Now, mother, please don't get excited.

ISOBEL: Why not?

JUDY: It doesn't *mean* anything.

ISOBEL: Oh yes, it does!

JUDY: It may not *lead* anywhere!

ISOBEL (*warm*): Oh, you don't know. This may be very important. Things develop.

JUDY: Well, I hope so certainly, but——

ISOBEL (*laughing, protesting*): But Judy——

JUDY: Mother! If there's going to be a lot of – *family fuss!* – I shall wish I hadn't told you!

ISOBEL (*still laughing*): Oh, Judy . . . (*Her laughter dies.*) Judy, you worry me.

Enter TOM *from hall.*

TOM: Hi, Jude. This thing's going to snap some day. (*Tries to straighten poker.*)

ISOBEL: Judy's been given the student award.

TOM struggles with poker.

JUDY: Stop it. Put it down – you'll strain yourself.

TOM: *I've* not got blood pressure.

By placing poker against edge of table, he partially straightens it; holds it up.

Tarra! Will you get paid?

JUDY: Of course.

TOM (*interested*): How much?

JUDY: Seventy-five pounds.

TOM (*disappointed*): Oh. Not bad . . .

JUDY: If one of the big firms takes up my designs it'll be a lot more. Oliver Wentworth-Blake got the award the year before last, De Lissers took him up straight away, he gets three thousand a year. (*They stare at her.*) About three thousand, anyway. It was the only time it happened. It was exceptional.

ISOBEL: That's a lot of money.

JUDY: I'm not expecting anything like that. Oliver Wentworth-Blake's one of the top textile designers in the country. I'm not expecting – oh, I wish you wouldn't get so excited.

ISOBEL (*her attitude to them is quite tilted by the news*): D'you know, if we sold everything we've got we shouldn't have much more than three thousand pounds.

TOM: Eh? The house, everything?

ISOBEL: Just about. (*Smiles at him rather anxiously.*) How much did you think we'd got?

TOM: Does that include my Oxford money?

ISOBEL: It's not yours, Tom, but that includes it.

TOM: For God's sake, I thought he'd been making money!

ISOBEL: He's made enough to keep us all alive for twenty years.

TOM: There are other ways of doing that. Why's he stuck it if they don't pay him?

ISOBEL (*uneasy*): They do pay him, of course.

TOM (*indicating the kitchen*): They can't pay him much.

ISOBEL: Not a lot, no.

JUDY: He likes the office.

ISOBEL: Don't be stupid, please.

JUDY: He does; he likes it.

ISOBEL: Judy, you keep your half-baked psychology for your own affairs!

JUDY: Thank you.

TOM (*in support of* JUDY's *theory*): Well, *I* don't get it.

ISOBEL: You? How should you?

TOM: Why didn't he clear out?

ISOBEL (*somewhat at bay against her own thoughts on the subject, she uses her most violent weapon against him*): You'll understand one day – when you've grown up.

TOM: I won't, you know!

ISOBEL: So you think!

TOM: Damn it, you've only got one life.

ISOBEL: Oh, how *very* profound!

TOM: Well, do you think he did resign today?

JUDY (*indifferent*): What's this?

TOM: He says he's turned it in, but I don't believe it.

ISOBEL: How *dare* you!

JUDY: Oh, that. I agree with Tom. I'll believe it when I see it.

ISOBEL: You agree? If your father says he resigned, he resigned!

JUDY: Come off it, mother.

ISOBEL: And what is that supposed to mean?

TOM: Well – come off it——

ISOBEL: I am speaking to Judy!

JUDY: I think you're being phoney, mother.

TOM: Exactly. Do *you* believe it?

ISOBEL: Certainly I believe it! Certainly I believe it! Your father wants to be a farmer. He hates the job; he's always wanted to be a farmer. You have no idea how much that means to him. He hates it and he's done it for you. For you, do you understand! He's been through a great deal and he's a fine man in all sorts of ways and you will treat him with respect! With respect! With respect! With respect!

She puts her face in her hands and weeps. TOM *and* JUDY *regard her guilty and embarrassed.*

TOM: Oh, Lord . . .

JUDY: Sorry, mother.

TOM: Yeh. Sorry . . .

There is a pause while she weeps silently.

JUDY: It isn't our fault.

TOM: Oh, shurrup, Judy.

JUDY: Well, facts are facts.

TOM (*inviting her to join his remorse*): It was a bit rough, though, all that.

JUDY: It's a bit tough on all of us.

TOM: 'Rough' not 'tough'.

JUDY: Rough, then.

TOM: Oh, shurrup . . .

JUDY (*shrugs*): Well. I'll have to go and meet the bus.

ISOBEL: Just a minute. . . ! (*Wipes her nose.*) I'm not at all sure about your taking a flat, Judy. And I shall want to meet Carol first.

JUDY: I'm going for her now.

ISOBEL: And, I shall have to discuss it with your father.

JUDY: Actually, mother, we've pretty well decided.

Exit JUDY *to hall.*

TOM: Judy reacts all wrong. . . . Are you O.K?

ISOBEL: Yes. Yes. I'm O.K. Read your book.

TOM: Right. (*Does so, then*) Mum.

ISOBEL: Yes?

TOM: No. O.K.

    ISOBEL *looks round and laughs.*

ISOBEL: What is it, then?

TOM: Nothing really, I wonder what she's like.

ISOBEL: There's a photo on Judy's dressing-table.

TOM: Yeh, but it's touched up.

    Bell rings.

    (*Eager.*) Front door! I'll go. (*Pauses fractionally before mirror.*) Hell, Mum, I need a new shirt.

ISOBEL: There are two in your drawer. Go on – go to the door.

    Exit TOM *to hall.* ISOBEL *leans against the sink, head bent.* TOM *and* BOWMAN *off. She listens, curious. The voices cease. Calls:*

Tom?

BOWMAN (*cheerfully, off*): Can I come in?

    Enter BOWMAN. *He is a tall, active man in early middle age with birdlike features and a countryman's complexion. His movements are slow and deft. Hatless, he wears a pepper-and-salt suit with bulging pockets. His expression is merry and determined. We see that* ISOBEL *is not what he expected. His manner becomes instantly more attentive.*

Good evening. Mrs Cherry?

ISOBEL (*wondering*): Yes. Good evening. (*Takes off apron.*)

BOWMAN: The young man went upstairs.

ISOBEL: Oh, yes, my son——

BOWMAN: I've come to see your husband, but I understand he's not in.

ISOBEL: I shouldn't think he'd be long. Can I help?

BOWMAN: I don't know. (*Sitting, then stops.*) May I sit down?

ISOBEL: Yes, of course. . . . Is it about his work?

BOWMAN: I represent Statham's in the West Country.

ISOBEL (*cautiously*): Statham's?

BOWMAN: Yes, I'm the West Country rep, but I happened to be
up today and I thought I'd better come and see your husband
personally. This is an awful time to call, by the way——

    Enter TOM, *right.*

TOM: Mother, where's my *green* shirt?

ISOBEL: Tom! . . . Your green shirt's in the basket.

    TOM *begins to search the laundry basket for his shirt.*

I'm sorry he's not here. He would be, normally. What do
you want to see him about?

BOWMAN (*as one confirming the obvious*): Oh, trees . . .

ISOBEL: Trees?

TOM: Apple trees?

BOWMAN: Yes. We're Statham's the growers.

    *He takes papers and pads from his pockets and spills them on to
the table.*

This paper defeats me. We've been in correspondence with
your husband for some time now and, as it's a biggish
number of plants, I thought I'd like to meet him personally.
Besides, I think your husband's making a mistake; he's
thinking in terms of bush trees and I want to get him to
consider half-standards.

ISOBEL: But——

BOWMAN: That isn't just sales talk; I honestly think it would
be to his advantage. In the first place, he wouldn't need so
many plants – it would cut the order by about seven hundred.
The cost, of course, depends again. At the moment, he's
talking of several rather fancy strains. (*Flips over a paper
on the table.*) Beauty of Bath, Sunset, Cornish Maiden,
Egremont Russet, Farmer's Fortune, and so on; very nice
fruit but all those aren't going to do well on the same soil,
and most of them are——

    He catches TOM *and* ISOBEL *exchanging a blank look, stops
and laughs at his own enthusiasm.*

Sorry – I'd better wait——

TOM: No, do go on, it's fascinating.

ISOBEL: Tom! I thought you wanted a shirt? Has Mr Cherry ordered these trees?

BOWMAN: Oh, not a firm order, but he obviously knows what he wants and – (*smiling*) – well, I'm hoping to make a deal this evening. I hope he won't mind my calling, I couldn't let him know because I wasn't sure I could make it this week. (*Consults another paper.*) Whereabouts in Somerset is this holding? He's sent us a sketch of the layout here; it looks a very good little property. I'm wondering what sort of soil you have.

　　TOM *has begun to change his shirt.*

ISOBEL (*to* TOM): Will you go and put your shirt on in your bedroom, please?

　　TOM *moves to the door, carrying the green shirt.*

I don't quite know what my husband has told you——

BOWMAN: Oh, nothing much; just that he wants to plant this property——

ISOBEL: We haven't got the property.

BOWMAN: Oh? (*Looks again, puzzled, at the letters.*)

ISOBEL: It – it's all rather in the air, you understand.

BOWMAN: Ah, the old story, eh? Right place, wrong price?

　　ISOBEL *makes a noncommittal gesture.*

Fifteen acres, isn't it?

ISOBEL (*reluctantly*): Yes.

TOM (*coming forward*): Hey, I didn't know anything about this.

ISOBEL (*having forgotten him, furious*): Is there any reason why you should?

　　Exit TOM *to hall.*

Look, Mr——

BOWMAN: Bowman.

ISOBEL: Mr Bowman – this inquiry of my husband's may not come to anything.

BOWMAN: Oh, we quite understand he's not made an order.

ISOBEL: No, but this place; we may never have it.

BOWMAN: Do you mind telling me what they're asking for it? . . . Quite right; it's no business of mine.

ISOBEL (*liking him*): No, it's not that——

BOWMAN: I see you've got a southerly slope to two hundred feet. Is that the Quantocks, by any chance?

ISOBEL: Really, I think it would be better to wait for my husband.

BOWMAN: Certainly! (*Rising.*) Well, it's a good life, if you can take it.

They have entered into a confusion together and move about spasmodically, watching each other.

And that's wonderful country down there.

ISOBEL: Yes. I don't know it myself but I've heard all about it; from my husband. It must be looking very fine now.

BOWMAN: It will be in a week or two when the blossom's out. I like the town, though.

ISOBEL: Do you?

BOWMAN: Yes. It's nice to see people moving quickly, for one thing. Down there everyone goes – (*with some exasperation*) – one foot after another – at funeral pace!

ISOBEL: I suppose they can afford to.

BOWMAN: That's just what they can't, if only they'd realize it! If you're in farming these days you're in business.

ISOBEL: Whatta pity.

BOWMAN (*politely*): Yes. I don't think I'd like to *live* in London. But I must say there's something about it. My wife loved it; she came from the town; she didn't like the country.

ISOBEL: Oh.

BOWMAN: Yes, I—— We . . .

ISOBEL (*quickly*): The town's very expensive.

BOWMAN: My God, isn't it! (*Moving over to a tray of small cacti in earthenware pots.*) Whose is this?

ISOBEL: Oh, that's mine.

BOWMAN: Nice. (*Picks one up.*) Do you get flowers on this?

ISOBEL: Yes. There's the bud just coming up.

BOWMAN: What's it like?

ISOBEL (*touching forehead*): Let me think . . . Oh, lovely.
Yellow, with bluey spots. Glorious ! – Rather horrible really.

BOWMAN (*laughs*): Yes. You've got green fingers; I could
never get mine to flower. (*Walks away.*) It's a good life if
you pull together. I envy your husband, Mrs Cherry – he's
on the right track.

ISOBEL: Do you have an orchard?

BOWMAN: No—— No, I like my job and I haven't got the
money.

   Enter TOM. *He wears a dark-green shirt, light-blue tie, jeans
and boxing pumps.*

TOM: Hi!

ISOBEL: You look absolutely hideous.

TOM: What this? The very thing!

BOWMAN: Look, if you can't buy this place, I could look out
for something else for you.

ISOBEL: Well – er – my husband——

BOWMAN: Yes, of course. I'll mention it to him.

ISOBEL: I wonder if you'd mind waiting in the front room.

BOWMAN: No, of course not.

ISOBEL: Oh, your papers.

   She pushes TOM, *who is reading them.*

   Tom!

BOWMAN: Yes, thanks. (*Gathers them up.*)

ISOBEL: Would you like this? (*Picks up magazine.*)

BOWMAN: Thanks, that's fine.

ISOBEL: There's an electric fire. I'll show you how to switch
it on.

   Exit ISOBEL. BOWMAN *catches* TOM's *eye – exit.*

   (*Off*) And I'll tell my husband you're here as soon as he
comes in.

BOWMAN (*off*): Yes, I expect we'll be able to sort it out
between us.

ISOBEL (*off*): This is the room. There are some books.

Re-enter ISOBEL.

TOM: Hey, Mum, is this on the level? Has he really left the——

ISOBEL: You look like a little spiv!

TOM: No, you don't get it. A spiv would look like a spiv, not me. It's a double take.

ISOBEL: Hideous.

TOM (*looking in mirror*): Very, very smart. A double take. (*Smooths hair.*) If she doesn't get it, she's dim. (*Straightens tie.*) If she's dim, I can't use her.

ISOBEL: You're a sweet little thing.

TOM: Huh! So are you . . . (*Jerks thumb to door of parlour.*) What gives with all this?

ISOBEL: For heaven's sake, Tom, what does it matter to you?

TOM: I'm curious, that's all.

ISOBEL: Yes, well stay curious.

　　　Enter CHERRY *through garden. He takes off his hat and looks at* TOM.

CHERRY: Hullo. Where's your barrow?

TOM (*not ready for another row but keeping his end up*): Oh, down the road.

CHERRY (*pushing back sleeves and washing at the sink*): What does he look like? (*Sniffs.*) Do I smell shepherd's pie?

ISOBEL: Yes . . .

CHERRY: Not kept you, have I?

ISOBEL: No. It's in the oven . . .

CHERRY: The evenings are drawing out, aren't they?

ISOBEL: Yes . . .

CHERRY: Soon be summer. Then autumn . . . Then Christmas, I suppose. (*Turns to face her, drying hands at a hanging towel.*) Well, now. (*She is looking at him; he turns to gaze at* TOM.) Where d'you say your barrow was? How's trade?

TOM: Pretty brisk. I've been selling apples from your orchard.

　　　CHERRY *turns instantly to the towel, still drying his hands, his back to them. He speaks mildly, reasonably.*

CHERRY: I wonder what the significance of *that* is supposed

to be? I mean apart from being a bit more of your impudence, is it supposed to mean something?

TOM (*made awkward by* CHERRY's *reasonable tone*): Well, you
began it.

CHERRY: Began what?

TOM (*now made silly*): You called me a barrow boy.

CHERRY (*swinging easily round*): Good Lord, boy! That was
only a bit of chaff; you'll have to learn to take a ragging
in the army. And you do look a bit of a sight – to my way of
thinking, anyway. Still, every man to his taste; you're old
enough to dress yourself.

His manner is of a just but weary father and TOM *is defeated; he
ducks out into garden.*

TOM: I'm going to get some cigarettes.

ISOBEL: Jim, I want to talk to you.

CHERRY (*catching her eye and not liking it, pats pocket rapidly*):
Just a jiffy, dear. (*Follows* TOM.) Tom! Tom! Get me an
ounce of tobacco, will you? I seem to be out. (*Hands him a
note from wallet.*) *Exit* TOM *through trellis.*

ISOBEL (*going into garden*): Jim, there's a man here for you;
he's in the front room.

CHERRY (*immediately moving to go in again*): Who is it?

ISOBEL: His name's Bowman. (*Stopping him.*) I don't want
him to hear.

CHERRY: Oh?

ISOBEL: From Statham's.

CHERRY: Oh, yes. (*Cheerfully.*) Wonder what he wants?

ISOBEL: He wants to sell you some fruit trees.

CHERRY: Yes. I thought we could use half a dozen bushes in
the back, what d'you think? I thought I might train a nice
peach against the wall of the coalhouse.

ISOBEL: He's talking in hundreds. He thinks you've got a
farm in Somerset.

CHERRY (*with a spluttering chuckle*): Me? Wish I had. (*Moves
towards door.*) Better go and put him straight.

ISOBEL: Look, Jim . . . (*Hopeless.*) Ah, well.

CHERRY: What is it, dear?

ISOBEL (*in a spasm of anger*): You told him – Oh well, what does it matter? . . . You sent him a plan of it!

CHERRY: Well, I just wanted to get an idea.

ISOBEL (*shaking her head*): Phooey.

CHERRY: Now don't take that tone, dear. I told him——

ISOBEL: Lies was what you told him.

CHERRY: I suppose I may write to a seedsman for some advice if I want to. I don't think we need a conference.

ISOBEL (*folding her arms*): Very well, what did you tell him?

CHERRY: I'm not going to be cross-questioned about it, dear . . . I told him – it's some time ago—— There's no harm in it!

ISOBEL: What kind of a fool does it make me look? I've been twenty minutes in there, twisting and dodging——

CHERRY: I'm sorry for that, dear; you should have told him.

ISOBEL: What? That I'm married to an infant? That my husband's an idiot who lives in a seed catalogue? Oh, no; you tell him.

CHERRY (*goes back indoors*): All right, I will.

ISOBEL: And tell him plainly. Finish it.

CHERRY: Well, of course.

ISOBEL (*follows him indoors*): 'Of course.' I don't want him back here! Tell him you haven't got an orchard!

CHERRY: All right.

ISOBEL: Tell him there's no such place!

CHERRY (*with dignity*): Very well . . . (*Pauses uncertainly at the door to hall.*)

ISOBEL: He's quite harmless. Go and tell him.

CHERRY: I must say, Isobel, I resent——

ISOBEL: You didn't give in notice today, did you?

CHERRY: – Resent your tone.

ISOBEL: You didn't, did you?

CHERRY: Oh, didn't I, though? You'll see at the end of the month. (*Makes to go through the door.*)

ISOBEL: I don't want to see at the end of the month. I want to know if you gave in notice today.

CHERRY: You wouldn't need to ask if you'd been at the office. The whole office heard me—— 'You keep the job,' I said, 'I despise it.' Straight from the shoulder.

ISOBEL: Jim! I want to know if you——

CHERRY: Goddammit, I'm telling you! 'Keep it!' I said. 'It's poisonous: it's unnatural; vile!'

ISOBEL: You didn't, then.

CHERRY: By God, I don't know what more I could have said!

ISOBEL: You could have said, 'Mr Burridge, I'm giving you a month's notice.' Did you?

CHERRY: I said more than that!

ISOBEL (*disgusted*): Oh, Jim . . . (*Turns away.*)

CHERRY: I'll say it before the month's out! Though I should have thought I'd made my feelings pretty plain today. I've had my bellyful of the Home Counties Insurance Society! I'll say it tomorrow, if that's what you want me to do!

ISOBEL: I don't want you to do anything.

CHERRY: Sorry, I thought you did.

ISOBEL: Yes, I suppose I do. But you can't do it.

CHERRY: Now I won't have this damned hinting! There may be this and that wrong, Bel, but for heaven's sake let's be honest!

ISOBEL (*stares at him*): Honest! Jim, I think you must be a bit mad.

CHERRY: I shouldn't be surprised. (*Sits.*) I'm not well, I know that. I had another turn today.

ISOBEL (*desperately*): No, Jim!

CHERRY: I did!

ISOBEL: Yes, but why mention it now?

CHERRY: Sorry. I thought you'd be interested.

ISOBEL: Well, I'm sorry, of course. You shouldn't drink so much. Especially that stuff.

CHERRY: I felt like ice from head to foot . . . I don't drink much.

ISOBEL: I expect you've had three or four pints since you came in!

CHERRY: There you go, you see! I haven't had anything like four pints! Anyway, what's four pints of scrumpy?

ISOBEL (*shrugs*): They're your arteries.

CHERRY (*coaxing*): Eh, Bel . . . cheer up, eh? . . . Come on, Bel.

ISOBEL (*weary*): Yes sure. Only tell this Bowman the truth, eh? Just for once, tell the truth! You haven't got an orchard; you never will have an orchard.

CHERRY: Don't be too sure about that. Orr, you make too much of things, Bel. I shall need this chap one day. All right, you'll see, one day I'll surprise you; one spring I'll surprise you. 'Come on,' I'll say, 'come and see what we've got,' and we'll leave the kids and drive down there. Then you'll see, Bel, a hundred trees in a row, and thirty rows – Egremont, Cornish Maiden, Farmer's Fortune, all in blossom, meeting over your head; it does, it meets over your head in a standard orchard; you can't see anything but blossom. By God, Bel, you'll see – that's the day I'm living for – (*He wags his finger at her.*) – And it may not be so far round the corner.

ISOBEL (*exhausted, manages a helpless shrug and smile*): It's nice dream, Jim.

CHERRY: Now why a dream?

ISOBEL: A nice, innocent dream; as a dream it's fine.

CHERRY: You know what they say; you've got to have one.

ISOBEL: They're right, too.

CHERRY (*impressed*): By Jingo, you sound fed up.

ISOBEL (*smiling coldly*): No dream.

CHERRY: O-o-oh, tell that to the marines.

ISOBEL: I haven't.

CHERRY (*roguish*): No? Venice? The little house by the Rialto? With the balcony and the yellow canvas awning?

ISOBEL (*genuinely surprised*): Good Lord . . . (*A little moved by this voice from the past, but sensible.*) I'd forgotten that.

CHERRY: Ha! Well, I hadn't. We'll spend the winter in Venice. As soon as the picking's over and the crop's marketed, we'll leave Somerset——

ISOBEL: But we're not in Somerset! Or Venice! Or the moon or the morning star! *This* is where we live!

CHERRY (*clinging to his whimsy*): Not for always.

ISOBEL: For the last twenty-five years! (*Earnestly.*) The middle cut Cherry! I was twenty when we came here! And what happens now? The prime of life? I don't think so. (*She sees that she has at last caught the centre of his attention and falls gratefully into the simply personal.*) How long . . . How long is it since we . . .

CHERRY: What?

ISOBEL: Slept together.

CHERRY: Eh?

ISOBEL: How long?

CHERRY (*alarmed*): Dash it all, Isobel! . . . We're not newly-weds!

ISOBEL: No, but I'm just asking how long. Do you know?

CHERRY (*looking away*): Yes.

ISOBEL: It's a long time.

CHERRY: Damnation, *you* didn't——

ISOBEL: – That's true.

CHERRY: It's not all that important.

ISOBEL: It is.

　　CHERRY *sits. There is a silence.*

CHERRY: I did have a row with Burridge today, but the boot was on the other foot. He was shouting at me.

ISOBEL: I wish you *had* done it.

CHERRY: *You* do? You don't.

ISOBEL: I don't know. It'd be something definite.

CHERRY: It'd be definite all right.

ISOBEL: That's all I want.

CHERRY: It's coming to a head between us, isn't it, Bel?

ISOBEL: Yes, Jim, I think it is.

CHERRY (*not exclaiming, quietly*): Ah, Christ, I'm sorry, Bel.

ISOBEL: This is my dream, Jim, if you want it. To have you come home on time and us have tea together and half an hour's talk without a single lie, or even half a lie; and a straight look from here to here (*she touches her eye then his*) and none of this glancing and winking and looking away. And then wash up together and no one leave any dirty bits for anyone else—— (*He commences a gesture of guilt.*) No, no, I mean for both of us, for both of us. And then – go to the pictures if we want to, not if we don't, and anything – have a row if we want a row, really want a real row, and then if we want to make love – (*gently*) – if we want to . . . Only no more cardboard prospects!

CHERRY: Yes, well, I deserved that.

ISOBEL: No, no – not like that!

CHERRY: No, but that's me all right. I'd better pull myself together. I could do that job left-handed . . . left-handed! (*Wry.*) I'll apologize to Burridge tomorrow.

ISOBEL: What was the row about?

> *Enter* TOM *and* CAROL *from hall.* CAROL *is one of those people who win raffles; with her, good luck is almost a visible attribute. She is a natural, sun-happy even in London. She bestows ad lib. a friendliness which costs her nothing. In appearance – complexion, hair, clothes – she is tawny, as though straight from a beach. She finds pleasure as water finds its level but like water can be decisive when she finds herself restrained. When she's had her run as a girl, she is going to make someone a remarkably unfaithful wife.*

TOM (*grinning*): Mother, this is Carol.

CAROL (*smiling*): Hullo.

ISOBEL (*smiling*): Hullo, Carol. How are you?

CAROL: I'm fine, thanks.

ISOBEL: My, you look fine. Have you been on holiday?

CAROL: No——

CHERRY (*smiling*): She's a country girl.

CAROL: I'm not!

> *She says it indignantly and they all laugh.*

TOM (*gracefully, he too wants the family to appear well*): This is my father.

CHERRY: How d'you do, my dear.

CAROL: Good evening. (*They shake hands.*) I hope I'm not late.

CHERRY: If you are, it's your prerogative.

CAROL: I don't carry the time.

CHERRY: Very sensible. I wish I didn't! Ha ha! . . .

> *They stand and smile at one another.*

ISOBEL: Jim, are you going to see Mr Bowman?

CHERRY (*easily*): Oh, yes! A little business matter to settle. You're not going, I hope.

CAROL: No, I don't think so.

CHERRY: I'll be seeing you later, then. (*To* ISOBEL, *for* CAROL'*s benefit, with assurance.*) I'll just settle this chap.

> *Exit* CHERRY. ISOBEL *looks after him.*

TOM: I found her in the road.

ISOBEL (*turns*): Where's Judy?

TOM: Oh, lord!

CAROL: Judy?

ISOBEL: You don't mean to say you left her——

> *Enter* JUDY *from garden. She marches up to the door and opens it with her customary air of efficiency in a world of fools. But when she sees* CAROL *she stops. And when she speaks it is gently, trustingly, almost shyly.*

JUDY: Hullo!

CAROL: Hullo, Judy.

JUDY: I've been waiting at the bus stop. (*She says this as though it were a comic mishap, and deserved.*)

CAROL: For me?

JUDY: That's what we arranged. Did you forget?

CAROL: I'm awfully sorry, darling. We went out and they got me a taxi.

JUDY: Gosh! Who?

CAROL: Peter and Wilfred got me the taxi.

JUDY: Was anyone else there?

CAROL: Yes; Suzie and Elspeth and Johnny Idasalski.

JUDY: What did you do?

CAROL: We went to the pictures. 'Clair de Lune'. (*Cool.*) You've seen it.

JUDY: I wouldn't have minded seeing it again. This is my mother.

CAROL: Yes, Tom just introduced us.

JUDY: Oh. Would you like to take your coat off?

CAROL: Thanks.

> TOM *has been sitting on the table but now is off it like a shot and helping her. It transpires that her arms and throat are of the same golden brown. They look at her.* ISOBEL *shuffles out of her slippers and into a pair of court shoes.*

ISOBEL: Well. So this is Carol.

CAROL: I'm afraid so.

ISOBEL (*laughing, protesting, lays a hand on her arm*): Oh, there's nothing to be afraid of! Have you eaten?

CAROL: Yes, thanks.

JUDY: Oh, Carol, you are awful. She hasn't, Mummy. I know she hasn't. She's slimming!

ISOBEL (*business at sink*): Don't *make* her eat, Judy. (*Sees her reflection in mirror, falls to examining herself despondently.*)

TOM: It's cottage pie. Pretty good.

CAROL: Well, I'll have some if it'll go round.

TOM: How did you like 'Clair de Lune'?

CAROL: I thought it was rather corny, you know.

TOM: *Le mot juste! C'est exact!* Corny.

CAROL: Everything so terribly significant all the time.

TOM: And so *dated*——
CAROL: Well, yes, it *is* dated——
TOM: Oh, the French have gone down the nick.
JUDY: It's all that other stuff I can't stand.
CAROL: What?
JUDY: All that sexy stuff.
CAROL: That's what I find pretty hard to take.
JUDY: That man was old enough to be her – he was a completely different generation!
CAROL (*without much interest*): Yes.
JUDY: You could see all the little marks on his face.
TOM (*without much interest*): Mm. Oh, it was corny all right.
ISOBEL: I thought it was rather a good film.
CAROL (*surprised*): Have you seen it?
ISOBEL: Well, yes, there's no age limit.
TOM: What was so good about it?
ISOBEL: It was gentle.
CAROL (*regarding her*): That's true.
TOM: Oh, there were some good bits in it.
CAROL: That scene in the Sunday School was gentle. It got me all right . . .
ISOBEL (*glances in mirror again, with decision*): Judy, I'm going upstairs. Turn the oven off if I'm not down. (*Going.*) I look a fright.
　　Exit to hall.
CAROL: Oh, you don't . . . Your mother's a real person!
JUDY: She's a very intelligent woman.
CAROL: She's good looking, isn't she? (*To* JUDY.) You ought to make her dress properly.
JUDY: She isn't interested in that.
CAROL: Really? What about your father? Frighteningly masculine, I thought.
TOM: No, he's a phoney.
CAROL: Are you sure?
TOM: He was decorated in the Great War.

JUDY: Joined up as a boy.

TOM: All that.

JUDY: But even so——

TOM: Oh, yes, he's a phoney. Unquestionably.

JUDY: I can't think why she married him.

TOM: There's nothing to him! Mind you, the twenties – they were all half batty anyway.

JUDY: She ought to have married someone completely different.

CAROL: Who?

JUDY: Someone of her own intellectual level.

TOM: Nah, that's not it.

CAROL (*lazily, with curiosity*): Judy, do you hate your father?

JUDY: No, I don't hate him . . . No——

CAROL: I wonder if this is why your work's so good.

TOM: She's good, is she?

CAROL: Haven't you told them?

JUDY: Yes. Don't start talking about it——

TOM: Oh, the student award; yes, terrific, isn't it?

JUDY: For heaven's sake, what does it matter?

    ISOBEL's *voice is heard calling indistinctly from upstairs.* JUDY *opens door and calls back.*

JUDY: Yes?

    ISOBEL *again.*

JUDY: It's in the top left-hand drawer of my dressing table . . . !

    ISOBEL *again.*

JUDY: Yes.

    ISOBEL *again.*

JUDY: Wait a minute. I'm coming.

    Exit JUDY.

TOM: So it turns out that Judy knows her stuff.

CAROL: Oh, yes. She'll be earning four figures before she's much older.

TOM: Go on! She's nutty about you.

CAROL: Me?

TOM: You going to show her around a bit? She doesn't get round enough, I don't think.

CAROL: Golly, *I* don't know.

TOM: I bet you do, though.

CAROL (*a demure, catlike smile*): Who's reading Eliot?

TOM: I am. Pretty corny really . . . (*Walks about excitedly.*) Could you stand the flicks again this evening?

CAROL: Why not?

TOM: Good . . . That's . . . good.

CAROL (*laughs at him softly*): You're going into the army, aren't you?

TOM: Yes. I don't want to.

CAROL: Will you get a commission?

TOM: Oh, I expect so.

    Enter JUDY *from hall.*

JUDY: It's all right, mother, Carol will have one.

    Enter ISOBEL.

ISOBEL: No, don't, Judy.

CAROL: What?

JUDY: Mother wants a pink lipstick.

ISOBEL: It really doesn't matter. Really.

CAROL: Yes, I've got one. I think. Yes, here it is.

ISOBEL: Oh, it doesn't matter a bit. (*Brisk.*) Come on, Judy: knives, forks, two spoons each. Tom! Tom! table mats.

TOM: Right!

    A to-ing and fro-ing breaks out as the table is lengthened, spread, and laid with crocks and cutlery, in a familiar domestic dance but today with a counterpoint of aroused vanity because of CAROL.

CAROL: No, look, do use it. (*Offers lipstick.*)

JUDY: Big spoons?

ISOBEL: What a lovely pink. (*To* JUDY.) One soup, one fruit. (*To* CAROL.) May I? (*Turns to mirror, uses lipstick.*)

CAROL: What can I do?

TOM: I dunno. Draw some cider – shall we have cider, Mum?

ISOBEL: Not for me, dear.

JUDY: Nor me, thank you.

TOM (*fetching glasses*): That's one – two——

CAROL: Mr Cherry?

TOM: And three's a crowd. Barrel's over here.

JUDY: There's no salt in the salt cellar.

TOM: No! Not like that. You've turned it off. Look——

CAROL: Oh, I get it.

JUDY: These soup spoons are dirty.

TOM (*throws tea towel to her*): Well polish them! Where are the other mats?

ISOBEL: In the cardboard box at the back.

JUDY: Not those. They're disgusting.

TOM: Hand-painted in the heart of – guess where! Somerset. Family joke!

CAROL: Oh.

ISOBEL (*inspecting herself*): No. It's too young.

CAROL: It isn't. Is it?

TOM: No – just the job.

JUDY: It's very nice, mother.

> *They gather round.* TOM *wolf-whistles.*

ISOBEL: Well, I don't know, I'm sure. How are we doing?

TOM: Fine. (*Regards table mat with distaste.*) We could do with some new mats——

ISOBEL (*not understanding*): These are practically new.

JUDY: And there's no salt in the salt cellar.

ISOBEL: I like your slacks, Carol.

CAROL: Do you really?

ISOBEL: Mmm.

CAROL: Forty-five shillings.

ISOBEL: Never!

> *The table is laid. The bustle stops. They all draw slowly round the armchairs.*

CAROL: It's a fact. I'll give you the address.

ISOBEL: Me? Now if you know a good place for little lace shawls——

CAROL: No, you're *just* the kind of person that ought to wear trews!

ISOBEL: Well, it's very nice of you to say so. Mr Cherry will draw his own.

TOM: Judy, Carol wants to go to the flicks.

CAROL: I should mention I'm flat broke.

TOM: I'll take care of that. How about it, Judy?

JUDY: Whose idea was that?

CHERRY (*off*): So what does Jesse do? He gets both his shoulders under her belly . . .

Enter CHERRY *from hall. He holds open the door and looks back.*

. . . gives a tremendous heave – and walks into the yard with the horse on his back!

Enter BOWMAN *from hall.*

BOWMAN (*politely*): Ha! What did your father do?

CHERRY: Couldn't do anything! ' 'Ere she be, gaffer!' says Jesse. 'I toald 'ee 'ee'd bought a cripple!'

BOWMAN (*glancing at* ISOBEL): Good lord.

CHERRY: Oh, he – he was a character. (*Sees the table.*) But you haven't set a place for my good friend, Mr Bowman!

BOWMAN: Oh, I can't possibly.

ISOBEL (*expressionless*): Will you stop to supper, Mr Bowman?

BOWMAN: There's nothing I should like better but——

CHERRY: That's right——

BOWMAN (*rather sharply*): I really can't . . . I should have started home an hour ago.

CHERRY: Well, then, well . . . Ah! D'you know where my grafting knife is, darling? Mr Bowman's going to have it sharpened for me.

ISOBEL: Yes, I think so. (*Produces it.*) Can't the ironmonger do it?

CHERRY: That's the item, squire.

BOWMAN: Oh, yes. An ironmonger could do it, you know.

CHERRY: Now you give it to your man and let him make a proper job of it – if it's not too much trouble, that is.

BOWMAN: Not at all.

CHERRY: You know what it is; you show that to these chaps up here, never seen one before. Now, a jar of scrumpy before you go?

BOWMAN: No, thank you, I've a long way to drive.

CHERRY: Wish I was coming with you. Still; there it is, then. I won't detain you.

BOWMAN: Good night, Mrs Cherry.

ISOBEL: Good night.

CHERRY (*escorting him to side door*): This way. It's quicker. And I'll think about what you say.

BOWMAN: Good.

CHERRY: I'm not convinced, mind you. I was brought up in a different school – bushes or standards I was taught – (*They go out. Opens the lattice.*) Well, cheerio, old man. It's been delightful meeting you. I'll see you some time soon?

BOWMAN: Er – yes.

CHERRY: We'll make an evening of it.

BOWMAN: Yes. (*Exit through lattice.*) Good night.

CHERRY: Good night, old man. Bon voyage. (*He goes back inside.*

Delightful chap, isn't he?

ISOBEL: Is he coming back?

CHERRY (*picks up one of the glasses of cider and holds it to the light*): Oh, oh, oh. Who drew the cider?

CAROL: I did. (*Winsomely.*) Isn't it all right?

CHERRY (*wags his finger at her*): You don't come from Somerset!

CAROL: No, I don't.

CHERRY: Now you come here and I'll show you. (*She does so. He puts the pint mug under the tap and demonstrates.*) Now. You put your finger over the spiggot, like this——

CAROL: Mine isn't big enough. (*She shows him.*)

CHERRY (*charmed*): Good heavens above, look at this child's hand! What's that good for?

CAROL: Nothing . . .

CHERRY: Ha ha! Well, if you can find someone with fingers like cucumbers, you can tell him this is the way to draw cider . . . See? (*He holds up his glass.*)

CAROL (*with great interest*): Oh, yes.

CHERRY: See?

TOM: Makes you wonder what they'll invent next, doesn't it?

CHERRY: Don't ask *him* to do it, mind. He'd get sucked through and drowned. (*He leans over* TOM's *chair.*)

ISOBEL: Supper's ready.

CHERRY: Are the plates hot?

ISOBEL: No, I forgot.

CHERRY (*fetches plates and puts them in the oven*): Must have hot plates for shepherd's pie.

He is about to rejoin the children but ISOBEL *detains him. Meanwhile,* CAROL *sits opposite* TOM *and they mime their own conversation as follows.* CAROL *speaks to* TOM, *who sulkily replies.* CAROL *sits right forward on her chair, flattering him. The three of them put their heads together and talk animatedly over the book,* TOM *rehabilitating himself.*

ISOBEL: Jim.

CHERRY: Hullo?

ISOBEL: Is he coming back?

CHERRY: I suppose so.

ISOBEL: Why?

CHERRY: Well, he's got my knife, hasn't he?

ISOBEL: He's coming all the way from Somerset with your knife?

CHERRY: No, of course not.

ISOBEL: *Did* you tell him?

CHERRY (*irritably*): Tell him what?

ISOBEL *looks after him malevolently.*

TOM (*reading*): 'For I have known them all already, know them all, Have known the evenings, mornings, afternoons, I have measured out my life with coffee spoons——'

CHERRY: With what?

JUDY: Coffee spoons.

CHERRY: Blimey! (*Winks at* CAROL.) Well, go on.

TOM: Let's go and eat! (*He closes the book.*)

CAROL: Did that man really carry a horse on his back?

CHERRY: He did, my dear.

CAROL: Hell, he must have been strong!

TOM (*with satirical awe*): He was so strong, he could bend that poker.

CAROL: Crikey!

TOM: You'll enjoy the film tonight. It's full of hairy marines.

CAROL: Good-oh.

JUDY (*giggling*): Carol, you are terrible.

CHERRY: Going to the pictures?

TOM (*anxious*): Yes.

CHERRY (*lofty, shrewd*): Er – have you got my tobacco, Tom? (TOM *produces it, looking anxiously at his father.*) Thank you . . . and the change . . .? (*At this,* ISOBEL *looks sharply and alarmed at* TOM. TOM *confusedly digs in his pockets.*) Oh, d'you need it?

TOM: Well . . .

CHERRY: That's all right, lad, keep it . . . only – mustn't forget to ask, you know.

    TOM *looks at* ISOBEL, *meets her angry glance, is further confused.*

TOM (*muttering*): Thank you.

CHERRY: Yes, this man, Carol – Hullo! (*Picks up the smaller poker.*) Who straightened this?

TOM (*glad*): I did!

CHERRY: *You* did? You must have used your feet.

TOM: No, I didn't! . . . I did it on the edge of the table.

CHERRY: Aha! (*Straightens it fully.*)

CAROL: Gosh! Can you do the big one?

CHERRY: No. No one in – (*contemptuous*) – London could. I might if I'd been doing the job I was born to. (*Significant.*) You come down to Somerset in a year's time and I might be able to show you something.

    ISOBEL *looks up sharply.*

CAROL (*playing up to* CHERRY): Oh?

CHERRY: Yes, I – well, let's just say I've taken certain steps today to terminate my present sedentary occupation.

ISOBEL (*horrified*): Oh – Jim!

    Exit swiftly to garden. She leans against garden trellis.

CHERRY (*rising, alarmed*): Where you going, Bel? (*To children, with forced comic surprise.*) Where's she's gone?

JUDY: Read us some more, Tom.

CAROL: He reads well, doesn't he?

JUDY: Yes, he does.

CHERRY: What, more coffee spoons? That's not poetry. 'Oh, for a muse of fire——'!

TOM: Go on then.

CHERRY: D'you think I can't? Eh?

TOM: All right, if you can——

CHERRY: He thinks he's the only man in England that knows any poetry!

TOM: All right, go on, then!

CHERRY (*powerful, deep, fluent, with emotion*):
  'Oh, for a muse of fire that would ascend
  The brightest heaven of invention,
  A kingdom for a stage, princes to act
  And monarchs to behold the swelling scene!
  Then should the warlike Harry like himself
  Assume the port of Mars . . .'

CAROL (*moved to genuine admiration*): *Pretty* good!

    ISOBEL *in the garden, unhearing, leaning against the gate, throws her head back, cries exhaustedly.*

CHERRY: Wait a tick——
  'Assume the port of Mars, and at his heels

Leashed in like hounds——'

ISOBEL: Oh, let me, let me, let me leave him!

CHERRY: 'Should famine, sword and fire crouch for employment . . .'

ISOBEL: Give me the strength; just for a moment!

CHERRY: 'But pardon, gentles all . . .'

ISOBEL: Just for long enough to walk out!

CHERRY: 'But pardon . . .'

ISOBEL: To get away from him! To get away from him for good!

CHERRY: 'But pardon . . .'

ISOBEL: Oh, let me, let me, let me leave him!

CHERRY: 'But pardon, gentles all . . .'

CURTAIN

ACT TWO

The scene is the same. The time is towards the end of the following month.

Empty stage: the clock chimes four.

Enter CHERRY *to the garden patch through the trellis gate, quietly. He hesitates, smothers a cough, places his hand on the knob of the door, consults his wrist-watch, hesitates again. He vanishes through the trellis and appears at the window, screwing his head to see right into the room. He goes back again, braces himself and opens the door with a manner which will look normally assured if there is someone in the kitchen but which makes no noise. Once inside, his step is stealthy but urgent. He closes the door quietly. He quickly opens a drawer, another and another, in which he finds what he wants: extracts a woman's handbag, opens it, takes out some notes, which he places in his own pocket-book, replaces it, closes the drawer; he is trembling. His glance falls on to the cider barrel. He hesitates, looks at the door, the barrel. He draws a mug of cider; then taking a glass flask from his pocket he laces it heavily with gin and drinks from it. Some of the urgency leaves him and he slowly approaches the table and puts down the mug. He makes a noise doing so and glances round uneasily. Silence prevails. He relaxes slightly; he is at the same time trying to think and using the drink to protect him from what he has to think about. There is a spray of blossom in a clean milk bottle on the table. He is about to drink again when he sees it; he lowers the mug, approaches his face and draws it across the petals, thinking. There is a clatter at the front door, off. He cocks his head sharply and a voice calls. Someone is coming. He is about to go out of the side door. He sees his mug on the table. He darts back for it and is about to go again.*

49

ISOBEL (*off*): Tom? (*Too late. He spins his hat on to a chair and assumes a nonchalant pose by the window. Enter from hall* ISOBEL, *carrying letters.*) Jim! What time is it?

CHERRY (*consults his watch*): I'm playing hookey.

ISOBEL (*this is evidently not the first time*): You've been coming home early a lot lately. Don't get into trouble again.

CHERRY: Cat's away, you know.

ISOBEL: Is Mr Burridge still on holiday?

CHERRY: Yes, he is.

ISOBEL: You are getting on better with him now, aren't you?

CHERRY: Oh, yes. Anything in the post?

ISOBEL: Oh. (*Handing it to him.*) There's an army letter for Tom. D'you think that's it?

CHERRY: *I* don't know.

ISOBEL: Jim, do you think he'll be all right?

CHERRY: He'll be fine. A credit to you.

ISOBEL (*pleased*): Really?

CHERRY: Sure of it. He is already. They both are.

ISOBEL (*sitting*): It's nice to have you home so early.

CHERRY (*sitting*): Nice to *be* home early.

ISOBEL (*smiling at him*): Jim, I think we're all right.

CHERRY: Oh, yes.

ISOBEL: Let's drink to it. (*She reaches for his glass.*)

CHERRY (*alarmed*): Hey! (*Snatches it away, turns a joke.*) Hands off my scrumpy!

ISOBEL: My!

CHERRY: Let me get you one. (*Doing so.*) No, you know, I never like anyone drinking my scrumpy.

ISOBEL: Don't fill it, Jim.

CHERRY: Well, here's to us, eh?

ISOBEL: May our dreams come true.

CHERRY: Right!

ISOBEL: I don't mean Venice, you know. I mean – us – Oh well, anyway! Cheers!

CHERRY: Cheers.

They drink.

ISOBEL (*puts down glass, little grimace*): I hope you're right about Tom. I don't think his character's at all formed.

CHERRY (*heavily*): If it isn't, heaven knows it isn't *your* fault, that's all I can say.

ISOBEL (*touched, protesting*): Or yours, Jim.

CHERRY (*wriggling – he unconsciously feels these to be coals of fire*): Well, I . . . hope not. Of course.

ISOBEL (*glances at letters*): More bills! This girl Carol. Do you think she's attractive?

CHERRY (*too loudly, and suddenly balancing his chair on two legs*): Attractive?

ISOBEL: I do.

CHERRY: She's got a nice nature.

ISOBEL: I wonder about that. These last few weeks since Tom's been seeing her . . . She makes him greedy. (*Opens letter.*) Oh, dear. (*Rises and goes to drawer.*) This is the third reminder. I'd better go round and pay.

CHERRY: What is it?

ISOBEL: Coal and coke. (*Looking in drawer.*) Do you know where my bag is?

CHERRY (*fascinated as she searches*): No.

ISOBEL (*opening another drawer*): I think she's good for Judy . . . Or is she . . . ? (*Returns to table with handbag.*)

CHERRY: Let me write you a cheque.

ISOBEL (*sitting*): No. It's only thirty-four shillings. (*Looking in handbag.*) I don't think Judy's all that plain, do you?

CHERRY (*watching helplessly*): No. A little awkward, perhaps. Over-fastidious. (*She turns to light and takes out purse. Her figure grows tense. Desperately.*) I think Judy's over-fastidious, Bel. (*She rummages quickly.*) . . . Fastidious . . .

ISOBEL (*leaning back*): O-o-o-o-oh, *God!*

CHERRY: What's up?

ISOBEL: I must make sure. (*Picks up bag, searches resolutely, replaces it on table; dejected.*) No. Gone . . . (CHERRY *stares in silence.*) Tom's stealing again.

CHERRY: Are you sure it's not there?

ISOBEL: Perfectly.

CHERRY: How much are you missing?

ISOBEL: Two pounds.

CHERRY: Notes?

ISOBEL: Yes.

CHERRY: You may have lost them.

ISOBEL: No. They've been taken from my bag. It's Tom.

CHERRY: Yes, I suppose so. (*A little twitch of pain.*) Must it be Tom?

ISOBEL: Who else? Who needs to?

CHERRY: You perhaps left it somewhere?

ISOBEL: I'm afraid not, Jim. He took some last week.

CHERRY (*covering surprise with a deadpan*): Last week?

ISOBEL: Two ten-shilling notes. And now two pounds. Oh, it's so disgusting! Why can't he ask for it? I thought we were past all this! What *is* going to become of the boy? Well, you'll have to lend it me now, Jim. D'you mind? Just a couple.

CHERRY: Cheque no good, eh? There we are, then. (*Gives money, laughs, shows empty pocket-book.*)

ISOBEL: Oh, I've cleaned you out. (*Takes it and lays it on table.*) I thought I might be wrong about it last week, but—— Oh, Jim, if we're going to *steal* from one another!

CHERRY: Now, Isobel, be careful. You may be mistaken.

ISOBEL: There's no mistake, dear. I marked the notes.

CHERRY: Marked them?

ISOBEL: Yes. That's the state we're reduced to. Wherever those notes are, they're marked!

Enter TOM *from hall.*

TOM: Hullo! (*The atmosphere hits him.*) Hullo! . . . You're home early, Dad . . . Uh . . .?

ISOBEL: Tom——

CHERRY: Now just a minute, dear——

ISOBEL: Tom, can I have my money back, please?

TOM (*stares for a moment, then steps back with a rather theatrical gesture of fatality*): Well, I'm damned. Of all the ruddy luck. Yes, I've got it.

ISOBEL: Kindly give it back.

TOM (*nervous*): Sure. (*Puts notes on table.*) I was going to. Look, Mum. I wanted it for——

ISOBEL: It doesn't matter what you wanted it for; give it back.

TOM (*pointing*): There it is.

ISOBEL: Tom, will you please give it back!

TOM (*puzzled, irritated*): That's it!

ISOBEL: I am asking you to return the money which you took from my purse!

TOM (*very distressed*): I have done, blast it! What's the matter with you?

ISOBEL: *All* of it!

TOM: That is all of it!

ISOBEL: It isn't!

TOM (*his voice trembling*): It is! Oh, blast it, mother, don't let's have a blasted row. I know I shouldn't have taken the blasted money. I wanted it to take Carol out, but I didn't; I was going to give it back; I've had it on me ever since; I've given it back! I'm sorry; I know I shouldn't . . . (*At this point he has to bite his lip.*)

ISOBEL: You've given me one pound.

TOM: Yes——?

ISOBEL: You took three.

TOM (*shakily indignant*): Took——? I didn't!

ISOBEL: You took three.

TOM: Eh?

ISOBEL: Don't *do* that! (*More calmly.*) Have you spent it?

TOM: Spent what? I took two ten-bobs and I've given you two ten-bobs – the same ones.

ISOBEL: Two pound notes have been taken from my purse; this morning, or last night.

TOM: Well, I can't help that.

CHERRY: Now just a bit, Bel——

TOM: I don't know what she's talking about!

ISOBEL: Tom, I warn you. If you don't give them back I shall find them!

TOM: She's off her head!

CHERRY: Now then!

TOM: Oh, to *hell* with that! One pound! That's what I took! (*Indicating notes on table.*)

ISOBEL: How can I believe that? Oh, Tom, it doesn't matter – you've admitted you took one; what difference does it make? Come on, let's have the whole thing cleared up now . . . Tom, I shall look through your things!

TOM: You'd better not!

ISOBEL: If you've spent them, darling, tell me. I don't mind.

TOM: That's very big of you! It so happens——

ISOBEL: Very well. I shall have to look for them.

    Exit to hall.

TOM: Mother! If you do – *Mother!*

    Exit to hall, following. CHERRY, *left alone on the stage, rubs his hands through his hair and over his flushed and puffy face.*

CHERRY: Oh, crikey! Oh, lor'! (*He retrieves his cider.*) Oh, you . . . you . . . (*He drinks and sits.*) You . . . (*He pulls a farming magazine from his pocket, opens it and studies its pages with fuddled care, bottom to top, left and right, like a child, drinking and talking meanwhile.*) That's a nice – holding. What's going to become of me . . . ? (*Takes a pencil and laboriously marks something in the paper; tearful.*) O-o-o-ooh, crikey! (*He drinks hastily.*) JUDY *enters through garden trellis,* CAROL *dawdling reluctantly after.*

JUDY: Oh, come on, Carol.

CAROL (*petulant*): I don't *want* to come in!

JUDY: Please, Carol.

CAROL: I don't *want* to!

JUDY (*sadly*): Don't you think you might do something because I want to?

CAROL: Not really, no.

JUDY: Oh, Carol, you *are* awful!

CAROL: You're always saying that.

JUDY (*admiring*): Well, everyone says you're moody.

CAROL (*interested*): Do they?

JUDY (*keeping it up*): It's all right for you, I suppose . . .

CAROL (*fishing*): Why? I'm no different from anyone else.

JUDY (*reproachful*): Oh, *Carol*! I don't know how your boys put up with you.

CAROL: 'Boys'? Men.

JUDY (*uncomfortable*): Boys – men – what's the difference?

CAROL: Men.

JUDY: Men makes them sound old.

CAROL: They're better old.

JUDY: You are awful.

CAROL: Oh, for Pete's sake!

JUDY: Gosh, you're moody. (*Brightly.*) When we have a flat we'll have to have a party every night, I can see that.

CAROL: That's what you're after, isn't it? Parties.

JUDY (*uneasy*): Well, I like parties . . .

CAROL: You don't go to them.

JUDY: I do—— I – I went to the end-of-term ball.

CAROL: That's not a *party*! (*A pause.*) Look: if we had a flat – and we had a party——

JUDY: Yes?

CAROL: And they all came——

JUDY: Yes?

CAROL: Well, look—— (*Quite gently.*) You'd have to do your own smooching.

JUDY (*small voiced*): I know that, Carol.

CAROL: Yes, but – I don't think you'd like it.

JUDY: I *would*! Oh, I would, Carol.

CAROL: Anyway, we're not getting the flat, are we?

JUDY: What d'you mean, Carol?

CAROL: You've been stringing me along, Judy. Johnny Idasalski's going to get that student award.

JUDY: Don't be silly, dear; I've practically got it. I've told you.

CAROL: Professor Herring was talking to Wilfred this morning and he said Johnny Idasalski would get it. Your work's pretty good but it's geometrical; it's *cold*.

JUDY (*turns away*): Cold. Did Professor Herring say that?

CAROL: Yes. I think so. Oh, crikey, don't start yelling.

JUDY: I'm not.

CAROL: I'll come inside, if you want me to.

JUDY: Yes. Righto. You are kind, Carol. I wanted to talk to you, you see. I was going to. It'll be all right. I'm sure it will. Even if I don't get this, I'm sure——

    CAROL *eyes her, calculates the intensity of her emotion, shrugs.*

CAROL: O.K. Take it easy.

JUDY: Yes, all right; I will; I don't mind, Carol; only just come inside; it's all right.

    She holds out her hand. CAROL *doesn't take it but does move forward and* JUDY, *satisfied, opens door. She sees* CHERRY, *checks.*

CHERRY: 'Lo, dear . . . I – er . . . (*Pulls himself together, frowning with drunken gravity.*)

JUDY (*whirls about in doorway*): He's drunk!

CAROL (*eager*): Is he?

    She pushes past and enters kitchen, followed by JUDY.

CHERRY (*rising, benign, dignified and helpless*): Hullo, Carol, Come in, Carol. Come in and sit down. (*In his drunkenness and care he is forced to a very simple method of reassuring them of his goodwill – a garden party style of speaking, very clear, considered and slow.*) How very charming you both look . . . It does me good to see you here . . . Can I persuade either, or both, of you to join me in a glass of country cider?

JUDY: No, thanks. (*Irritated.*) You know I can't stand it!

CHERRY: I'm sorry. I had forgotten. (*To* CAROL.) Now what are you contemplating so intently? (*He raises his hand to his head with the innocent smile of the simple-hearted drunk.*) I hope I am not still wearing my hat.

CAROL: No. Your hair's a bit rumpled.

CHERRY (*stroking it, absently*): That may be . . . that may be . . .

CAROL: I'll have some cider.

CHERRY: Ah, yes. (*Gets a glass for her.*) I have had – (*fills it*) – an extremely distressing day.

CAROL: Oh, what a pity. What's been the matter?

CHERRY: I should like very much to be able to confide in you, my dear. But I cannot. (*Carries cider to her.*) And Judy, my dear, what kind of day have your talents brought to you?

JUDY: Father, really.

CHERRY: Is it offensive? Don't be offended.

JUDY: I'm not.

    Enter TOM.

TOM: Oh——

CAROL: Hi, Tom!

TOM: Hi, Er, Dad . . .

CHERRY (*longing for some easy way to make amends; eager*): Yes, son?

TOM (*embarrassed*): I suppose you couldn't lend me——?

CHERRY (*hopeless*): Tom, I'm awfully sorry; I don't seem to—— (*He pats his pockets smiling frozenly.* TOM *turns angrily away.*)

    Enter ISOBEL.

ISOBEL: Tom, what are you doing?

TOM: I'm trying to borrow your two lousy quid!

ISOBEL: And what possible purpose can that serve? Kindly come back, I'm not nearly satisfied yet. (*Exit* TOM.) And you too, Judy.

JUDY: Me? Why?

ISOBEL: Because I ask you to.

JUDY: Why, what's going on?

ISOBEL (*going*): Will you please come?

> *Exit* ISOBEL, *and we hear her angry voice receding.*

JUDY: Carol, don't go.

CAROL: O.K.

JUDY (*going*): Really, mother, I don't know what——

> *Exit* JUDY, *and we hear her protests receding to silence.*

CHERRY: I dislike intensely this atmosphere of tumult in a house. I am fastidious, you know.

CAROL: You don't have to tell me that, Mr Cherry.

CHERRY (*encouraged*): No, but I wish you'd tell Judy. You understand a great deal for your age. (*Holding her arm.*) It's pleasant having you here. (*Releasing her*) – I'm not intending to be familiar.

CAROL: I don't mind.

CHERRY (*nodding with a wise, sad smile*): To you I must seem as repulsively old as you are . . . young.

CAROL: No. You don't seem old. You just seem – well – a man.

CHERRY (*as one who admits a point*): One does learn *something* as one lives; there's that, I suppose.

CAROL: What's this about two pounds? Has Tom lifted it?

CHERRY (*desperately*): No! . . . I'd rather say nothing about it, if you don't mind, Carol. Tom is deeply under your spell. We all are.

CAROL (*admiring*): Your generation is terribly smooth.

CHERRY: 'Smooth' doesn't sound altogether . . .?

CAROL: Oh, it is. Altogether. (*She sips his cider.*) Phew! (*Sips again.*) Gin!

CHERRY (*disconcerted*): Gin?

CAROL (*playfully reproachful*): Mr Cherry.

CHERRY (*reassured*): You've discovered my little secret.

CAROL (*sipping it*): You must have a constitution like a bull!

CHERRY (*yields entirely to her flattery; laughs*): I'm well seasoned! Yes, I wish I had a shilling for every pint of this I've sunk. (*Drinks.*)

CAROL (*sitting on table*): What would you do with it?

CHERRY (*puts down glass and wipes lips*): I might buy you a nice present.

CAROL: No, seriously.

CHERRY: Well, why not?

CAROL (*laughs*): Mrs Cherry mightn't like it.

CHERRY: Oh . . . (*Laughs.*) Well . . . (*Sits.*) Seriously then, if I had the money, I'd buy that. (*Slapping his magazine.*)

CAROL *leans towards him. He looks up as her face approaches but she stops short.*

CAROL: What is it?

CHERRY: It's a farm.

CAROL (*twisting her head to look at the advertisement*): I can't read it. What does it say?

CHERRY: Oh. (*Embarrassed, mumbling rapidly.*) 'Fifteen acres orchard and grass in ring fence with two hundred and fifty yards frontage on metalled road——'

CAROL: No. Slowly. What's it mean?

CHERRY: Well: 'Two hundred and fifty yard frontage on metalled road' – that's very handy for getting your stuff shifted. If you've only got a narrow frontage it means every-thing's got to be brought in from the fields to the same gate, you see. And that means either you're up to your eyes in mud half the year or you make a paved drive, which costs money. Then 'tyings for six'. That's cows, of course. I shouldn't bother with that. Cows are a great responsibility. I might keep a little Jersey or Guernsey on just to supply the house. But I don't know even about that. I can't stand them killing the calves. 'Walled garden' – that's useful——

CAROL: Is this in Somerset?

CHERRY: Mendip. That's the best of Somerset . . .! (*Suddenly moved, gloomy.*) I talk about it too much.

CAROL: You talk awfully well about it.

CHERRY: I don't know about that. Course, I was born there . . . Quite near where I think this is but bigger, oh, a big farm, with twelve men working for us at harvest time, real men, real characters.

CAROL: That one who carried the horse?

CHERRY: That's right. He was the Lord of the Harvest, as they used to call him in those days. Oh, harvest time was something glorious then, the horses and the men. They used to bring up huge parcels of bread from the farm, a perfect mountain of bread, and real Cheddar cheese, and cold boiled bacon under the hedge on a tablecloth; the dogs used to sit round in a circle with their tongues hanging out, the dogs the men brought, terriers and collies, they came from miles for the rats, the hares and rabbits in the corn. The dogs my father had were beautiful.

From our big field you looked right over the Plain of Somerset; nothing but pasture and orchards, it's too wet for crops, it's not much above sea level; green and blue as far as you could see. The men were a rough lot and I wasn't much better than the men, but the place was something all right . . . The way those old-time squires planted trees – there was an avenue of elm trees two miles long that didn't go anywhere; it's still there, I'll bet; ecclesiastical property, they won't have cut it down. That's another thing we could see up there, the old cathedral. They used to set their watches by the bells and my father said, 'Allow nine seconds for the distance.' It's a noble pile, that building, a gem of architecture; yes, many's the time; you could bend down and look between your legs – (*he does it*) – with the sweat running into your eyes – (*he rises*) – and see this thing the Normans built, crumbling away like something soft in the sunshine we had then . . . We were as brown as – pieces of furniture!

CAROL (*speculative*): You must have been rather smashing.

CHERRY: As a matter of fact, I was! (*He takes off his coat, rolls up his shirt-sleeves and drinks; reasonable.*) I was big, you know. (*Carried away again.*) I was feared in the village! (*Reasonable.*) By the lads, that is, by the boys.

CAROL: What about the girls?

CHERRY: Believe it or not, I was a bit fancied by the girls.

CAROL (*eyeing him, deep-chested and with some remnants of animal poise as he drinks*): You were strong, weren't you?

CHERRY: Had to be! Well, depends what you mean by strong. You'd have appreciated old Jesse. I've seen that man take a bar of iron like this and just – (*seizes the big poker*) – bend it. With his two hands.

CAROL: He must have been a bit of a dream.

CHERRY: What, to look at? Oh, my dear, incredible.

CAROL: Can't you bend it, Mr Cherry?

CHERRY: By Jiminy! I've a good mind to try! Come on, let's drink up and—— (*He drinks.*)

CAROL: All right. (*She steps forward and takes his glass.*)

CHERRY: Hey! (*She looks at him over the glass as she sips it.*) Like it?

CAROL: Mm. (*She goes on looking and sipping. They are standing close.*)

CHERRY (*attempting to take it*): Hey, steady. (*She resists. They hold the glass betweem them.*) Steady . . . steady, Carol . . .

CAROL (*softly*): Are you going to kiss me, Mr Cherry? (*He wavers.*) You can, if you bend that poker.

CHERRY: I – I can't . . . Well, all right! I'll have a go! (*He seizes it at either end.*) I shall keep you to it, mind!

CAROL: Of course.

CHERRY: Wait a bit. (*Excited, laughing.*) This is how Jesse used to. (*Puts it behind his neck.*) Let's see, now. (*Eyes it.*) I don't think – (*He places it against his knee and pulls at either end.*) I don't think I can! (*Pulling hard, gasping.*) Wait, now!

CAROL: You're strong!

CHERRY: Wait! (*He begins to tremble with strain.*) Wait!

His face suffuses with colour, his whole body shakes. He ceases, drops the poker, head lowered, arms wrapped about his constricted chest, his face vacant and alarmed.

CAROL: Hard luck. (*He gropes to a chair.*) What's the matter . . .?

He sits heavily.

CHERRY (*whispering*): Will you get my coat?

CAROL: Yes. (*Does so.*)

    CHERRY *feebly plucks it round his shoulders. She helps.*

CHERRY: Thank you.

CAROL: Poor Mr Cherry. (*Alarmed.*) Are you all right . . .? (*Sharply.*) Mr Cherry?

    CHERRY *nods without speaking, and in the silence there is a noise of altercation from a distant part of the house,* ISOBEL *angry, the children indignant; it ends sharply as the front door slams.*

CHERRY: Yes. (*Straightens up a little.*)

CAROL: Sure?

CHERRY: Yes. (*Straightens up and blows.*)

CAROL: Well, you tried, anyway. (*She kisses him lightly on the forehead.*)

CHERRY: Oh. (*Turns away.*) Yes; I can't do it.

CAROL: I reckon the man who could bend that could do anything.

    Enter ISOBEL.

ISOBEL (*flatly*): Oh – Carol. (*Looks at* CHERRY.) Jim . . .? Have you had a dizzy spell?

CHERRY: No.

ISOBEL (*glances at him, is sufficiently reassured to let it go*): Well – (*sitting*) – I'm defeated——

CHERRY: Bel, I think you ought to let it drop. That's what I think.

ISOBEL: Jim, I can't!

CHERRY (*drinking*): For heaven's sake, it's only two pounds, for heaven's sake! (*Indicating* CAROL.) Anyway, they'll be gone in no time, won't they? Tom's going into the army, isn't he? Judy's going to live with Carol——

CAROL (*with significant blankness*): Oh.

ISOBEL: What?

CAROL: I'm afraid that's off. I thought you knew. We shan't be able to afford it.

ISOBEL: No, I didn't know that.

CAROL: Yes; Judy hasn't got the student award.

ISOBEL: She *hasn't*?

CAROL: Uh-uh.

ISOBEL: But she told me definitely.

CAROL (*smiling, preparing to go*): Yes, me too; I can't think why. It is a pity. She's a very nice girl, Mrs Cherry. Someone's going to be crazy about her some day. It's awfully disappointing, isn't it...? Well... (*Drifts towards the door.*)

ISOBEL: But has someone else got it?

CAROL (*at door*): Mm. 'Byee. 'Bye, Mr Cherry; I hope you feel better.

She goes out into garden.

ISOBEL: Jim! You have had a turn!

CHERRY (*nodding, breathless*): Oh, no, it's all right. Really.

She puts her hand on his. In the garden, CAROL *is arrested at the trellis by* TOM.

TOM (*smiling*): Hey. Come and say good-bye to Judy.

CAROL: Oh screw Judy.

TOM: She's waiting for you in the Moca Berry.

CAROL (*smiles, shrugs; indifferently*): Oh, Lord! Are you coming?

TOM: I'll walk down with you, but I'm not coming in. Come on, you don't have to let yourself in for anything.

Exit TOM *and* CAROL *through trellis.*

ISOBEL (*sees large poker misplaced*): Jim – you've never been trying that! Darling, you promised.

CHERRY: I didn't really try; don't worry.

ISOBEL: Jim, I couldn't bear it.

CHERRY: What about Judy, eh?

ISOBEL: Oh yes ... poor Judy ... But you see, Jim? She's got . no money; she *might* have taken it.

CHERRY: No! I – I am confident that if one of them has, there would be extenuating circumstances.

ISOBEL: Ah, Jim ... (*Sits close by him.*)

CHERRY: I am confident of that.

ISOBEL: You're a much nicer person than I am. You are.

CHERRY (*rising and going to door, vehemently, almost weeping*):
No! It's just that I'm confident there would be extenuating
circumstances!

ISOBEL (*following him to door*): Shall we let it slide?

CHERRY (*huskily, not looking at her*): I think that would be best.

ISOBEL: Are you going out? (*Anxious but playful.*) Jim, you've
been drinking an awful lot lately, darling, haven't you?

The trellis gate opens and TOM *walks swiftly through the
garden to the door of the house.*

CHERRY: Yes, perhaps. (*He opens the door to go out just as* TOM
gets to it, and TOM *lounges straight in. This is the catalyst for his
distress. He vibrates with irritation.*) Oh, excuse me.

TOM: Is the investigation still going forward?

ISOBEL: No.

CHERRY: You were a bit handy when I opened the door,
weren't you? He's been listening.

ISOBEL: Oh, Jim——

TOM: No, that's quite right. Some people like going through
drawers, other people like listening through keyholes. It's
entirely a matter of taste. (*He turns away.*)

CHERRY: Now your mother has very kindly agreed to drop
the whole business——

TOM: Good. We can keep it going indefinitely that way, can't
we? Well, I don't want it (*raises hand in air and gesticulates*)
releasing into the atmosphere to join our other little –
domestic pets up there. (*He looks at* ISOBEL.) *I* didn't steal
that money, and *Judy* didn't. Now, do you know that or
don't you . . .? (*She is unwilling.*) . . . Well, do you believe it
or not?

ISOBEL: Tom, I don't think you should——

CHERRY (*alarmed, blustering*): Perhaps *I* stole it!

TOM: Why not?

*CHERRY starts towards him, stops, turns and staggers out to
garden. Exit.*

ISOBEL: Jim! (*Goes to door as he is going through trellis.*) Jim! (*He waves her back, not turning, and exit.*) Tom, of all the mean, vicious——

TOM: Why? Why vicious?

ISOBEL: That was unpardonable!

TOM: Why? Explain why it's worse to suspect him than me. (*Picking up letter.*) Is this my call-up?

ISOBEL: I hope so!

TOM (*opens it*): Congratulate yourself. It is.

ISOBEL (*a little faint*): Oh, Tom. Is it?

TOM *shows it.*

TOM: Don't spoil it! I'm *half* emancipated now – keep it up a bit and you'll have a man in the house.

ISOBEL (*sitting, suddenly tired*): Oh, Tom! Stop it.

TOM (*also strained*): Me stop it, by God!

ISOBEL: Kindly moderate your language. You're not in the army yet.

TOM (*comforted by the parental rebuke, relaxes, smiles*): O.K., Mum?

ISOBEL (*sighs*): I suppose so, Tom. But, oh, I *wish* you hadn't taken those ten-shilling notes.

TOM: Well, let me tell you about that. No, let me, because I think this is pretty good. I was outside with Carol. And Carol wanted me to take her to the flicks. O.K.? So I said, 'Wait a bit; I've got some inside,' and I came back in here and – took it – out of your purse. *But*, when I went out I said I didn't seem to have any, and we went for a walk in the park. And believe me, walks in the park are not Carol's cup of tea, and I had the money in my pocket – (*taps his pocket*) – all the time. And I've had it there ever since. Now I know I should have put it back and I don't know why I didn't—— Yes, I do; I suppose I've just got sticky fingers; I'll have to watch it. But I would never have spent it, and I *think* I would have put it back . . . Now that's not bad, is it?

ISOBEL (*warmly*): No, Tom, that's not bad.

TOM: I don't want to be that kind of person.

    ISOBEL *gives a sigh of relief and puts her head happily between her hands, like a person who has come ashore after a long swim.*

ISOBEL: Oh, that's good, Tom. When have you got to go? (*And she asks this question now quite calmly.*)

TOM (*consults letter*): The seventh. A fortnight.

ISOBEL: You underestimate your father, Tom. He loves you.

TOM: Some love.

ISOBEL: He does! He was defending you just now against me! He wouldn't believe it!

TOM (*after a pause*): Yes?

ISOBEL: Yes. (*Severe.*) You hurt him.

TOM: Now I said forget it! And I repeat, why was it worse to suspect——

ISOBEL: Don't be absurd! Why should your father want two pounds?

TOM: I dunno. Buy gin . . . Didn't you know?

ISOBEL: I didn't know what it was.

TOM: It's gin. And it costs thirty-five bob a bottle.

ISOBEL: Do you think I'm going to stand here and discuss your father with you in terms like these? He just *gave* me two pounds out of his own pocket!

TOM: All right; but why me? Why couldn't someone have come in through that door – (*indicates door to garden*) – found your purse, taken the money and left?

ISOBEL (*looks from drawer to door, delighted*): Tom!

TOM: Ah yes, but that didn't occur to us; we'd rather keep it in the family.

ISOBEL (*terribly relieved*): That's what happened. Why didn't you say so?

TOM: I've only just thought of it; you're the detective round here. But as soon as a bit of money goes, you don't stop to think – it's out with the fingerprint powder, mark the notes – that's what I find pretty hard to take, laying little traps for us for a measly bit of money!

ISOBEL (*contemptuous*): The money!

TOM: Oh yes, the money! (*From the far side of the stage he points an accusing finger.*)

    ISOBEL *takes the notes from the pocket of her dress, tears them across and lets them drop without looking at them.* TOM *stops short and smiles in admiration.* That was nice . . . That was dignified.

ISOBEL: It wasn't the money, Tom. (*She looks at door.*) But I should have thought of that.

TOM (*forgiving, dismissary*): Yes. Anyway——

ISOBEL: No, I should have thought of it. There was no need to – Am I usually as unpleasant as this?

TOM: Mm. I'll tell you one thing – I can use these even if you can't. (*Goes on his knees and pieces together the torn notes.*) You can do a lot with this stuff.

ISOBEL (*mocking*): *Not* very dignified.

TOM: Oh, well, if you can afford to chuck it about, I reckon I can afford to pick it up.

    His attention is caught by something on the notes. He cocks his head and looks again, sits back on his heels and grins up at her.

How did you mark them?

ISOBEL (*stares at him; after a pause*): I——

TOM: Was it a bloody great cross in the corner? (*Shows the notes.*)

    ISOBEL *speechless, nods.*

TOM (*getting up, with gusty relief*): Why, you silly woman, you had them! (*He sees her face and the truth falls on him. He gets up quickly.*) Are those the ones he gave you? (*He stuffs notes in pocket, wipes his nose with his hand. Door bell rings. She nods.*) Someone at the door . . . (*Softly.*) Do you want them? (*Gives them.*) Jesus, I'm sorry, Mum. (*Bell repeated.*) I'll get it.

    Exit TOM *to hall.* ISOBEL *sits at table, rests her chin on one hand and with the other she pushes the torn notes into place on the surface of the table, intensely considering, approaching a decision. Enter* TOM, *stands at door.*

TOM: It's that chap Bowman. D'you want to see him?

    ISOBEL *shakes head. Enter* BOWMAN, *behind* TOM.

BOWMAN: Good afternoon.

TOM: Now just a minute——!

ISOBEL (*rousing herself*): All right, Tom.

BOWMAN (*coming right in*): I've called to see Mr Cherry about the trees.

ISOBEL: My husband isn't here.

TOM: I told him that.

    BOWMAN *looks expectantly at* ISOBEL.

ISOBEL (*a shade impatient*): I'm afraid *I* can't help you.

BOWMAN: May I wait?

ISOBEL: Mr Bowman, don't you *know* you're on a wild goose chase?

BOWMAN: In what way, exactly?

ISOBEL: My husband is – Tom, would you——? (*Exit* TOM.) Mr Bowman, there is no orchard. I should have thought you might have guessed. It's a kind of hobby of my husband's. He thinks about it and makes plans about it . . . but it isn't a bit serious. He writes these letters to people. It's a kind of . . .

BOWMAN: A kind of hallucination.

ISOBEL: Well, then; if you know?

BOWMAN (*hurriedly, walks away*): I wanted to ask you for something.

ISOBEL: Me?

BOWMAN: I – er – (*it is on the spur of the moment*) – I wondered if you'd let me have one of your plants. (*Indicates tray of cacti.*)

ISOBEL: Of course. Which one?

BOWMAN: Er – (*at random*) – this one. (*Puts it on table before her.*)

ISOBEL: Yes, certainly. You can get those anywhere.

BOWMAN (*hurried*): And I've brought Mr Cherry's knife back. (*Puts a small parcel on table.*)

ISOBEL: That's very kind of you. Couldn't you have posted it?

BOWMAN: I did take that round to his office – but of course he wasn't there – so I thought – I'd come round here.

ISOBEL: What do you mean, 'of course he wasn't there'?

BOWMAN: At the office.

ISOBEL: Why shouldn't he be at the office?

BOWMAN: Well, he's left, hasn't he?

ISOBEL: Left?

BOWMAN: Left his job.

ISOBEL: Did they say so?

BOWMAN: Didn't you know?

ISOBEL: Did they *say* so?

BOWMAN: Yes. Some time ago, I gathered.

ISOBEL: Some time ago?

BOWMAN: Look – I'm sorry if I've . . .

ISOBEL: No, that's all right.

BOWMAN: I was thinking about whether to come, all the way up in the car . . .

ISOBEL: Did they say when?

BOWMAN: No, I don't think they did. I got the impression it was the beginning of the month.

ISOBEL: Beginning of the month! But that's impossible! That's three weeks! He's been going every day.

BOWMAN: Not to the office, Mrs Cherry.

ISOBEL: Then what has he been doing?

BOWMAN: Killing time?

ISOBEL (*looking at notes*): . . . I see . . . yes, I see.

BOWMAN: I shouldn't have come, should I?

ISOBEL (*hardly hearing*): What?

BOWMAN: You don't even know what I'm talking about, do you?

ISOBEL (*uneasy*): Well, I don't know.

BOWMAN: No – I shouldn't.

ISOBEL (*amazed*): Why, did you come to see me?

BOWMAN (*nods*): Mmm.

ISOBEL (*gives a sharp laugh*): No, I don't think you should.

BOWMAN: Can I help?

ISOBEL (*looking at him, startled; with absolute incomprehension*):
You?

BOWMAN *grimaces a little and picks up his hat. Enter* CHERRY
*from garden, noisy, breathless, crimson, unsteady; he carries a
small bottle wrapped in tissue paper.*

CHERRY: There you are! (*Collapses into a kitchen chair at the
table and fights for breath.*) Oof! . . . Saw your car . . . Oof!
. . . Ran all the way from the pub! Oof! . . . Wait a tick! (*Puts
his head between his knees and breathes noisily.*) O-o-o-f . . .
Good of you to come, old man. (*Puts bottle on table.*) Drop
of this makes all the difference to a gill of scrumpy. (*Half
attempts to rise, sits again.*) Bel, let's have two glasses . . . Oof!
Well now, how are you, squire? I've been thinking about
what you say. (*Taking much handled sketch map from inside
pocket and unfolding it.*) And I think there's something in it –
not everything, but something. (*A little irritably.*) Come on,
Bel, let's have a drink. Now Beauty of Bath: all right – out.
But what about Sunset and Farmer's——?

BOWMAN: There's your knife. It's been back to Trapman's.

CHERRY: Oh. Well, that *is* good of you. They'll have made a
job of it. Now, what do I owe you? (*Pats his pockets.*) Oh.

BOWMAN (*going*): 'S all right.

CHERRY: No, now – you're not going?

BOWMAN: Yes, 'fraid so. I've got——

Exit.

CHERRY (*rises, surprised*): But I want to talk——!

BOWMAN *shuts door behind him.* CHERRY *turns from door, his
mouth making a half-framed question. He returns, sees the marked
notes on table. He puts out a hand to them. Scared.*

You found your notes, then?

ISOBEL: Yes. You gave them to me. (*He sits abruptly.*) Why did
you, Jim? (*He reaches out unconsciously for his toy, symbol, com-
forter, the wrapped grafting knife. Cries out.*) Don't look at your
knife *now*! (*He leaves it.*) Why did you take it, Jim?

CHERRY: I – er-um . . . er-um . . . wanted it. For . . . for . . .

ISOBEL: But why like that? Why not ask for it? It's your money – you earned it.

CHERRY (*straightening a little but avoiding her eye*): Well, I just – (*he is still out of breath*) – just happened to need it.

ISOBEL: So you took it!

CHERRY (*with even a soupçon of defiance now*): Yes.

ISOBEL: And you let me think Tom had stolen it!

CHERRY: He stole the other, didn't he?

ISOBEL: He gave it back! And you sat there and let me go on and on and on——

CHERRY: I couldn't tell you then!

ISOBEL: Why not?

CHERRY: I don't know. You were – (*desperately*) – I couldn't!

ISOBEL: And never would.

CHERRY (*as one who, though humble, must insist on minimal rights*): Oh yes, oh yes, I would, Bel.

ISOBEL (*approaching, quietly coaxing*): Jim, tell me the truth about one thing. *Why* did you take it?

CHERRY: Well, I was short. (*Bracing a little.*) There's none in the bank, Bel.

ISOBEL (*gently*): No?

CHERRY (*bracing a little more*): Bel, I——

ISOBEL (*encouraging, hopeful*): Yes?

CHERRY (*failing*): We've overspent, I suppose.

ISOBEL: The *truth*, Jim! Oh, why can't you say – (*She cries out*) – 'I lost my job!'

CHERRY (*stares at her in silence*): You know? (*He sits, puts one hand before his face. He speaks with the tremulous weak happiness that follows confession.*) Thank God, thank God you know. (*He puts the other hand over his face, sobs.*) O-o-o-o-o-o-oh.

ISOBEL *walks jerkily up and down behind him, regarding his shaking back, moved to him, but too tired to be certain.*

ISOBEL (*cautious*): Jim?

CHERRY (*controls his eagerness for reconciliation*): Yes?

He half peeps behind his fingers. He sniffs. One hand moves out automatically for the little parcel.

ISOBEL (*springing upon him and knocking it off the table*): LEAVE your knife alone! (*It clatters to the floor.*) (*Rages.*) You see? You can't even weep! You're lying now! Everything you do is a lie! You're lying all the time! There's absolutely *nothing* you have any respect for! Nothing! Your apples and orchards; your dreams; your one dream – it's nothing but a lie and an excuse for lies and lies! You can't even weep!

Her own control gives way. Her face distorts sharply. She thrusts her knuckles into her mouth and exits to hall.

CHERRY (*rising, calling after her, desperately*): I am! Look at my tears! (*He stands glaring at the open door.*)

ISOBEL *returns slowly on to the stage. He takes a hesitant step towards her, putting a finger to his face. Hesitant, injured:*
Look.

ISOBEL (*crosses to him*): You've been unhappy, haven't you?

CHERRY: Oh, yes.

ISOBEL: You left every morning at half-past eight?

CHERRY: I know. I thought I'd tell you I'd got the sack during the day, but when I got home I – I like the evenings, Bel. I never could.

ISOBEL: All right, Jim, we'll find out. (*Crosses to get coat.*) We'll find out where you really stand, really. We'll find out today.

CHERRY: What are you going to do, Bel?

ISOBEL: We can't go on like this, Jim. We've got to find out, haven't we?

CHERRY: What are you going to do?

The curtain falls here briefly to indicate the passage of two hours. The house lights do not go up. The curtain rises on the same scene. CHERRY sits at the table, fidgeting with his mug of cider, back bent, head sagging, an image of defeat, staring at the table or at nothing. TOM sits with a book, looking from time to time at his father with interest and some pity. Neither speaks and CHERRY, *becoming aware of it, grows increasingly restless.*

CHERRY (*conversational*): Do you know where your mother went, Tom?

TOM: No, Dad.

    A short pause.

CHERRY: She didn't say where she was going?

TOM: Not to me . . .

    A longer pause. They go back to their initial state.

CHERRY (*brightly*): What's your book, Tom?

TOM: Coffee spoons.

CHERRY (*abashed*): Oh.

TOM (*making amends*): It's a poem by T. S. Eliot. Called 'The Love Song of J. Alfred Prufrock'. It's a kind of satire, you know, on the twenties. Well, on Eliot himself in the twenties, I suppose.

CHERRY: Really? That sounds interesting, Tom. (*He drinks.*) (TOM *looks at him, falls silent, returns to the book.* CHERRY *casts round desperately.*) He's thought a great deal of, isn't he now, by – er – younger – or have I got it wrong?—— T. S. Eliot, that's the chap, isn't it?

TOM: Oh, yes; most people regard him as the best living poet.

CHERRY: Yes, I thought that was the name . . . (*His head sinks lower into his shoulders.*)

    TOM *looks at him compassionately.*

TOM (*brightly*): I bet those two girls are still sinking coffee in the Moca Berry.

    Grateful, he quickly drags his chair the length of the table to Tom's end of the room. TOM *shuts his book.*

CHERRY: Yes? Is it good, that expresso stuff?

TOM: Not bad (*stilted*). A bit of all right, isn't she?

CHERRY (*too loudly*): Carol?

TOM: Ye-e-es.

CHERRY (*too loudly*): Rather a *common* type of girl, I think.
Something rather – rather *common* there.

TOM: Perhaps that's it.

CHERRY: Ah! Ah! Now, d'you know the one thing that
matters in these – er – matters – *affaires du coeur* – affairs,
matters of the heart, whatever it is they call them? Admiration. Shall we have a drink, Tom? (*He really waits for* TOM'*s
permission.*)

TOM: Yes, let's.

    CHERRY *goes for the drinks from the barrel.*

CHERRY: Yes, admiration, it's the one thing you need.

TOM: I thought you needed to be good in bed.

CHERRY: Now I will tell you something that will surprise
you; man to man; since you're going into the army. You
can't even have much fun in bed with someone if you don't
admire them. That surprises you, doesn't it?

TOM: No.

CHERRY: Oh, yes, it does; you thought it was all – Jean
Harlow! Diana Dors! I know . . . Respect! Admiration!
Upstairs and downstairs! Ha ha. Drink up, old man!

TOM (*rather tickled by the invitation to equality*): All right.
What's to stop me admiring Carol?

CHERRY: Oh! Well! It's as clear as it could be to me. Cheerio,
Tom – we'd better call you Tommy Atkins now – Ha ha.

TOM: Cheerio.

    They drink.

CHERRY: Mmm – how can I put it? It's like a taste for anything – for cheese, say——

    Enter ISOBEL *from hall, wearing hat and coat which she takes
off.* CHERRY *breaks off. His aplomb drains out of him. He watches
her apprehensively.*

CHERRY (*experimental*): Hullo, dear.

ISOBEL (*warmly*): Hullo, Jim.

CHERRY (*immediately confident*): Where on earth have you
been?

ISOBEL: Down the High Street. (*Kisses him on the head.*) What's like a taste for cheese?

TOM: A taste for Carol, he says.

ISOBEL (*smiles*): Oh, Tom, I want to talk to Daddy.

CHERRY (*blustering*): Now just a minute, dear, I'm talking to Tom.

ISOBEL (*gently*): Sorry. (*She sits with him.*)

CHERRY: He wants to get married. (*From this point, the drink in him is more and more evident.*)

TOM (*glances at* ISOBEL, *laughs awkwardly*): I don't know about that——

CHERRY: Now don't back down! Stand your ground!

TOM: It's not a matter of——

CHERRY: Have some guts, man! You've no guts, Tom.

TOM: Nice of you to say so.

CHERRY: Well, have you?

　　ISOBEL *indicates to* TOM *to go.*

TOM (*going*): I've the guts I was born with, I suppose. (*Indignation makes his voice rise high.*)

CHERRY (*mimicking his inflection, loose and ugly*): Waapa waapa waapa waaaaaapa! (*Exit* TOM.) My goodness, if I had my time over again with that boy——

ISOBEL: He was being very nice, Jim——

CHERRY: He was being damned insolent!

ISOBEL: He's not been rude about the money?

CHERRY: The money? D'you mean to say you told him?

ISOBEL (*gentle*): He found the notes, Jim.

CHERRY: Oh, did he! That's very nice! Very nice! (*He drinks.*) Very discreet, very forbearing! (*Raises mug again.*)

ISOBEL: Darling, I want to—— (*Tentatively restraining his arm.*)

CHERRY: Don't! I may say, if you and Tom and Judy and – anyone else, if you think I'm going to eat humble pie the rest of my life because of what's happened today, you're very much mistaken! If anyone thinks because I've lost my job they can patronize and sneer and look down and *forgive* me, they'd better think again! Because I give you notice I shan't put up with it!

ISOBEL: Oh, that's *fine*, Jim! That's *right*!

CHERRY (*a little put off by this response*): Well, that's the way I feel. I don't want anyone's pity. That's not my way.

ISOBEL: Oh, that is fine, Jim. (*Takes an envelope from pocket of raincoat hanging on door and returns quickly to table.*)

CHERRY: What have you got there?

ISOBEL (*carefully*): Jim, I've been to the estate agent. They're going to sell the house for us. And with the money, we can buy your orchard.

CHERRY: Buy——? Buy? (*A good deal sobered, blows his nose.*)

ISOBEL: We can get two thousand five hundred for the house easily – you've always said you can buy an orchard for two thousand.

CHERRY: A small one——

ISOBEL: But big enough to make a living.

CHERRY: Not much of a living——

ISOBEL: But a living.

CHERRY: But it isn't necessary, Bel——

ISOBEL: It *is*, Jim.

CHERRY: It may not be; Gilbert Grass is trying to get me an agency——

ISOBEL: We'll do it together. I've got green fingers, you know that——

CHERRY: Listen! (*Explanatory.*) Gilbert's got my job and he's trying to get——

ISOBEL: If you could find a place, we could move down now. Straight away.

CHERRY (*protesting, defensive, alarmed, astonished*): But what about the agency?

A pause. ISOBEL *rethinks her approach. She begins again, without indignation, like a fact-finding commission.*

ISOBEL: Why? Why do you want an agency?

CHERRY: For the money, of course. If there's another reason for being an insurance agent, I don't know it.

ISOBEL (*again without bias either way*): But what do we want with money?

CHERRY: Oh, that's all very well, dear, when you're Tom's age. We're adults and we're not getting any younger——

ISOBEL: We've still got time. You can teach me what to do . . . (*She permits herself to urge him.*) Why not, Jim? Why not?

CHERRY: You're not being sensible – what about the children?

ISOBEL (*emotion begins to break through*): We've done all right by the children. We've done them proud.

CHERRY: They're still going to need help. It seems Judy hasn't got this job——

ISOBEL (*hard*): Then she can get another.

CHERRY: And is Tom to live on his grant?

ISOBEL (*hard*): It's been done before.

CHERRY: But if I can get an agency? I may not be much good in the office – in fact, I'll admit I'm damn bad in the office – but I've got a knack with the customers – no one's ever denied that. There's good money in selling insurance.

ISOBEL: But you don't like insurance!

CHERRY (*sage*): We can't all do just as we like, dear.

ISOBEL (*with much emotion*): But it's made us unhappy! *Another pause.*

CHERRY (*shaking his head*): It probably goes deeper than that.

ISOBEL: Perhaps; perhaps not. Why don't we try?

CHERRY: You know the old tag? – 'I change my skies but not my heart.' People have run to the other side of the world before now; it never does any good. No, I don't think that's the answer, Bel. (*With conscious heroism.*) I think we must stand our ground.

ISOBEL: 'Stand our ground.' (*Almost shouting.*) For heaven's sake, will you be serious? (*Goes and kneels by his chair, looking into his face anxiously.*) What's the matter, Jim? Can't you see how serious it is? What is it? Are you too drunk?

CHERRY: That's a nice thing to say.

ISOBEL (*nearly exhausted*): Oh, Lord, I'm tired . . .

CHERRY (*making hay, as so often before, with facile sympathy*): No wonder; I've given you a pretty filthy day. Now listen, dear; from this minute we'll have a fresh start. I mean it; I'm absolutely determined; we're going to turn over a new leaf.

ISOBEL (*quiet, but drearily bitter*): There are no leaves left in my book. . . . And there've been no leaves in your book for a long time. So don't sit there making promises we both know neither of us can carry out. Let's cut off and root up and go and do what you've always *wanted*! (*Another pause.*) (*Getting a bit desperate.*) Jim . . . Look, Jim . . . I don't know whether you remember, but from the first time I ever heard you speak, the first time I ever *saw* you, you were talking about Somerset.

CHERRY (*indignant*): I remember.

ISOBEL: I thought you were a bit of a poet. I wondered then why you didn't go back; but I thought you were like a fox or something in a kennel or somewhere. And I've thought so since when you've let me down, and you've let me down so often all my bones are tender . . . ! I've always thought: 'It isn't fair. He wants something. Just not having it takes it out of him so much, he wants it so much.' – And you've known that's what I've thought, Jim, because whenever it's happened and you've let me down you've always talked about the country – so now – let's go to it, Jim. Let's have it. Please!

CHERRY (*after a pause while he makes the withdrawal to another line of defence*): . . . Well, let me think about it. Give me time!

ISOBEL (*harsh*): Time. How much time? Jim, Jim, I want to know tonight.

CHERRY: Tonight? Why? Why tonight? Now that's just wilful, Isobel. Tonight's the same as any other night.

ISOBEL: That's why I want to know tonight. I mean every night's the same as any other night: but some nights people get born, don't they? Some nights——

TOM (*off*): Come on, Judy – come away!

JUDY (*off*): Let me go, Tom, leave me alone!

    TOM *enters garden ahead of* JUDY. TOM *stands on step.*

TOM: Go away, Judy. Go on, go away!

JUDY: I want Mummy.

TOM: I know what you want and you're not going in. (*Comes down persuasive.*) You don't need Carol, Jude . . . Look, let's make up a foursome. You bring one of the girls from the art school and I'll bring Sam Flemming.

JUDY: No! (*Attempts to get to door.*)

TOM (*intercepting*): Now I'm telling you, Judy, leave Dad alone.

JUDY: He did it. He drove her away!

TOM: Now listen – you haven't got that job and she's dropped you. It's as simple as that!

JUDY: No! It was father. You don't know what he's like to a woman.

    JUDY *darts to the door;* TOM *stops her; they scuffle.*

ISOBEL: Tom! Judy! What are you doing? (*Opens door.*)

JUDY (*crosses to her*): Mummy! Carol's gone!

TOM: Oh, crikey!

ISOBEL: Judy, Judy, I will not have hysterics. Daddy and I are very busy.

JUDY: Oh, yes. Daddy's been busy.

TOM: Shurrup!

JUDY: She left me because of – Daddy.

TOM: Hot air! Hot air!

JUDY: He kissed her! Mummy, he mauled her about!

TOM (*with profound disapproval, disgust*): Ah, Judy – Judy, you drive yourself. (*Exit* JUDY *to hall.*) Look . . . Mum—— (*The parents have been immobilized, incapacitated by all this.*

Now CHERRY *looks up.*) Half that was hot air.

CHERRY (*furious, choking*): Go and attend to your sister!

TOM (*firing at once*): Oh, drop dead, will you!

    Exit TOM. *Husband and wife sit side by side, a pause, at either end of the table, their faces expressing on the whole nothing more than exhaustion. It is the nadir of their marriage.* ISOBEL *clears her throat and speaks.*

ISOBEL: Now let me see . . .

CHERRY: Look, I hope you didn't believe that——

ISOBEL (*mild*): Why not? Wasn't it true?

CHERRY: Not like that! I did kiss her, yes – well, more like she kissed me, really——

ISOBEL: Assaulted you, did she?

CHERRY (*protesting, really anxious*): No! It was just foolery! We – I suppose – I dunno – we were larking about in here and she said if I could bend the big poker I could give her a kiss——

ISOBEL: And you tried. Silly chump. (*Looks at it.*) No one could bend that.

CHERRY: No, I suppose not. Jesse Bishop could.

ISOBEL (*flatly*): Was there ever such a person? Did he ever really exist?

CHERRY: Jesse Bishop? Why, yes, he lived in this little old cottage – with this big bed and the old clock ticking. He used to grow purple flowering broccoli. He could have bent it.

ISOBEL (*pursed*): Well, you can't; and if you take my advice, you won't try again.

CHERRY: No, I won't, I won't. (*Sentimental.*) I could bend it for you, Bel.

ISOBEL: I'm not asking you to do the impossible. (*Draws one of his magazines towards her.*) Come on, let's find an orchard.

CHERRY: You do understand about Carol, don't you?

ISOBEL: Yes, I think so . . . I know I haven't had to share you with a *woman*, Jim. God knows what it is that's had the best

of you! *This*, I think! (*Slapping the magazine.*) I hope! So
now let's go to it! . . . While there's still just a chance.

   CHERRY *begins to understand her, looks at magazine, turns
   a page mindlessly, looks up at her.*

CHERRY: You don't know what it'd be like! You'd hate it,
   Bel.

ISOBEL: I wouldn't. I promise.

CHERRY: We'd never make a success of it!

ISOBEL: That wouldn't matter.

CHERRY: Oh, be *reasonable*, Bel.

   Enter TOM *from hall.*

TOM: It's Mr Grass. He says it's important.

CHERRY (*out of his seat, at the hall door, calling*): Mr Grass?
   Come through, won't you? *Very* good – That's it.

   Enter GRASS. *He looks straight at* ISOBEL, *the underbred little
   conqueror, his lips pursed over a smile of the deepest satisfaction.*

GRASS: Good evening, Mrs Cherry.

   ISOBEL *turns away her head.*

CHERRY: *Very* good of you to drop by, Mr Grass.

GRASS: Oh, I haven't dropped by. I made a special journey.

CHERRY: Well, that *is* good of you. (*Deprecating.*) I suppose
   I can't get you to take a glass of this stuff?

GRASS (*an amused, disgusted smile at* CHERRY'*s cider*): Thank
   you, no. Well, we have an agency for you, Jim. Not mine,
   I'm afraid – that's gone to Hetherington – his district will
   be vacant now, of course, and we've decided to give you a
   crack at that.

CHERRY (*disappointed*): Oh. Well, that's a fair district. It's a
   good district, Bel. (*To* GRASS.) Isn't it?

GRASS: I don't know about it being good . . . (*With insolent
   solicitude.*) Have I come at an inconvenient time, Mrs
   Cherry?

ISOBEL (*bitterly*): You've come. (*Rouses herself slightly.*) Are
   you going to take it, Jim?

CHERRY (*as though she had broached an entirely new possibility in even raising the question*): Oh. Oh. Well now, dear, we can hardly pass it up.

ISOBEL (*rising*): And the orchard?

CHERRY: I'm afraid that'll have to wait a bit.

ISOBEL (*in a tone of complete finality*): I see. (*Going.*)

CHERRY: In another year or two——

ISOBEL (*turning*): Oh, no. Oh, no, no, no, no, no! (*Going.*)

CHERRY: Bel!

ISOBEL: I'm going, Jim. (*Walking through door.*) I'm leaving you.

    Exit ISOBEL.

TOM: Go on, Dad. Chuck him out!

CHERRY: What are you talking about?

TOM: You go after Mum.

CHERRY: Are you referring to Mr Grass?

TOM (*aghast*): For crying out loud!

CHERRY (*his breath begins to come short*): I've asked you a question! Ridiculous . . . I must apologize, Gilbert. As you can imagine, it's been a trying time for us all. Not that that excuses the behaviour of my son——

TOM (*gently*): Unless you're absolutely starkers, you'll get after Mum!

CHERRY (*begins to shake and raises his voice*): Not, I say, that it excuses the behaviour of my son!

GRASS (*subdued*): Is she serious?

CHERRY: Good heavens, no! I'm sorry you should have seen this, Gilbert. My wife's rather given . . . rather given . . .

TOM: Dad. Daddy, go and talk to her. Please!

CHERRY (*looks sightlessly towards* TOM): Ridiculous!

GRASS (*scared*): Well, I'll be off, Jim.

CHERRY (*smiling helplessly, his chest heaving*): No, don't go; there's no need. (*In tone of reassurance.*) She won't go . . . she's too sensitive, you know, always has been . . .

GRASS: I think I ought to——

Enter ISOBEL *with case. She takes mac from back of door.*

CHERRY (*lips trembling*): She's not going . . . to go. (GRASS *sidles quickly out of the side door.* CHERRY *turns on him suddenly.*) Little rat! (*And* GRASS *exits through trellis exactly like one. Soothing.*) Bel——

ISOBEL: I'm going, Jim. (*Begins to put on mac.*)

CHERRY: What've you got in your case? (*Infantile craftiness.*) They may be things of mine! You're not going to walk off with things of mine, Isobel; that's not fair! (*He looks round with idiotic satisfaction at this point he has made.*)

ISOBEL: Nothing of yours.

CHERRY (*paternal, implying a willingness to make any reasonable concession*): What's the matter?

ISOBEL: The matter? You, I suppose. Nothing particular. The whole of you.

CHERRY: It's that orchard, isn't it?

TOM (*tremulously striving to sound considered*): I don't think there's any need to go, mother.

ISOBEL (*tremulous too*): I'm sorry, Tom. I'll write you to-morrow.

Exit TOM *abruptly, closing hall door after him.* ISOBEL *turns slowly away.*

CHERRY (*seized by a new awareness*): All right, we'll buy an orchard, Bel!

ISOBEL (*harshly*): I don't want an orchard! I want——! (*Keeping back her tears.*) And neither do you! Your dream – you don't even have that!

CHERRY (*desperation seizes him*): I'm sorry! Bel, I'm sorry!

ISOBEL: You don't believe I'm going now! Do you? You're waiting for me to feel sorry for you—— (*She picks up her case.*)

CHERRY: (*panic-stricken*): No, Bel!

ISOBEL: Well, I'm not going to.

CHERRY: No, Bel!

ISOBEL: I'm not going to!

CHERRY: N-n-n-n-now, Bel—— What d'you want——?
Don't go. I'll do anything if you'll stay—— (*He darts away
and seizes the big poker.*) I'll bend it for you! (*Smiles idiotically.*)

ISOBEL: You see? You think I'm playing!

*She turns to get past him to the garden door; he dodges grotesquely
before her.*

CHERRY: All right – go, if you like; but watch me bend it,
Bel. I'll do it for you. You'll stay and watch, Isobel? (*She
makes a gesture of contemptuous dismissal.*) That's all very
well – this is made of five-eighths iron rod!

ISOBEL: Let me out! (*She goes into garden, turns. With steady
indignation.*) If your dream had been a real dream——

CHERRY: Bel!

ISOBEL: If you'd really wanted that – blossom.

CHERRY: Bel!

ISOBEL: But there – wasn't – even – that!

Exit.

CHERRY: Isobel! I'm going to bend the big one. Stay! Stay!
(*He stumbles down steps without poker and shouting after her.*)
I'll do it for you! Isobel, watch me! (*Goes back inside, seizes
poker, gabbling.*) *Watch* me! Watch me! Wait! Wait! Wait!
(*He puts the poker over the back of his neck and, seizing it at either
end, strains at it. He tugs at it savagely; staggers, steadies himself,
and tugs again, his breath very audible.*) I can't! I can't! (*He
puts out an abnormal effort and reels across the stage, smashing into
the table and chairs, some of which go over.* CHERRY *resumes
his desperate tugging at the bar.*) Oh God, it's hard! . . . Oh
God, it's hard! . . . It's too strong for me! . . . It's too . . . It's . . .
(*Breathing like a bellows, he stands centre stage, straddled, and
the bar begins to bend. The rear wall – scrim – begins to dissolve
into light. He struggles on. Through the scrim is seen an orchard
whose receding rows of black trunks support a bright cloud of
blossom reaching to the top of the set. The light on the blossom
increases and* CHERRY *stumbles, grotesque and earthy, before
his vision.*) Isobel! . . . I've done it! . . . I've done it! Isobel!

Isobel! Here – here – here – Oh! Beauty of Bath – Farmer's
Fortune – Sunset – You can smell it! And Cornish Maiden –
Isobel – Beauty – Cornish Maid – Sunset – Fortune—— (*He
crashes spread-eagled to the floor; he turns once over on to his back
and lies absolutely still with his eyes staring open while the vision
fades.*)

CURTAIN

A Man for all Seasons

SIR THOMAS MORE

More is a man of an angel's wit and singular learning; I know not his fellow. For where is the man of that gentleness, lowliness, and affability? And as time requireth a man of marvellous mirth and pastimes; and sometimes of as sad gravity: a man for all seasons

Robert Whittinton

He was the person of the greatest virtue these islands ever produced.

Samuel Johnson

PREFACE

THE BIT of English History which is the background to this play is pretty well known. Henry VIII, who started with everything and squandered it all, who had the physical and mental fortitude to endure a lifetime of gratified greeds, the monstrous baby whom none dared gainsay, is one of the most popular figures in the whole procession. We recognise in him an archetype, one of the champions of our baser nature, and are in him vicariously indulged.

Against him stood the whole edifice of medieval religion, founded on piety, but by then as moneyed, elaborate, heaped high and inflexible as those abbey churches which Henry brought down with such a satisfying and disgraceful crash.

The collision came about like this: While yet a Prince, Henry did not expect to become a King, for he had an elder brother, Arthur. A marriage was made between this Arthur and a Spanish Princess, Catherine, but Arthur presently died. The Royal Houses of Spain and England wished to repair the connection, and the obvious way to do it was to marry the young widow to Henry, now heir in Arthur's place. But Spain and England were Christian Monarchies and Christian law forbade a man to marry his brother's widow.

To be a Christian was to be a Churchman and there was only one Church (though plagued with many heresies) and the Pope was its head. At the request of Christian Spain and Christian England the Pope dispensed with the Christian law forbidding a man to marry his brother's widow, and when in due course Prince Henry ascended the English throne as Henry VIII, Catherine was his Queen.

For some years the marriage was successful; they respected and liked one another, and Henry took his pleasures elsewhere but lightly. However, at length he wished to divorce her.

The motives for such a wish are presumably as confused, inaccessible and helpless in a King as any other man, but here are three which make sense: Catherine had grown increasingly plain and intensely religious; Henry had fallen in love with Anne Boleyn; the Spanish alliance had become unpopular. None of these absolutely necessitated a divorce but there was a fourth that did. Catherine had not been able to provide Henry with a male child and was now presumed barren. There was a daughter, but competent statesmen were unanimous that a Queen on the throne of England was unthinkable. Anne and Henry were confident that between them they could produce a son; but if that son was to be Henry's heir, Anne would have to be Henry's wife.

The Pope was once again approached, this time by England only, and asked to declare the marriage with Catherine null, on the grounds that it contravened the Christian law which forbade marriage with a brother's widow. But England's insistence that the marriage had been null was now balanced by Spain's insistence that it hadn't. And at that moment Spain was well placed to influence the Pope's deliberations; Rome, where the Pope lived, had been very thoroughly sacked and occupied by Spanish troops. In addition one imagines a natural disinclination on the part of the Pope to have his powers turned on and off like a tap. At all events, after much ceremonious prevarication, while Henry waited with a rising temper, it became clear that so far as the Pope was concerned, the marriage with Catherine would stand.

To the ferment of a lover and the anxieties of a sovereign Henry now added a bad conscience; and a serious matter it was, for him and those about him.

The Bible, he found, was perfectly clear on such marriages as he had made with Catherine; they were forbidden. And the threatened penalty was exactly what had befallen him, the failure of male heirs. He was in a state of sin. He had been thrust into a state of sin by his father with the active help of the Pope. And the Pope now proposed to keep him in a state of sin. The man who would do that, it began to seem to Henry, had small claim to being the Vicar of God.

And indeed, on looking into the thing really closely, Henry found – what various voices had urged for centuries off and on – that the supposed Pope was no more than an ordinary Bishop, the Bishop of Rome. This made everything clear and everything possible. If the Pope was not a Pope at all but merely a bishop among bishops, then his special powers as Pope did not exist. In particular of course he had no power to dispense with God's rulings as revealed in Leviticus 18, but equally important, he had no power to appoint other Bishops; and here an ancient quarrel stirred.

For if the Pope had not the power to appoint bishops, then who did have, if not the King himself – King by the Grace of God? Henry's ancestors, all those other Henries, had been absolutely right; the Bishops of Rome, without a shadow of legality, had succeeded over the centuries in setting up a rival reign within the reign, a sort of long drawn usurpation. The very idea of it used to throw him into terrible rages. It should go on no longer.

He looked about for a good bishop to appoint to Canterbury, a bishop with no ambitions to modify God's ruling on deceased brothers' wives, yet sufficiently spirited to grant a divorce to his sovereign without consulting the Bishop of Rome. The man was to hand in Thomas Cranmer; Catherine was divorced, Anne married, and the Established Church of England was off on its singular way.

That, very roughly indeed, is the political, or theological, or politico-theological background to the play. But what of the social, or economic, or socio-economic, which we now think more important?

The economy was very progressive, the religion was very reactionary. We say therefore that the collision was inevitable, setting Henry aside as a colourful accident. With Henry presumably we set aside as accidents Catherine and Wolsey and Anne and More and Cranmer and Cromwell and the Lord Mayor of London and the man who cleaned his windows; setting indeed everyone aside as an accident, we say that the collision was inevitable. But that, on reflection, seems only to repeat that it happened. What is of interest is the way it happened, the way it was lived. For lived such collisions are. 'Religion' and 'economy' are abstractions which describe the way men live. Because men work we may speak of an economy, not the other way round. Because men worship we may speak of a religion, not the other way round. And when an economy collides with a religion it is living men who collide, nothing else (they collide with one another and within themselves).

Perhaps few people would disagree with that, put like that, and in theory. But in practice our theoreticians seem more and more to work the other way round, to derive the worker *from* his economy, the thinker *from* his culture, and we to derive even ourselves from our society and our location in it. When we ask ourselves 'What am I?' we may answer 'I am a Man' but are conscious that it's a silly answer because we don't know what kind of thing that might be; and feeling the answer silly we feel it's probably a silly question. We can't help asking it, however, for natural curiosity makes us ask it all the time of everyone else, and it would seem artificial to make ourselves the sole exception, would indeed envelop the mental image of our self in a unique silence and thus raise the question in a particularly disturbing way. So we answer of ourselves as we should of any other: 'This man here is a qualified surveyor, employed but with a view to partnership; this car he is driving has six cylinders and is almost new; he's doing all right; his opinions . . . ' and so on, describing ourselves to ourselves in terms more appropriate to somebody seen through a window. We think of ourselves in the Third Person.

To put it another way, more briefly; we no longer have, as past societies have had, any picture of individual Man (Stoic Philosopher, Christian Religious, Rational Gentleman) by which to recognise ourselves and against which to measure ourselves; we are anything. But if anything, then nothing, and it is not everyone who can live with that, though it is our true present position. Hence our willingness to locate ourselves from something that is certainly larger than ourselves, the society that contains us.

But society can only have as much idea as we have what we are about, for it has only our brains to think with. And the individual who tries to plot his position by reference to our society finds no fixed points, but only the vaunted absence of them, 'freedom' and 'opportunity'; freedom for what, opportunity to do what, is nowhere indicated. The only positive he is given is 'get and spend' ('get and spend – if you can' from the Right, 'get and spend – you deserve it' from the Left) and he did not need society to tell him that. In other words we are thrown back by our society upon ourselves at our lowest, that is at our least satisfactory to ourselves. Which of course sends us flying back to society with all the force of rebound.

Socially, we fly from the idea of an individual to the professional describers, the classifiers, the men with the categories and a quick ear for the latest sub-division, who flourish among us like priests. Individually, we do what we can to describe and classify ourselves and so assure ourselves that from the outside at least we do have a definite outline. Both socially and individually it is with us as it is with our cities – an accelerating flight to the periphery, leaving a centre which is empty when the hours of business are over.

That is an ambitious style of thinking, and pride cometh before a fall, but it was with some such ideas in mind that I started on this play. Or else they developed as I wrote it. Or else I have developed them in defence of it now that it is written. It is not easy to know what a play is 'about' until it is finished, and by then what it is 'about' is incorporated in it irreversibly and is no more to be separated from it than the shape of a statue is to be separated from the marble. Writing a play is thinking, not thinking about thinking; more like a dream than a scheme – except that it lasts six months or more, and that one is responsible for it.

At any rate, Thomas More, as I wrote about him, became for me a man with an adamantine sense of his own self. He knew where he began and left off, what area of himself he could yield to the encroachments of his enemies, and what to the encroachments of those he loved. It was a substantial area in both cases for he had a proper sense of fear and was a busy lover. Since he was a clever man and a great lawyer he was able to retire from those areas in wonderfully good order, but at length he was asked to retreat from that final area where he located his self. And there this supple, humorous, unassuming and sophisticated person set like metal, was overtaken by an absolutely primitive rigour, and could no more be budged than a cliff.

This account of him developed as I wrote: what first attracted me was a person who could not be accused of any incapacity for life, who indeed seized life in great variety and almost greedy quantities, who nevertheless found something in himself without which life was valueless and when that was denied him was able to grasp his death. For there can be no doubt, given the circumstances, that he did it himself. If, on any day up to that of his execution, he had been willing to give public approval to Henry's marriage with Anne Boleyn, he could have gone on living. Of course the marriage was associated with other things – the attack on the abbeys, the whole Reformation policy – to which More was violently opposed, but I think he could have found his way round that; he showed every sign of doing so. Unfortunately his approval of the

marriage was asked for in a form that required him to state
that he believed what he didn't believe, and required him to
state it on oath.

This brings me to something for which I feel the need to explain, perhaps apologise. More was a very orthodox Catholic
and for him an oath was something perfectly specific; it was
an invitation to God, an invitation God would not refuse, to
act as a witness, and to judge; the consequence of perjury was
damnation, for More another perfectly specific concept. So
for More the issue was simple (though remembering the out-
come it can hardly have been easy). But I am not a Catholic nor
even in the meaningful sense of the word a Christian. So by
what right do I appropriate a Christian Saint to my purposes?
Or to put it the other way, why do I take as my hero a man who
brings about his own death because he can't put his hand on an
old black book and tell an ordinary lie?

For this reason: A man takes an oath only when he wants
to commit himself quite exceptionally to the statement, when
he wants to make an identity between the truth of it and his
own virtue; he offers himself as a guarantee. And it works.
There is a special kind of shrug for a perjurer; we feel that the
man has no self to commit, no guarantee to offer. Of course it's
much less effective now that for most of us the actual words of
the oath are not much more than impressive mumbo-jumbo
than it was when they made obvious sense; we would prefer
most men to guarantee their statements with, say, cash rather
than with themselves. We feel – we know – the self to be an
equivocal commodity. There are fewer and fewer things
which, as they say, we 'cannot bring ourselves' to do. We can
find almost no limits for ourselves other than the physical, which
being physical are not optional. Perhaps this is why we have
fallen back so widely on physical torture as a means of
bringing pressure to bear on one another. But though few of
us have anything in ourselves like an immortal soul which we
regard as absolutely inviolable, yet most of us still feel some-

thing which we should prefer, on the whole, not to violate. Most men feel when they swear an oath (the marriage vow for example) that they have invested something. And from this it's possible to guess what an oath must be to a man for whom it is not merely a time-honoured and understood ritual but also a definite contract. It may be that a clear sense of the self can *only* crystallize round something transcendental in which case, our prospects look poor, for we are rightly committed to the rational. I think the paramount gift our thinkers, artists, and for all I know, our men of science, should labour to get for us is a sense of selfhood without resort to magic. Albert Camus is a writer I admire in this connection.

Anyway, the above must serve as my explanation and apology for treating Thomas More, a Christian Saint, as a hero of selfhood.

Another thing that attracted me to this amazing man was his splendid social adjustment. So far from being one of society's sore teeth he was, like the hero of Camus' *La Chute*, almost indecently successful. He was respectably not nobly born, in the merchant class, the progressive class of the epoch, distinguished himself first as a scholar, then as a lawyer, was made an Ambassador, finally Lord Chancellor. A visitors' book at his house in Chelsea would have looked like a Sixteenth Century *Who's Who*: Holbein, Erasmus, Colet, everybody. He corresponded with the greatest minds in Europe as the representative and acknowledged champion of the New Learning in England. He was a friend of the King, who would send for More when his social appetites took a turn in that direction and once walked round the Chelsea garden with his arm round More's neck. ('If my head would win him a castle in France, it should not fail to fall', said More.) He adored and was adored by his own large family. He parted with more than most men when he parted with his life, for he accepted and enjoyed his social context.

One sees that there is no necessary contradiction here; it is society after all which proffers an oath and with it the opportunity for perjury. But why did a man so utterly absorbed in his society, at one particular point disastrously part company from it? How indeed was it possible – unless there was some sudden aberration? But that explanation won't do, because he continued to the end to make familiar and confident use of society's weapons, tact, favour, and above all, the letter of the law.

For More again the answer to this question would be perfectly simple (though again not easy); the English Kingdom, his immediate society, was subservient to the larger society of the Church of Christ, founded by Christ, extending over Past and Future, ruled from Heaven. There are still some for whom that is perfectly simple, but for most it can only be a metaphor. I took it as a metaphor for that larger context which we all inhabit, the terrifying cosmos. Terrifying because no laws, no sanctions, no *mores* obtain there; it is either empty or occupied by God and Devil nakedly at war. The sensible man will seek to live his life without dealings with this larger environment, treating it as as a fine spectacle on a clear night, or a subject for innocent curiosity. At the most he will allow himself an agreeable *frisson* when he contemplates his own relation to the cosmos, but he will not try to live in it; he will gratefully accept the shelter of his society. This was certainly More's intention.

If 'society' is the name we give to human behaviour when it is patterned and orderly, then the Law (extending from empirical traffic regulations, through the mutating laws of property, and on to the great tabus like incest and patricide) is the very pattern of society. More's trust in the law was his trust in his society; his desperate sheltering beneath the forms of the law was his determination to remain within the shelter of society. Cromwell's contemptuous shattering of the forms of law by an unconcealed act of perjury showed how fragile for any individual is that shelter. Legal or illegal had no further meaning, the social references had been removed. More was offered to be sure, the chance of slipping back into the society which had thrust him out into the warring cosmos, but even in that solitude he found himself able to repeat, or continue, the decision he had made while he still enjoyed the common shelter.

I see that I have used a lot of metaphors. I know no other way to treat this subject. In the play I used for this theme a poetic image. As a figure for the superhuman context I took the largest, most alien, least formulated thing I know, the sea and water. The references to ships, rivers, currents, tides, navigation, and so on, are all used for this purpose. Society by contrast figures as dry land. I set out with no very well formed idea of the kind of play it was to be, except that it was not to be naturalistic. The possibility of using imagery, that is of using metaphors not decoratively but with an intention, was a side effect of that. It's a very far from new idea, of course. Whether it worked I rather doubt. Certainly no-one noticed. But I comfort myself with the thought that it's the nature of imagery to work, in performance at any rate, unconsciously. But if, as I think, a play is more like a poem than a straight narration, still less a demonstration or lecture. then imagery ought to be important. It's perhaps necessary to add that by a poem I mean something tough and precise, not something dreamy. As Brecht said, beauty and form of language are a primary alienation device. I was guaranteed some beauty and form by incorporating passages from Sir Thomas More himself. For the rest my concern was to match with these as best I could so that the theft should not be too obvious.

In two previous plays, *Flowering Cherry* and *The Tiger and the Horse*, I had tried, but with fatal timidity, to handle contemporaries in a style that should make them larger than life; in the first mainly by music and mechanical effects, in the second mainly by making the characters unnaturally articulate and unnaturally aware of what they 'stood for'. Inevitably these plays looked like what they most resembled, orthodox fourth wall

dramas with puzzling, uncomfortable, and, if you are un-
charitable, pretentious overtones. So for this one I took a his-
torical setting in the hope that the distance of years would give
me Dutch courage, and enable me to treat my characters in a
properly heroic, properly theatrical manner.

The style I eventually used was a bastardized version of the
one most recently associated with Bertolt Brecht. This is not the
place to discuss that style at any length, but it does seem to me
that the style practised by Brecht differs from the style taught by
Brecht, or taught to us by his disciples. Perhaps they are more
Royalist than the King. Or perhaps there was something
dæmonic in Brecht the artist which could not submit to Brecht
the teacher. That would explain why in the *Chalk Circle*, which
is to demonstrate that goodness is a terrible temptation, goodness triumphs very pleasantly. And why in *Mother Courage*,
which is to demonstrate the unheroic nature of war, the climax
is an act of heroism which Rider Haggard might have balked
at. And why in *Galileo*, which is to demonstrate the social and
objective value of scientific knowledge, Galileo, congratulated
on saving his skin so as to augment that knowledge, is made to
deny its value on the grounds that he defaulted at the moment
when what the world needed was for one man to be true to
himself. I am inclined to think that it is simply that Brecht was
a very fine artist, and that life is complicated and ambivalent.
At all events I agree with Eric Bentley that the proper effect of
alienation is to enable the audience *reculer pour mieux sauter*, to
deepen, not to terminate, their involvement in the play.

Simply to slap your audience in the face satisfies an austere
and puritanical streak which runs in many of his disciples and
sometimes, detrimentally I think, in Brecht himself. But it is a
dangerous game to play. It has the effect of shock because it is
unexpected. But it is unexpected only because it flies in the face
of a thoroughly established convention. (A convention which
goes far beyond naturalism; briefly, the convention that the
actors are there as actors, not as themselves.) Each time it is done

it is a little less unexpected, so that a bigger and bigger dosage will be needed to produce the same effect. If it were continued indefinitely it would finally not be unexpected at all. The theatrical convention would then have been entirely dissipated and we should have in the theatre a situation with one person, who used to be an actor, desperately trying to engage the attention – by rude gestures, loud noises, indecent exposure, fireworks, anything – of other persons, who used to be the audience. As this point was approached some very lively evenings might be expected, but the depth and subtlety of the notions which can be communicated by such methods may be doubted. When we use alienation methods just for kicks, we in the theatre are sawing through the branch on which we are sitting.

I tried then for a 'bold and beautiful verbal architecture', a story rather than a plot, and overtly theatrical means of switching from one locale to another. I also used the most notorious of the alienation devices, an actor who addresses the audience and comments on the action. But I had him address the audience in character, that is from within the play.

He is intended to draw the audience into the play, not thrust them off it. In this respect he largely fails, and for a reason I had not foreseen. He is called 'The Common Man' (just as there is a character called 'The King') and the word 'common' was intended primarily to indicate 'that which is common to us all'. But he was taken instead as a portrayal of that mythical beast The Man In The Street. This in itself was not so bad; after all he was intended to be something with which everyone would be able to identify. But once he was identified as common in that sense, my character was by one party accepted as a properly belittling account of that vulgar person, and by another party bitterly resented on his behalf. (Myself I had meant him to be attractive, and his philosophy impregnable.) What both these parties had in common – if I may use the word – is that they thought of him as somebody else. Wherever he might have been, this Common Man, he was certainly not in the theatre. He is harder to find than a unicorn. But I must modify that. He was not in the Stalls, among his fashionable detractors and defenders. But in the laughter this character drew down from the Gallery, that laughter which is the most heartening sound our Theatre knows, I thought I heard once or twice a rueful note of recognition.

September 1960

A Man For All Seasons *was first presented in London at the Globe Theatre on 1st July 1960 by H. M. Tennent Ltd, with the following cast:*

THE COMMON MAN	Leo McKern
THOMAS MORE	Paul Scofield
RICHARD RICH	John Bown
THE DUKE	Alexander Gauge
ALICE MORE	Wynne Clark
MARGARET MORE	Pat Keen
THE CARDINAL	Willoughby Goddard
THOMAS CROMWELL	Andrew Keir
THE AMBASSADOR	Geoffrey Dunn
HIS ATTENDANT	Brian Harrison
WILLIAM ROPER	John Carson
THE KING	Richard Leech
A WOMAN	Beryl Andrews
THE ARCHBISHOP	William Roderick

The play directed by
NOËL WILLMAN

Scenery and costumes by
MOTLEY

PEOPLE IN THE PLAY

THE COMMON MAN: Late middle age. He wears from head to foot black tights which delineate his pot-bellied figure. His face is crafty, loosely benevolent, its best expression that of base humour.

SIR THOMAS MORE: Late forties. Pale, middle-sized, not robust. But the life of the mind in him is so abundant and debonair that it illuminates the body. His movements are open and swift but never wild, having a natural moderation. The face is intellectual and quickly delighted, the norm to which it returns serious and compassionate. Only in moments of high crisis does it become ascetic – though then freezingly.

RICHARD RICH: Early thirties. A good body unexercised. A studious unhappy face lit by the fire of banked down appetite. He is an academic, hounded by self-doubt to enter the world of affairs, and longing to be rescued from himself.

DUKE OF NORFOLK: Late forties. Heavy, active, a sportsman and soldier held together by rigid adherence to the minimal code of conventional duty. Attractively aware of his moral and intellectual insignificance, but also a great nobleman, untouchably convinced that his acts and ideas are important because they are his.

ALICE MORE: Late forties. Born into the merchant class, now a great lady, she is absurd at a distance, impressive close to. Overdressed, coarsely fashioned, she worships society; brave, hot-hearted, she worships her husband. In consequence, troubled by and defiant towards both.

MARGARET MORE: Middle twenties. A beautiful girl of ardent moral fineness; she both suffers and shelters behind a reserved stillness which it is her father's care to mitigate.

CARDINAL WOLSEY: Old. A big decayed body in scarlet. An almost megalomaniac ambition unhappily matched by an excelling intellect, he now inhabits a lonely den of self-indulgence and contempt.

THOMAS CROMWELL: Late thirties. Subtle and serious; the face expressing not inner tension but the tremendous out-going will of the renaissance. A self-conceit that can cradle gross crimes in the name of effective action. In short an intellectual bully.

CHAPUYS: Sixties. A professional diplomat and lay ecclesiastic dressed in black. Much on his dignity as a man of the world he in fact trots happily along a mental footpath as narrow as a peasant's.

CHAPUYS' ATTENDANT: An apprentice diplomat of good family.

WILLIAM ROPER: Early thirties; a stiff body and an immobile face. Little imagination, moderate brain, but an all con-suming rectitude which is his cross, his solace, and his hobby.

THE KING: *Not* the Holbein Henry, but a much younger man, clean-shaven, bright-eyed, graceful and athletic. The Golden Hope of the New Learning throughout Europe. Only the levity with which he handles his absolute power fore-shadows his future corruption.

A WOMAN: Middle fifties. Self-opinionated, self-righteous, selfish, indignant.

CRANMER: Late forties. Sharp-minded, sharp-faced. He treats the Church as a job of administration and theology as a set of devices, for he lacks personal religiosity.

THE SET is the same throughout but capable of varied lightings, as indicated. Its form is finally a matter for the designer, but to some extent is dictated by the action of the play. I have visualised two galleries of flattened Tudor arches, one above the other, able to be entered from off-stage. A flight of stairs leading from the upper gallery to the stage. A projection which can suggest an alcove or closet, with a tapestry curtain to be drawn across it. A table and some chairs, sufficiently heavy to be congruous indoors or out.

THE COSTUMES are also a matter for the designer, but I have visualised no exact reproductions of the elaborate style of the period. I think plain colours should be used, thus scarlet for the Cardinal, grey for More, gold for the King, green for the Duke, blue for Margaret, black and pinstripe for the administrators Rich and Cromwell, and so on.

ACT ONE

When the curtain rises, the set is in darkness but for a single spot which descends vertically upon the COMMON MAN, *who stands in front of a big property basket.*

COMMON MAN: It is perverse! To start a play made up of Kings and Cardinals in speaking costumes and intellectuals with embroidered mouths, with me.

If a King, or a Cardinal had done the prologue he'd have had the right materials. And an intellectual would have shown enough majestic meanings, coloured propositions, and closely woven liturgical stuff to dress the House of Lords! But this!

Is this a costume? Does this say anything? It barely covers one man's nakedness! A bit of black material to reduce Old Adam to the Common Man.

Oh, if they'd let me come on naked, I could have shown you something of my own. Which would have told you without words——! . . . Something I've forgotten . . . Old Adam's muffled up.

(Backing towards basket.) Well, for a proposition of my own, I need a costume. *(Takes out and puts on the coat and hat of* STEWARD.*)*

Matthew! The Household Steward of Sir Thomas More! *(Lights come up swiftly on set. He takes from the basket five silver goblets, one larger than the others, and a jug with a lid, with which he furnishes the table. A burst of conversational merriment off; he pauses and indicates head of stairs.)* There's company to dinner. *(Finishes business at table.)*

All right! A Common Man! A Sixteenth-Century Butler!
(*He drinks from the jug.*) All right – the Six—— (*Breaks off,
agreeably surprised by the quality of the liquor, regards the jug
respectfully and drinks again.*) The Sixteenth Century is the
Century of the Common Man. (*Puts down the jug.*) Like all
the other centuries. (*Crossing right.*) And that's my proposition.

    *During the last part of the speech, voices off. Now, enter, at head
of stairs,* SIR THOMAS MORE.

STEWARD: That's Sir Thomas More.

MORE: The wine please, Matthew?

STEWARD: It's there, Sir Thomas.

MORE (*looking into jug*): Is it good?

STEWARD: Bless you, sir! *I* don't know.

MORE (*mildly*): Bless you too, Matthew.

    Enter RICH *at head of stairs.*

RICH (*enthusiastically pursuing an argument*): But every man has
his price!

STEWARD (*contemptuous*): Master Richard Rich.

RICH: But yes! In money too.

MORE (*gentle impatience*): No no no.

RICH: Or pleasure. Titles, women, bricks-and-mortar, there's
always something.

MORE: Childish.

RICH: Well, in suffering, certainly.

MORE (*interested*): Buy a man with suffering?

RICH: Impose suffering, and offer him – escape.

MORE: Oh. For a moment I thought you were being profound.
    (*Gives cup to* RICH.)

RICH (*to* STEWARD): Good evening, Matthew.

STEWARD (*snubbing*): 'Evening, sir.

RICH: No, not a bit profound; it then becomes a purely
practical question of how to make him suffer sufficiently.

MORE: Mm. . . . (*Takes him by the arm and walks with him.*) And
. . . who recommended you to read Signor Machiavelli?

(RICH *breaks away laughing; a fraction too long.* MORE *smiles.*)
No, who? (*More laughter.*) . . . Mm?

RICH: Master Cromwell.

MORE: Oh. . . . (*Back to the wine jug and cups.*) He's a very able
man.

RICH: And so he is!

MORE: Yes, I say he is. He's very able.

RICH: And he will do something for me, he says.

MORE: I didn't know you knew him.

RICH: Pardon me, Sir Thomas, but how much do you know
about me?

MORE: Whatever you've let me know.

RICH: I've let you know everything!

MORE: Richard, you should go back to Cambridge; you're
deteriorating.

RICH: Well, I'm not used! . . . D'you know how much I have
to show for seven months' work——

MORE: – Work?

RICH: – Work! Waiting's work when you wait as I wait,
hard! . . . For seven months, that's two hundred days, I have
to show: the acquaintance of the Cardinal's outer doorman,
the indifference of the Cardinal's inner doorman, and the
Cardinal's chamberlain's hand in my chest! . . . Oh – also
one half of a Good Morning delivered at fifty paces by the
Duke of Norfolk. Doubtless he mistook me for someone.

MORE: He was very affable at dinner.

RICH: Oh, everyone's affable *here*. . . . (MORE *is pleased.*) Also
of course, the friendship of Sir Thomas More. Or should I
say acquaintance?

MORE: Say friendship.

RICH: Well, there! 'A friend of Sir Thomas and still no office?
There must be something wrong with him.'

MORE: I thought we said friendship. . . . (*Considers; then.*) The
Dean of St Paul's offers you a post; with a house, a servant
and fifty pounds a year.

RICH: What? What post?

MORE: At the new school.

RICH (*bitterly disappointed*): A teacher!

MORE: A man should go where he won't be tempted. Look, Richard, see this. (*Hands a silver cup.*) Look.... Look....

RICH: Beautiful.

MORE: Italian.... Do you want it?

RICH: Why——?

MORE: No joke; keep it; or sell it.

RICH: Well I—— Thank you of course—— Thank you! Thank you! But——?

MORE: You'll sell it, won't you?

RICH: Yes, I think so. Yes, I will.

MORE: And buy, what?

RICH (*sudden ferocity*): Some decent clothes!

MORE (*with sympathy*): Ah.

RICH: I want a gown like yours.

MORE: You'll get several gowns for that I should think. It was sent to me a little while ago by some woman. Now she's put a lawsuit into the Court of Requests. It's a bribe, Richard.

RICH: Oh.... (*Chagrined.*) So you give it away of course.

MORE: Yes!

RICH: To me?

MORE: Well, I'm not going to keep it, and you need it. Of course – if you feel it's contaminated ...

RICH: No, no. I'll risk it. (*Both smile.*)

MORE: But, Richard, in office they offer you all sorts of things. I was once offered a whole village, with a mill, and a manor house, and heaven knows what else – a coat of arms I shouldn't be surprised. Why not be a teacher? You'd be a fine teacher. Perhaps, a great one.

RICH: And if I was who would know it?

MORE: You, your pupils, your friends, God. Not a bad public, that.... Oh, and a *quiet* life.

RICH (*laughing*): *You* say that!

MORE: Richard, I was commanded into office; it was inflicted on me. . . . (RICH *regards him.*) Can't you believe that?

RICH: It's hard.

MORE (*grimly*): Be a teacher.

Enter at head of stairs NORFOLK.

STEWARD (*to audience*): The Duke of Norfolk. A lord.

NORFOLK: I tell you he stooped from the clouds! (*Breaks off, irritable.*) Alice!

Enter instantly at head of stairs ALICE.

ALICE (*irritable*): Here!

STEWARD (*to audience*): Lady Alice. My master's wife.

NORFOLK: I tell you he stooped——

ALICE: – He didn't——

NORFOLK: – Goddammit he did——

ALICE: – Couldn't——

NORFOLK: – He *does*——

ALICE: – Not possible——

NORFOLK: – But *often*——

ALICE: Never.

NORFOLK: Well, damn my soul! (*Takes wine.*) Thank you, Thomas.

MORE (*to* MARGARET, *having appeared on gallery*): Come down, Meg.

STEWARD (*to audience, soapy*): Lady Margaret, my master's daughter, lovely; really lovely.

ALICE (*glances suspiciously at* STEWARD): Matthew, get about your business. (*Exit* STEWARD.) We'll settle this, my lord, we'll put it to Thomas. Thomas, no falcon could stoop from a cloud, could it?

MORE: I don't know, my dear; it sounds unlikely. I have seen falcons do some very splendid things.

ALICE: But how could he stoop from a cloud? He couldn't see where he was going.

NORFOLK: You see, Alice – you're ignorant of the subject; a real falcon don't *care* where he's going! Anyway, I'm talking to Meg. (*A sportsman's story*.) 'Twas the very first cast of the day, Meg; the sun was behind us. And from side to side of the valley like the roof of a tent, was solid mist——

ALICE: Oh, mist.

NORFOLK: Well, mist is cloud isn't it?

ALICE: No.

RICH: The opinion of Aristotle is that mists are an exhalation of the earth whereas clouds——

NORFOLK: He stooped five hundred feet! Like *that*! Like an Act of God isn't he, Thomas?

MORE: He's tremendous.

NORFOLK (*to* ALICE): Tremendous.

MARGARET: Did he kill the heron?

NORFOLK: Oh, the *heron* was *clever*. (*Very discreditable evidently*.) It was a royal stoop though. (*Sly*.) If you could ride, Alice, I'd show you.

ALICE (*hotly*): I can ride, my lord!

MORE: No, no, you'll make yourself ill.

ALICE: And I'll bet – twenty-five – no thirty shillings I see no falcon stoop from no cloud!

NORFOLK: Done.

MORE: Alice – you can't ride with *them*.

ALICE: God's body, Thomas, remember who you are. Am I a City Wife?

MORE: No indeed, you've just lost thirty shillings I think; there *are* such birds. And the heron got home to his chicks, Meg, so everything was satisfactory.

MARGARET (*smiling*): Yes.

MORE: What was that of Aristotle's, Richard?

RICHARD: Nothing, Sir Thomas – 'twas out of place.

NORFOLK (*to* RICH): I've never found much use in Aristotle myself, not practically. Great philosopher of course. Wonderful mind.

RICH: Exactly, Your Grace!

NORFOLK (*suspicious*): Eh?

MORE: Master Rich is newly converted to the doctrines of Machiavelli.

RICH: Oh *no*. . . !

NORFOLK: Oh, the Italian. Nasty book, from what I hear.

MARGARET: Very practical, Your Grace.

NORFOLK: You read it? Amazing girl, Thomas, but where are you going to find a husband for her?

MORE (MORE *and* MEG *exchange a glance*): Where indeed?

RICH: The doctrines of Machiavelli have been largely mistaken I think; indeed properly apprehended he has no doctrine. Master Cromwell has the sense of it I think when he says——

NORFOLK: You know Cromwell?

RICH: . . . Slightly, Your Grace. . .

NORFOLK: The Cardinal's Secretary. (*Exclamations of shock from* MORE, MARGARET *and* ALICE.) It's a fact.

MORE: When, Howard?

NORFOLK: Two, three days.

They move about uneasily.

ALICE: A *farrier's* son?

NORFOLK: Well, the Cardinal's a butcher's son, isn't he?

ALICE: It'll be up quick and down quick with Master Cromwell.

NORFOLK *grunts.*

MORE (*quietly*): Did you know this?

RICH: No!

MARGARET: Do you *like* Master Cromwell, Master Rich?

ALICE: He's the only man in London if he does!

RICH: I think I do, Lady Alice!

MORE (*pleased*): Good. . . . Well, you don't need *my* help now.

RICH: Sir Thomas, if only you knew how much, much rather I'd yours than his!

Enter STEWARD *at head of stairs. Descends and gives letter to* MORE *who opens it and reads.*

MORE: Talk of the Cardinal's Secretary and the Cardinal appears. He wants me. Now.

ALICE: At this time of the night?

MORE (*mildly*): The King's business.

ALICE: The Queen's business.

NORFOLK: More than likely, Alice, more than likely.

MORE (*cuts in sharply*): What's the time?

STEWARD: Eleven o'clock, sir.

MORE: Is there a boat?

STEWARD: Waiting, sir.

MORE (*to* ALICE *and* MARGARET): Go to bed. You'll excuse me, Your Grace? Richard? (*Kisses wife and daughter.*) Now you'll go to bed. . . . (*The* MORE *family, as a matter of routine, put their hands together and:*)

MORE ⎫ Dear Lord give us rest tonight, or if we must
ALICE ⎬ be wakeful, cheerful. Careful only for our
MARGARET ⎭ soul's salvation. For Christ's sake. Amen.

MORE: And Bless our Lord the King.

ALICE ⎫ And Bless our Lord the King.
MARGARET ⎭

ALL: Amen.

    And then immediately a brisk leave-taking, MORE *moving off below, the others mounting the stairs.*

MORE: Howard, are *you* at Richmond?

NORFOLK: No, down the river.

MORE: Then good night! (*Sees* RICH *disconsolate.*) Oh, Your Grace, here's a young man desperate for employment. Something in the clerical line.

NORFOLK: Well, if you recommend him.

MORE: No, I don't recommend him; but I point him out. (*Moving off.*) He's at the New Inn. You could take him there.

NORFOLK (*to* RICH *mounting stairs*): All right, come on.

RICH: My Lord.

NORFOLK: We'll hawk at Hounslow, Alice.

ALICE: Wherever you like. (ALICE *and* MARGARET *follow* NORFOLK.)

RICH (*at foot of stairs*): Sir Thomas! . . . (MORE *turns.*) Thank you.

MORE: Be a teacher. (*Moving off again.*) Oh—— The ground's hard at Hounslow, Alice!

NORFOLK: Eh? (*Delighted roar.*) That's where the Cardinal crushed his bum!

MORE ⎫
NORFOLK ⎬ Good night! Good night!
ALICE ⎪
RICH ⎭

They process off along the gallery.

MORE (*softly*): Margaret!

MARGARET: Yes?

MORE: Go to bed.

MARGARET *exits above,* MORE *exits below. After a moment* RICH *walks swiftly back down stage, picks up the goblet and is going off with it.*

STEWARD: Eh!

RICH: What——! Oh. . . . It's a gift, Matthew. Sir Thomas gave it to me. (STEWARD *takes it and regards it silently.*) He gave it to me.

STEWARD (*returns it*): Very nice present, sir.

RICH (*backing away with it*): Yes. Good night, Matthew.

STEWARD: Sir Thomas has taken quite a fancy to you, sir.

RICH: Er, here—— (*Gives money and goes.*)

STEWARD: Thank you, sir. . . . (*To audience.*) That one'll come to nothing. (*Begins packing props into basket. Pauses with cup in hand.*) My master Thomas More would give anything to anyone. Some say that's good and some say that's bad, but I say he can't help it – and that's bad . . . because some day someone's going to ask him for something that he wants to keep; and he'll be out of practice. (*Puts cloth with papers, ink, etc., on table.*) There must be something that he wants to keep. That's only Common Sense.

Enter WOLSEY. *He sits at table and immediately commences writing, watched by* COMMON MAN *who then exits. Enter* MORE.

WOLSEY (*writing*): It's half-past one. Where've you been? (*Bell strikes one.*)

MORE: One o'clock, Your Grace. I've been on the river.

WOLSEY *writes in silence, while* MORE *waits standing.*

WOLSEY (*still writing, pushes paper across table*): Since you seemed so violently opposed to the Latin dispatch, I thought you'd like to look it over.

MORE (*touched*): Thank you, Your Grace.

WOLSEY: Before it goes.

MORE (*smiles*): Your Grace is very kind. (*Takes and reads.*) Thank you.

WOLSEY: Well, what d'you think of it? (*He is still writing.*)

MORE: It seems very well phrased, Your Grace.

WOLSEY (*permits himself a chuckle*): The devil it does! (*Sits back.*)

And apart from the style, Sir Thomas?

MORE: I think the Council should be told before that goes to Italy.

WOLSEY: Would you tell the Council? Yes, I believe you would. You're a constant regret to me, Thomas. If you could just see facts flat on, without that moral squint; with just a little common sense, you could have been a statesman.

MORE (*little pause*): Oh, Your Grace flatters me.

WOLSEY: Don't frivel. . . . Thomas, are you going to help me?

MORE (*hesitates, looks away*): If Your Grace will be specific.

WOLSEY: Ach, you're a plodder! Take you altogether, Thomas, your scholarship, your experience, what are you? (*A single trumpet calls, distant, frosty and clear.* WOLSEY *gets up and goes and looks from window.*) Come here. (MORE *joins him.*) The King.

MORE: Yes.

WOLSEY: Where has he been? D'you know?

MORE: I, Your Grace?

WOLSEY: Oh, spare me your discretion. He's been to play in the muck again.

MORE (*coldly*): Indeed.

WOLSEY: Indeed! Indeed! Are you going to oppose me? (*Trumpet again.* WOLSEY *visibly relaxes.*) He's gone in. . . . (*Leaves window.*) All right, we'll plod. The King wants a son; what are you going to do about it?

MORE (*dry murmur*): I'm very sure the King needs no advice from me on what to do about it.

WOLSEY (*from behind grips his shoulder fiercely*): Thomas, we're alone. I give you my word. There's no one here.

MORE: I didn't suppose there was, Your Grace.

WOLSEY: Oh. (*Goes to table, sits, signs* MORE *to sit.* MORE *unsuspectingly obeys. Then, deliberately loud.*) Do you favour a change of dynasty, Sir Thomas? D'you think two Tudors is sufficient?

MORE (*starting up in horrified alarm*): – For God's sake, Your Grace——!

WOLSEY: Then the King needs a son; I repeat what are you going to do about it?

MORE (*steadily*): I pray for it daily.

WOLSEY (*snatches up candle and holds to* MORE'S *face. Softly*): God's death, he means it. . . . That thing out there's at least fertile, Thomas.

MORE: But she's not his wife.

WOLSEY: No, Catherine's his wife and she's as barren as brick. Are you going to pray for a miracle?

MORE: There *are* precedents.

WOLSEY: Yes. All right. Good. Pray. Pray by all means. But in addition to Prayer there is Effort. My effort's to secure a divorce. Have I your support or have I not?

MORE (*sits*): A dispensation was given so that the King might marry Queen Catherine, for state reasons. Now we are to ask the Pope to – dispense with his dispensation, also for state reasons?

WOLSEY: – I don't *like* plodding, Thomas, don't make me plod longer than I have to—— Well?

MORE: Then clearly all we have to do is approach His Holiness and ask him.

The pace becomes rapid.

WOLSEY: – I think we might influence His Holiness' answer——

MORE :– Like this? – (*The dispatch.*)

WOLSEY: – Like that and in other ways——

MORE: – I've already expressed my opinion on this——

WOLSEY: – Then, good night! Oh, your conscience is your own affair; but you're a statesman! Do you *remember* the Yorkist Wars?

MORE: Very clearly.

WOLSEY: Let him die without an heir and we'll have them back again. Let him die without an heir and this 'peace' you think so much of will go out like that! (*Extinguishes candle.*) Very well, then England needs an heir; certain measures, perhaps regrettable, perhaps not – (*pompous*) there is much in the Church that *needs* reformation, Thomas—— (MORE *smiles.*) All right, regrettable! But necessary, to get us an heir! Now explain how you as Councillor of England can obstruct those measures for the sake of your own, private, conscience.

MORE: Well . . . I believe, when statesmen forsake their own private conscience for the sake of their public duties . . . they lead their country by a short route to chaos. (*During this speech he relights the candle with another.*) And we shall have my prayers to fall back on.

WOLSEY: You'd like that, wouldn't you? To govern the country by prayers?

MORE: Yes, I should.

WOLSEY: I'd like to be there when you try. Who *will* deal

with all this – paper, after me? You? Fisher? Suffolk?

MORE: Fisher for me.

WOLSEY: Aye, but for the King. What about my Secretary, Master Cromwell?

MORE: Cromwell!

WOLSEY: You'd rather do it yourself?

MORE: Me rather than Cromwell.

WOLSEY: Then come down to earth. . . . And until then, allow for an enemy, here!

MORE: As Your Grace pleases.

WOLSEY: As God wills!

MORE: Perhaps, Your Grace. (*Mounting stairs.*)

WOLSEY: More! You should have been a cleric!

MORE (*amused, looking down from gallery*): Like yourself, Your Grace?

Exit MORE. WOLSEY *is left staring, then exits through the lower arches with candle, taking most of the light from the stage as he does so. But the whole rear of the stage now patterns with webbed reflections thrown from brightly moonlit water, so that the structure is thrown into black relief, while a strip of light descends along the front of the stage, which is to be the acting area for the next scene.*

An oar and a bundle of clothing are lowered into this area from above. Enter COMMON MAN; *he unties the bundle and dons the coat and hat of* BOATMAN.

MORE (*off*): Boat! (*Approaching.*) Boat!

BOATMAN (*donning coat and hat*): Here, sir!

MORE (*off*): A boatman please!

BOATMAN: Boat here, sir! (*He seizes the oar.*)

Enter MORE.

MORE (*peering*): Boatman?

BOATMAN: Yes, sir. (*To audience, indicating oar.*) A boatman.

MORE: Take me home.

BOATMAN (*pleasantly*): I was just going home myself, sir.

MORE: Then find me another boat.

BOATMAN: Bless you, sir – that's all right! (*Comfortably.*) I expect you'll make it worth my while, sir.

    CROMWELL *steps from behind arch, left.*

CROMWELL: Boatman, have you a licence?

BOATMAN: Eh? Bless you, sir, yes; I've got a licence.

CROMWELL: Then you know that the fares are fixed—— (*Turns to* MORE. *Exaggerated pleasure.*) Why, it's Sir Thomas!

MORE: Good morning, Master Cromwell. You work very late.

CROMWELL: I'm on my way to the Cardinal. (*He expects an answer.*)

MORE: Ah.

CROMWELL: You have just left him I think.

MORE: Yes, I have.

CROMWELL: You left him . . . in his laughing mood, I hope?

MORE: On the whole I would say, not. No, not laughing.

CROMWELL: Oh, I'm sorry. (*Backing to exit.*) I am one of your *multitudinous* admirers, Sir Thomas. A penny ha'penny to Chelsea, Boatman.

    Exit CROMWELL.

BOATMAN: The coming man they say, sir.

MORE: Do they? Well, where's your boat?

BOATMAN: Just along the wharf, sir.

    They are going, when enter CHAPUYS *and* ATTENDANT *from archway, Right.*

CHAPUYS: Sir Thomas More!

MORE: Signor Chapuys? You're up very late, Your Excellency.

CHAPUYS (*significantly*): So is the Cardinal, Sir Thomas.

MORE (*closing up*): He sleeps very little.

CHAPUYS: You have just left him, I think.

MORE: You are correctly informed. As always.

CHAPUYS: I will not ask you the subject of your conversation. . . . (*He waits.*)

MORE: No, of course not.

CHAPUYS: Sir Thomas, I will be plain with you . . . plain, that is, so far as the diplomatic decencies permit. (*Loudly.*) My master Charles, the King of Spain! (*Pulls* MORE *aside, discreet.*) My master Charles, the King of Spain, feels himself concerned in anything concerning his blood relation! He would feel himself insulted by any insult offered to his father's sister! I refer of course to Queen Catherine. (*Regards* MORE, *keenly.*) The King of Spain would feel himself insulted by any insult offered to Queen Catherine.

MORE: His feeling would be natural.

CHAPUYS (*consciously sly*): Sir Thomas, may I ask if you and the Cardinal parted, how shall I say, amicably?

MORE: Amicably. . . . Yes.

CHAPUYS (*a shade indignant*): In agreement?

MORE: Amicably.

CHAPUYS (*warmly*): Say no more, Sir Thomas; I understand.

MORE (*a shade worried*): I hope you do, Your Excellency.

CHAPUYS: You are a good man.

MORE: I don't see how you deduce that from what I've told you.

CHAPUYS (*holds up hand*): A nod is as good as a wink to a blind horse. I understand. You are a good man. (*Turns to exit.*) Dominus vobiscum.

Exit CHAPUYS. MORE *looks after him. Then:*

MORE (*abstracted*): . . . spiritu tuo . . .

BOATMAN (*mournful; he is squatting on the ground*): People seem to think boats stay afloat on their own, sir, but they don't; they cost money. (MORE *is abstractedly gazing over the audience.*) Take anchor rope, sir, you may not believe me for a little skiff like mine, but it's a penny a fathom. (MORE *is still abstracted.*) And with a young wife, sir, as you know. . . .

MORE (*abstracted*): I'll pay what I always pay you. . . . The river looks very black tonight. They say it's silting up, is that so?

BOATMAN (*joining him*): Not in the middle, sir. There's a channel there getting deeper all the time.

MORE: How is your wife?

BOATMAN: She's losing her shape, sir, losing it fast.

MORE: Well, so are we all.

BOATMAN: Oh yes, sir; it's common.

MORE (*going*): Well, take me home.

 Exit MORE.

BOATMAN: That I will, sir! (*Crossing to basket and pulling it out.*) From Richmond to Chelsea, downstream, a penny halfpenny . . . coat, hat . . . coat, hat (*goes for table-cloth*) from Chelsea to Richmond, upstream, a penny halfpenny. Whoever makes the regulations doesn't row a boat. Cloth. . . . (*Puts cloth in basket, takes out slippers.*) Home again.

 Lighting changes to MORE'S *house interior.*

 Enter MORE *on stairs. Sits wearily. Takes off hat, half takes off coat, but is too tired. It chimes three.* STEWARD *kneels to put on his slippers for him.*

MORE: Ah, Matthew. . . . Thank you. Is Lady Alice in bed?

STEWARD: Yes, sir.

MORE: Lady Margaret?

STEWARD: No, sir. Master Roper's here.

MORE (*surprised*): At this hour? . . . Who let him in?

STEWARD: He's a hard man to keep out, sir.

MORE: Where are they?

 Enter MARGARET *and* ROPER.

MARGARET: Here, Father.

MORE (*regarding them, resignedly*): Good morning, William. It's a little early for breakfast.

ROPER (*solidly*): I haven't come for breakfast, sir.

 MORE *looks at him and sighs.*

MARGARET: Will wants to marry me, Father.

MORE: Well, he can't marry you.

ROPER: Sir Thomas, I'm to be called to the Bar.

MORE (*warmly*): Oh, congratulations, Roper!

ROPER: My family may not be at the palace, sir, but in the City——

MORE: The Ropers were advocates when the Mores were selling pewter; there's nothing wrong with your family. There's nothing wrong with your fortune – there's nothing wrong with you – (*sourly*) except you need a clock——

ROPER: I can buy a clock, sir.

MORE: Roper, the answer's 'no'. (*Firmly.*) And will be 'no' so long as you're a heretic.

ROPER (*firing*): That's a word I don't like, Sir Thomas!

MORE: It's not a likeable word. (*Coming to life.*) It's not a likeable thing!

 MARGARET *is alarmed, and from behind* MORE *tries to silence* ROPER.

ROPER: The Church is heretical! Doctor Luther's proved that to my satisfaction!

MORE: Luther's an excommunicate.

ROPER: From a heretic Church! Church? It's a shop—— Forgiveness by the florin! Joblots now in Germany! . . . Mmm, and divorces.

MORE (*expressionless*): Divorces?

ROPER: Oh, half England's buzzing with that.

MORE: 'Half England.' The Inns of Court may be buzzing, England doesn't buzz so easily.

ROPER: It will. And is that a Church? Is that a Cardinal? Is that a Pope? Or Antichrist! (MORE *looks up angrily.* MARGARET *signals frantically.*) Look, what I know I'll say!

MARGARET: You've no sense of the *place*!

MORE (*rueful*): He's no sense of the time.

ROPER: I—— (*But* MORE *gently holds up his hand and he stops.*)

MORE: Listen, Roper. Two years ago you were a passionate Churchman; now you're a passionate – Lutheran. We must just pray, that when your head's finished turning your face is to the front again.

ROPER: Don't lengthen your prayers with *me*, sir!

MORE: Oh, one more or less. . . . Is your horse here?

ROPER: No, I walked.

MORE: Well, take a horse from the stables and get back home. (ROPER *hesitates*.) Go along.

ROPER: May I come again? (MORE *indicates* MARGARET.)

MARGARET: Yes. Soon.

ROPER: Good night, sir.

    Exit ROPER.

MARGARET: Is that final, Father?

MORE: As long as he's a heretic, Meg, that's absolute. (*Warmly*.) Nice boy. . . . Terribly strong principles though. I told you to go to bed.

MARGARET: Yes, why?

MORE (*lightly*): Because I intended you to *go* to bed. You're very pensive?

MARGARET: You're very gay. Did he talk about the divorce?

MORE: Mm? You know I think we've been on the wrong track with Will—— It's no good arguing with a Roper——

MARGARET: Father, did he?

MORE: *Old* Roper was just the same. Now let him think he's going *with* the current and he'll turn round and start swimming in the opposite direction. What we want is a really substantial attack on the Church.

MARGARET: We're going to get it, aren't we?

MORE: Margaret, I'll not have you talk treason. . . . And I'll not have you repeat lawyer's gossip. I'm a lawyer myself and I know what it's worth.

ALICE (*off. Indignant and excited*): Thomas——!

MORE: Now look what you've done.

    Enter ALICE *at head of stairs in nightgown.*

ALICE: Young Roper! I've just seen young Roper! On *my* horse.

MORE: He'll bring it back, dear. He's been to see Margaret.

ALICE: Oh – why you don't beat that girl!

MORE: No no, she's full of education – and it's a delicate commodity.

ALICE: Mm! And more's the pity!

MORE: Yes, but it's there now and think what it cost. (*He sneezes.*)

ALICE (*pouncing*): Ah! Margaret – hot water.

Exit MARGARET.

MORE: I'm sorry you were awakened, chick.

ALICE: I wasn't sleeping very deeply, Thomas – what did Wolsey want?

MORE (*innocent*): Young Roper asked for Margaret.

ALICE: What! Impudence!

MORE: Yes, wasn't it?

ALICE: Old fox! What did he want, Thomas?

MORE: He wanted me to read a dispatch.

ALICE: Was that all?

MORE: A Latin dispatch.

ALICE: Oh! Won't you talk about it?

MORE (*gently*): No.

Enter MARGARET *with cup which she takes to* MORE.

ALICE: Norfolk was speaking for you as Chancellor before he left.

MORE: He's a dangerous friend then. Wolsey's Chancellor, God help him. We don't want another. (MARGARET *takes cup to him; he sniffs it.*) I don't want this.

ALICE: Drink it. Great men get colds in the head just the same as commoners.

MORE: That's dangerous, levelling talk, Alice. Beware of the Tower. (*Rises.*) I will, I'll drink it in bed.

All move to stairs and ascend, talking.

MARGARET: Would you want to be Chancellor?

MORE: No.

MARGARET: That's what I said. But Norfolk said if Wolsey fell——

MORE (*no longer flippant*): If Wolsey fell, the splash would swamp a few small boats like ours. There will be no new Chancellors while Wolsey lives.

Exit above.

The light is dimmed there and a bright spot descends below. Into this bright circle from the wings is thrown the great red robe and the Cardinal's hat. The COMMON MAN *enters from the opposite wing and roughly piles them into his basket. He then takes from his pocket a pair of spectacles and from the basket a book. He reads:*

COMMON MAN (*reading*): 'Whether we follow tradition in ascribing Wolsey's death to a broken heart, or accept Professor Larcomb's less feeling diagnosis of pulmonary pneumonia, its effective cause was the King's displeasure. He died at Leicester on 29 November 1530 while on his way to the Tower under charge of High Treason.

'England's next Lord Chancellor was Sir Thomas More, a scholar and, by popular repute, a saint. His scholarship is supported by his writings; saintliness is a quality less easy to establish. But from his wilful indifference to realities which were obvious to quite ordinary contemporaries, it seems all too probable that he had it.'

Exit COMMON MAN. *As he goes, lights come up and a screen is lowered depicting Hampton Court.* CROMWELL *is sitting half-way up the stairs.*

Enter RICH, *crossing.*

CROMWELL: Rich! (RICH *stops, sees him, and smiles willingly.*) What brings you to Hampton?

RICH: I came with the Duke last night, Master Cromwell. They're hunting again.

CROMWELL: It's a kingly pastime, Master Rich. (*Both smile.*) I'm glad you found employment. You're the Duke's Secretary are you not?

RICH (*flustered*): My work *is* mostly secretarial.

CROMWELL (*as one making an effort of memory*): Or is it his librarian you are?

RICH: I do look after His Grace's library, yes.

CROMWELL: Oh. Well, that's something. And I don't suppose you're bothered much by His Grace – in the library? (RICH *smiles uncertainly*.) It's odd how differently men's fortunes flow. My late master died in disgrace, and here I am in the King's own service. There you are in a *comparative* backwater – yet the new Lord Chancellor's an old friend of yours.

(*He looks at him directly*.)

RICH (*uncertainly*): He isn't really my *friend*. . . .

CROMWELL: Oh, I thought he was. (*Gets up, prepares to go*.)

RICH: – In a sense he is.

CROMWELL (*reproachful*): Well, I always understood he set you up in life.

RICH :Master Cromwell – what *is* it that you do for the King?
         Enter CHAPUYS.

CHAPUYS (*roguish*): Yes, *I* should like to know that, Master Cromwell.

CROMWELL: Ah, Signor Chapuys. You've met His Excellency Rich? (*Indicates* CHAPUYS.) The Spanish Ambassador. (*Indicates* RICH.) The Duke of Norfolk's librarian.

CHAPUYS: But how should we introduce *you*, Master Cromwell, if we had the happiness?

CROMWELL: Oh sly! Do you notice how sly he is, Rich? (*Walks away*.) Well, I suppose you would call me (*suddenly turns*) 'The King's Ear'. . . . (*Deprecating shrug*.) It's a useful organ, the ear. But in fact it's even simpler than that. When the King wants something done, I do it.

CHAPUYS: Ah. (*Mock interest*.) But then why these Justices, Chancellors, Admirals?

CROMWELL: Oh, *they* are the constitution. Our ancient, English constitution. I merely do things.

CHAPUYS: For example, Master Cromwell. . . .

CROMWELL (*admiring*): Oho – beware these professional diplomats. Well now, for example; next week at Deptford we are launching the *Great Harry* – one thousand tons, four masts, sixty-six guns, an overall length of one hundred and seventy-five feet, it's expected to be very effective – all this you probably know. However you may not know that the King himself will guide her down the river; yes, the King himself will be her pilot. He will have assistance of course but he himself will be her pilot. He will have a pilot's whistle upon which he will blow, and he will wear in every respect a common pilot's uniform. Except for the material, which will be cloth of gold. These innocent fancies require more preparation than you might suppose and someone has to do it. (*He spreads his hands.*) Meanwhile, I do prepare myself for, higher things. I stock my mind.

CHAPUYS: Alas, Master Cromwell, don't we all? This ship for instance – it has fifty-six guns by the way, not sixty-six and only forty of them heavy—— After the launching I understand, the King will take his barge to Chelsea. (CROMWELL'S *face darkens during this speech.*)

CROMWELL (*sharply*): Yes——

CHAPUYS: – To——

CROMWELL ⎱ (*together*): Sir Thomas More's.
CHAPUYS ⎰

CHAPUYS (*sweetly*): Will you be there?

CROMWELL: Oh no – they'll talk about the divorce. (*It is* CHAPUYS' *turn to be shocked:* RICH *draws away uneasily.*) The King will ask him for an answer.

CHAPUYS (*ruffled*): He has given his answer!

CROMWELL: The King will ask him for another.

CHAPUYS: Sir Thomas is a good son of the Church!

CROMWELL: Sir Thomas is a man.

Enter STEWARD. *Both* CROMWELL *and* CHAPUYS *look towards him sharply, then back at one another.*

CHAPUYS (*innocently*): Isn't that his Steward now?

CROMWELL: I believe it is. Well, good day, Your Excellency.

CHAPUYS (*eager*): Good day, Master Cromwell. (*He expects him to go.*)

CROMWELL (*standing firm*): Good day. (*And* CHAPUYS *has to go.*)

    CROMWELL *walks side stage, with furtive and urgent beckonings to* STEWARD *to follow.* RICH *follows but hangs off. Meanwhile* CHAPUYS *and his* ATTENDANT *have gone behind screen, beneath which their legs protrude clearly.*

STEWARD (*conspiratorial*): Sir, Sir Thomas doesn't talk about it. (*He waits but* CROMWELL *remains stony.*) He doesn't talk about it, to his wife, sir. (*He waits again.*)

CROMWELL: This is worth nothing.

STEWARD (*significant*): But he doesn't talk about it to Lady Margaret – that's his daughter, sir.

CROMWELL: So?

STEWARD: So he's worried, sir. . . (CROMWELL *is interested.*) Frightened. . . . (CROMWELL *takes out a coin but pauses suspiciously.*) Sir, he goes *white* when it's mentioned!

CROMWELL (*hands coin*): All right.

STEWARD (*looks at coin; reproachful*): Oh, sir——!

CROMWELL (*waves him away*): Are you coming in my direction, Rich?

RICH (*still hanging off*): No no.

CROMWELL: I think you should, you know.

RICH: *I* can't tell you anything!

    Exit RICH *and* CROMWELL *left and right.* CHAPUYS *and* ATTENDANT *come from behind screen.*

CHAPUYS (*beckons* STEWARD): Well?

STEWARD: Sir Thomas rises at six, sir, and prays for an hour and a half.

CHAPUYS: Yes?

STEWARD: During Lent, sir, he lived entirely on bread and water.

CHAPUYS: Yes?

STEWARD: He goes to confession twice a week, sir. Parish priest. Dominican.

CHAPUYS: Ah. He is a true son of the Church.

STEWARD (*soapy*): That he is, sir.

CHAPUYS: What did Master Cromwell want?

STEWARD: Same as you, sir.

CHAPUYS: No man can serve two masters, Steward.

STEWARD: No indeed, sir; I serve *one*. (*He pulls to the front an enormous cross until then hanging at his back on a length of string – a caricature of the ebony cross worn by* CHAPUYS.)

CHAPUYS: Good, simple man. Here. (*Gives coin. Going.*) Peace be with you.

STEWARD: And with you, sir.

CHAPUYS: Our Lord watch you.

STEWARD: You too, sir. (*Exit* CHAPUYS.) That's a very religious man.

   Enter RICH.

RICH: What does Signor Chapuys want, Matthew?

STEWARD: I've no idea, sir.

RICH (*gives coin*): What did you tell him?

STEWARD: I told him that Sir Thomas says his prayers and goes to confession.

RICH: Why that?

STEWARD: That's what he wanted to know, sir. I mean I could have told him any number of things about Sir Thomas – that he has rheumatism, prefers red wine to white, is easily sea-sick, fond of kippers, afraid of drowning. But that's what he wanted to know, sir.

RICH: What did he say?

STEWARD: He said that Sir Thomas is a good churchman, sir.

RICH (*going*): Well, that's true, isn't it?

STEWARD: I'm just telling you what he said, sir. Master Cromwell went that way, sir.

RICH (*furious*): Did I ask you which way Master Cromwell went?

   Exit RICH *opposite*.

STEWARD (*to audience, thoughtfully*): The great thing's not to get out of your depth. . . . What I can tell them's common

knowledge! But now they've given money for it and everyone wants value for his money. They'll make a secret of it
now to prove they've not been bilked. . . . They'll make it
a secret by making it dangerous. . . . Mm. . . . Oh, when I
can't touch the bottom I'll go deaf, blind and dumb. (*Holds
out coins.*) And that's more than I *earn* in a fortnight!

*On this; a fanfare of trumpets; plainsong; the rear of the stage
becomes a source of glittering blue light; Hampton Court is hoisted
out of sight, and other screens are lowered one after the other, each
masking the rest, bearing respectively sunflowers, hollyhocks, roses,
magnolias. When the fanfare ceases the plainsong goes on quietly,
and the screens throw long shadows like the shadows of trees, and*
NORFOLK, ALICE, MARGARET, *erupt on to the stage.*

ALICE (*distressed*): No sign of him, my lord!
NORFOLK: God's body, Alice, he must be found!
ALICE (*to* MEG): He *must* be in the house!
MARGARET: He's *not* in the house, Mother!
ALICE: Then he must be here in the garden!

They 'search' among the screens.
NORFOLK: He takes things too far, Alice.
ALICE: Do I not know it?
NORFOLK: It will end badly for him!
ALICE: I know that too!

They 'notice' the STEWARD.
MARGARET ⎫   ⎧ Matthew! Where's my father?
ALICE   ⎬ (*together*): ⎨ Where is Sir Thomas?
NORFOLK ⎭   ⎩ Where's your master?

Fanfare, shorter but nearer.
NORFOLK (*despairing*): Oh my God.
ALICE: Oh Jesus!
STEWARD: My lady – the King?
NORFOLK: Yes, fool! (*Threatening.*) And if the King arrives
and the Chancellor's not here——
STEWARD: Sir, my lady, it's not *my* fault!
NORFOLK (*quietly displeased*): Lady Alice, Thomas'll get no

good of it. This is not how Wolsey made himself great.

ALICE (*stiffly*): Thomas has his own way of doing things, my lord!

NORFOLK (*testy*): Yes yes, Thomas is unique; but where *is* Thomas?

STEWARD *swings onstage small gothic door. Plainsong. All run to the door.* NORFOLK *opens it.*

ALICE: Thomas!

STEWARD: Sir!

MARGARET: Father!

NORFOLK (*indignant*): My Lord Chancellor!

Enter MORE *through the doorway. He blinks in the light. He is wearing a cassock. Shuts door behind him.*

What sort of fooling is this? Does the King visit you every day.

MORE: No, but I go to Vespers most days.

NORFOLK: He's here!

MORE: But isn't this visit *meant* to be a surprise?

NORFOLK (*grimly*): For you, yes, not for him.

MARGARET: Father. . . . (*Indicates cassock.*)

NORFOLK: Yes – d'you propose to meet the King disguised as a parish clerk? (*They fall upon him and drag the cassock over his head.*) A parish clerk, my lord Chancellor! You dishonour the King and his office!

MORE (*appearing momentarily in the folds of the cassock*): The service of God is not a dishonour to any office. (*The cassock is pulled off.*) Believe me, my friend, I do not belittle the honour His Majesty is doing me. (*Briskly.*) Well! That's a lovely dress, Alice; so's that, Margaret. (*Looks at* NORFOLK.) I'm a dowdy bird, aren't I? (*Looks at* ALICE.) Calm yourself, Alice, we're all ready now.

He turns about and we see that his gown is caught up behind him revealing his spindly legs in long hose laced up at the thighs.

ALICE: Thomas!

MARGARET *laughs.*

MORE: What's the matter? (*Turns round again and his women folk pursue him to pull down the gown while* NORFOLK *throws his hands in the air. Expostulation, explanation, exclamation, overlapping in a babble.*)

NORFOLK: – By God you can be hare-brained——!

MARGARET: – Be still——!

ALICE: – Oh, Thomas! Thomas!——

NORFOLK: – What whim possessed you——

MORE: – 'Twas not a whim——!

ALICE: – Your second best stockings——!

MARGARET: – Father, be still——!

NORFOLK: – Oh, enough's enough——!

MORE: – Haven't you done——!

    HENRY, *in a cloth of gold, runs out of the sunlight half-way down the steps, and blows a blast on his pilot's whistle. All kneel. In the silence he descends slowly to their level, blowing softly . . .*

MORE: Your Majesty does my house more honour than I fear my household can bear.

HENRY: No ceremony, Thomas! No ceremony! (*They rise.*) A passing fancy – I happened to be on the river. (*Holds out shoe, proudly.*) Look, mud.

MORE: We do it in better style, Your Grace, when we come by the road.

HENRY: Oh, the road! There's the road for me, Thomas, the river; *my* river. . . . By heaven what an evening! I fear we come upon you unexpectedly, Lady Alice.

ALICE (*shocked*): Oh no, Your Grace – (*remembering*) that is yes, but we are ready for you – ready to entertain Your Grace that is.

MORE: This is my daughter Margaret, sir. She has not had the honour to meet Your Grace. (*She curtseys low.*)

HENRY (*looks her over, then*): Why, Margaret, they told me you were a scholar.

    MARGARET *is confused.*

MORE: Answer, Margaret.

MARGARET: Among women I pass for one Your Grace.
(NORFOLK *and* ALICE *exchange approving glances.*)

HENRY: Antiquone modo Latine loqueris, an Oxoniensi?
[Is your Latin the old Latin, or Oxford Latin?]

MARGARET: Quem me docuit pater, Domine.
[My father's Latin, Sire.]

HENRY: Bene. Optimus est. Graecamne linguam quoque te docuit?
[Good. That is the best. And has he taught you Greek too?]

MARGARET: Graecam me docuit non pater meus sed mei patris amicus, Johannes Coletus, Sancti Pauli Decanus. In litteris Graecis tamen, non minus quam Latinis, ars magistri minuitur discipuli stultitia.
[Not my father, Sire, but my father's friend, John Colet, Dean of St Paul's. But it is with the Greek as it is with the Latin; the skill of the master is lost in the pupil's lack of it.]
Her Latin is better than his; he is not altogether pleased.

HENRY: Ho! (*He walks away from her, talking; she begins to rise from her curtsey,* MORE *gently presses her down again before the King turns.*) Take care, Thomas: 'There is no end to the making of books and too much reading is a weariness of the flesh.' (*Back to* MARGARET.) Can you dance, too?

MARGARET: Not well, Your Grace.

HENRY: Well, *I* dance superlatively! (*Plants his leg before her face.*) That's a dancer's *leg,* Margaret! (*She has the wit to look straight up and smile at him. All good humour he pulls her to her feet; sees* NORFOLK *grinning the grin of a comrade.*) Hey, Norfolk? (*Indicates* NORFOLK'S *leg with much distaste.*) Now *that's* a wrestler's leg. But I can throw him. (*Seizes* NORFOLK.) Shall I show them, Howard? (NORFOLK *is alarmed for his dignity. To* MARGARET.) Shall I?

MARGARET (*looking at* NORFOLK, *gently*): No, Your Grace.

HENRY (*releases* NORFOLK, *seriously*): You are gentle. (*To* MORE, *approving.*) That's good. (*To* MARGARET.) You shall read to me. (MARGARET *is about to demur.*) No no, you shall read to me. Lady Alice, the river's given me an appetite.

ALICE: If Your Grace would share a very simple supper.

HENRY: It would please me to. (*Preparing to lead off, sees* MARGARET *again.*) I'm something of a scholar too; did you know?

MARGARET: All the world knows Your Grace's Book, asserting the seven sacraments of the Church.

HENRY: Ah yes. Between ourselves, your father had a hand in that; eh, Thomas?

MORE: Here and there, Your Grace. In a minor capacity.

HENRY (*looking at him*): He seeks to shame me with his modesty. . . . (*Turns to* ALICE.) On second thoughts we'll follow, Lady Alice, Thomas and I will follow. (*He waves them off. They bow, withdraw, prepare for second bow.*) Wait! (*Raises whistle to lips; then:*) Margaret, are you fond of music?

MARGARET: Yes, Your Grace.

HENRY (*beckons her to him; holds out whistle*): Blow. (*She is uncertain.*) Blow. (*She does.*) Louder! (*She does and at once music without, stately and oversweet. Expressions of pleasure all round.*) I brought them with me, Lady Alice; take them in! (*Exit all but* MORE *and* HENRY. *The music continues receding.*) Listen to this, Thomas. (*He walks about, the auditor, beating time.*) Do you know it?

MORE: No, Your Grace, I——

HENRY: Sh! (MORE *is silent;* HENRY *goes on with his listening.*) . . . I launched a ship today, Thomas.

MORE: Yes, Your Grace, I——

HENRY: *Listen*, man, *listen*. . . . (*A silence.*) . . . The *Great Harry* . . . I steered her, Thomas, under sail.

MORE: You have many accomplishments, Your Grace.

HENRY (*holds up a finger for silence. . . . A silence*): A great experience. (MORE *keeps silent.*) . . . A great experience, Thomas.

MORE: Yes, Your Grace.

The music is growing fainter.

HENRY: I am a fool.

MORE: How so, Your Grace?

HENRY (*a silence, during which the music fades to silence*): . . . What else but a fool to live in a Court, in a licentious mob – when I have friends, with gardens.

MORE: Your Grace——

HENRY: No courtship, no ceremony, Thomas. Be seated. You *are* my friend are you not? (MORE *sits*.)

MORE: Your Majesty.

HENRY: And thank God I have a friend for my Chancellor. (*Laughing*.) Readier to be friends I trust than he was to be Chancellor.

MORE: My own knowledge of my poor abilities——

HENRY: I will judge of your abilities, Thomas. . . . Did you know that Wolsey named you for Chancellor?

MORE: Wolsey!

HENRY: Aye; before he died. Wolsey named you and Wolsey was no fool.

MORE: He was a statesman of incomparable ability, Your Grace.

HENRY: Was he? Was he so? (*Rises*.) Then why did he fail me? Be seated – it was villainy then! Yes villainy. I was right to break him; he was all pride, Thomas; a proud man; pride right through. And he failed me! (MORE *opens his mouth*.) He failed me in the one thing that mattered! The one thing that matters, Thomas, then or now. And why? He wanted to be Pope! Yes, he wanted to be the Bishop of Rome. I'll tell you something, Thomas, and you can check this for yourself – it was never merry in England while we had Cardinals amongst us. (*He nods significantly at* MORE *who lowers his eyes*.) But look now – (*walking away*) – I shall forget the feel of that . . . great tiller under my hands . . . I took her down to Dogget's Bank, went about and brought her up in Tilbury Roads. A man could sail clean round the world in that ship.

MORE (*affectionate admiration*): Some men could, Your Grace.

HENRY (*off-hand*): Touching this matter of my divorce, Thomas; have you thought of it since we last talked?

MORE: Of little else.

HENRY: Then you see your way clear to me?

MORE: That you should put away Queen Catherine, sire? Oh, alas (*thumps table in distress*), as I think of it I see so clearly that I can *not* come with Your Grace that my endeavour is not to think of it at all.

HENRY: Then you have not thought enough! . . . (*With real appeal.*) Great God, Thomas, why do you hold out against me in the desire of my heart – the very wick of my heart?——

MORE (*draws up sleeve, baring his arm*): There is my right arm. (*A practical proposition.*) Take your dagger and saw it from my shoulder, and I will laugh and be thankful, if by that means I can come with Your Grace with a clear conscience.

HENRY (*uncomfortably pulls at the sleeve*): I know it, Thomas, I know. . . .

MORE (*rises, formally*): I crave pardon if I offend.

HENRY (*suspiciously*): Speak then.

MORE: When I took the Great Seal your Majesty promised not to pursue me on this matter.

HENRY: Ha! So I break my word, Master More! No no, I'm joking . . . I joke roughly. . . . (*Wanders away.*) I often think I'm a rough fellow. . . . Yes, a rough young fellow. (*Shakes his head indulgently.*) Be seated. . . . That's a magnolia. We have one like it at Hampton – not so red as that though. Ha – I'm in an excellent frame of mind. (*Glances at the magnolia.*) Beautiful. (*Reasonable, pleasant.*) You must consider, Thomas, that I stand in peril of my soul. It was no marriage; she was my brother's widow. Leviticus: 'Thou shalt not uncover the nakedness of thy brother's wife.' Leviticus, Chapter 18, Verse 16.

MORE: Yes, Your Grace. But Deuteronomy——

HENRY (*triumphant*): Deuteronomy's ambiguous!

MORE (*bursting out*): Your Grace, I'm not fit to meddle in these matters – to me it seems a matter for the Holy See——

HENRY (*reproving*): Thomas, Thomas, does a man need a Pope to tell him when he's sinned? It was a sin, Thomas; I admit it; I repent. And God has punished me; I have no son. . . . Son after son she's borne me, Thomas, all dead at birth, or dead within the month; I never saw the hand of God so clear in anything. . . . I have a daughter, she's a good child, a well-set child—— But I have no son. (*Flares up.*) It is my bounden *duty* to put away the Queen and all the Popes back to St Peter shall not come between me and my duty! How is it that you cannot see? Everyone else does.

MORE (*eagerly*): Then why does Your Grace need my poor support?

HENRY: Because you are honest. What's more to the purpose, you're known to be honest. . . . There are those like Norfolk who follow me because I wear the crown, and there are those like Master Cromwell who follow me because they are jackals with sharp teeth and I am their lion, and there is a mass that follows me because it follows anything that moves – and there is you.

MORE: I am sick to think how much I must displease Your Grace.

HENRY: No, Thomas, I respect your sincerity. Respect? Oh, man it's water in the desert. . . . How did you like our music? That air they played, it had a certain – well, tell me what you thought of it.

MORE (*relieved at this turn; smiling*): Could it have been Your Grace's own?

HENRY (*smiles back*): Discovered! Now I'll never know your true opinion. And that's irksome, Thomas, for we artists, though we love praise, yet we love truth better.

MORE (*mildly*): Then I will tell Your Grace truly what I thought of it.

HENRY (*a little disconcerted*): Speak then.

MORE: To me it seemed – delightful.

HENRY: Thomas – I chose the right man for Chancellor.

MORE: I must in fairness add that my taste in music is reputedly deplorable.

HENRY: Your taste in music is excellent. It exactly coincides with my own. Ah music! Music! Send them back without me, Thomas; I will live here in Chelsea and make music.

MORE: My house is at Your Grace's disposal.

HENRY: Thomas, you understand me; we will stay here together and make music.

MORE: Will your Grace honour my roof at dinner?

HENRY (*has walked away, blowing moodily on his whistle*): Mm? Yes; I expect I'll bellow for you. . . .

MORE: My wife will be more——

HENRY: Yes, yes. (*He turns, his face set.*) Touching this other business, mark you, Thomas, I'll have no opposition.

MORE (*sadly*): Your Grace?

HENRY: No opposition I say! No opposition! Your conscience is your own affair; but you are my Chancellor! There, you have my word – I'll leave you out of it. But I don't take it kindly, Thomas, and I'll have no opposition! I see how it will be; the Bishops will oppose me. The full-fed, hypocritical, 'Princes of the *Church*'! Ha! As for the Pope! – Am I to burn in Hell because the Bishop of Rome with the Emperor's knife to his throat, mouths me Deuteronomy? Hypocrites! They're all hypocrites! Mind they do not take you in, Thomas! Lie low if you will, but I'll brook no opposition – no words, no signs, no letters, no pamphlets – mind that, Thomas – no writings against me!

MORE: Your Grace is unjust. I am Your Grace's loyal minister. If I cannot serve Your Grace in this great matter of the Queen——

HENRY: I have no Queen! Catherine is not my wife and no priest can make her so, and they that say she is my wife are not only liars . . . but Traitors! Mind it, Thomas!

MORE: Am I a babbler, Your Grace? (*But his voice is unsteady.*)

HENRY: You are stubborn. . . . (*Wooingly.*) If you could come with me, you are the man I would soonest raise – yes, with my own hand.

MORE (*covers his face*): Oh, Your Grace overwhelms me!
    A complicated chiming of little bells is heard.

HENRY: What's that?

MORE: Eight o'clock, Your Grace.

HENRY (*uneasily eyeing* MORE): Oh, lift yourself up, man – have I not promised? (MORE *braces.*) Shall we eat?

MORE: If Your Grace pleases. (*Recovering.*) What will Your Grace sing for us? (*They approach the stairs.*)

HENRY: Eight o'clock you said? Thomas, the tide will be changing. I was forgetting the tide. I'd better go.

MORE (*gravely*): I'm sorry, Your Grace.

HENRY: I must catch the tide or I'll not get back to Richmond till. . . . No, don't come. Tell Norfolk. (*He has his foot on the bottom stair when enter* ALICE *and* STEWARD *above.*) Oh, Lady Alice, I must go. (ALICE *descends, her face serious.*) I want to catch the tide. To tell the truth, Lady Alice, I have forgotten in your haven here how time flows past outside. Affairs call me to court and so I give you my thanks and say Good night.

(*He mounts.*)

MORE ⎫
       ⎬ (*bowing*): Good night, Your Grace.
ALICE ⎭

    Exit HENRY, *above.*

ALICE: What's this? You crossed him.

MORE: Somewhat.

ALICE: Why?

MORE (*apologetic*): I couldn't find the other way.

ALICE (*angrily*): You're too nice altogether, Thomas!

MORE: Woman, mind your house.

ALICE: I *am* minding my house!

MORE (*takes in her anxiety*): Well, Alice. What would you *want* me to do?

ALICE: Be ruled! If you won't rule him, be ruled!

MORE (*quietly*): I neither could nor would rule my King. (*Pleasantly.*) But there's a little . . . little, area . . . where I must rule myself. It's very little – less to him than a tennis court. (*Her face is still full of foreboding: he sighs.*) Look; it was eight o'clock. At eight o'clock, Lady Anne likes to dance.

ALICE (*relieved*): Oh?

MORE: I think so.

ALICE (*irritation*): And *you* stand between them!

MORE: I? What stands between them is a sacrament of the Church. I'm less important than you think, Alice.

ALICE (*appealing*): Thomas, stay friends with him.

MORE: Whatever can be done by smiling, you may rely on me to do.

ALICE: You don't know *how* to flatter.

MORE: I flatter very well! My recipe's beginning to be widely copied. It's the basic syrup with just a soupçon of discreet impudence. . . .

ALICE (*still uneasy*): I wish he'd eaten here. . . .

MORE: Yes – we shall be living on that 'simple supper' of yours for a fortnight. (*She won't laugh.*) Alice. . . . (*She won't turn.*) Alice. . . . (*She turns.*) Set your mind at rest – this (*tapping himself*) is not the stuff of which martyrs are made.

    Enter above, quickly, ROPER.

ROPER: Sir Thomas!

MORE (*winces*): Oh, no. . . !

ALICE: Will Roper, what d'you want?

    Enter after ROPER, MARGARET.

MARGARET: William, I told you not to!

ROPER: I'm not easily 'told', Meg.

MARGARET: I *asked* you not to.

ROPER: Meg, I'm full to here! (*Indicates throat.*)

MARGARET: It's not convenient!

ROPER: Must everything be made convenient? I'm not a convenient man, Meg – I've got an inconvenient conscience!

  MARGARET *gestures helplessly to* MORE.

MORE (*laughs*): Joshua's trumpet. One note on that brass conscience of yours and my daughter's walls are down.

ROPER (*descending*): You raised her, sir.

MORE (*a bit puzzled*): How long have you been here? Are you in the King's party?

ROPER: No, sir, I am *not* in the King's party! (*Advancing.*) It's of that I wish to speak to you. My spirit is perturbed.

MORE (*suppressing a grin*): Is it, Will? Why?

ROPER: I've been offered a seat in the next Parliament. (MORE *looks up sharply.*) Ought I to take it?

MORE: No ... Well that depends. With your views on Church Reformation I should have thought you could do yourself a lot of good in the next Parliament.

ROPER: My views on the Church – I must confess—— Since last we met my views have somewhat modified. (MORE *and* MARGARET *exchange a smile.*) I modify nothing concerning the *body* of the Church – the money-changers in the temple must be scourged from thence – with a scourge of fire if that is needed! ... But an attack on the Church herself! No, I see behind that an attack on God——

MORE: – Roper——

ROPER: The Devil's work!

MORE: – Roper——!

ROPER: To be done by the Devil's ministers!

MORE: For heaven's sake remember my office!

ROPER: Oh, if you stand on your office——

MORE: I don't stand on it, but there are certain things I may not hear!

ROPER: 'Sophistication. It is what I was told. The Court has corrupted you, Sir Thomas; you are not the man you were; you have learnt to study your 'convenience'; you have learnt to flatter!

MORE: There, Alice; you see? I have a reputation for it.

ALICE: God's Body, young man, if I was the Chancellor I'd have you whipped!

Enter STEWARD.

STEWARD: Master Rich is here, Sir Thomas.

RICH *follows him closely.*

RICH: Good evening, sir.

MORE: Ah, Richard?

RICH: Good evening, Lady Alice. (ALICE *nods, non-committal.*) Lady Margaret.

MARGARET (*quite friendly but very clear*): Good evening, Master Rich.

A pause.

MORE: Do you know——? (*Indicates* ROPER.) William Roper, the younger.

RICH: By reputation, of course.

ROPER: Good evening, Master . . .

RICH: Rich.

ROPER: Oh. (*Recollecting something.*) Oh.

RICH (*quick and hostile*): You have heard of me?

ROPER (*shortly*): Yes.

RICH (*excitedly*): In what connection? I don't know what you can have heard—— (*Looks about: hotly.*) I sense that I'm not welcome here! (*He has jumped the gun; they are startled.*)

MORE (*gently*): Why, Richard, have you done something that should make you not welcome?

RICH: Why, do you suspect me of it?

MORE: I shall begin to.

RICH (*draws closer to him and speaks hurriedly*): Cromwell is asking questions. About you. About you particularly. (MORE *is unmoved.*) He is continually collecting information about you!

MORE: I know it. (STEWARD *begins to slide out.*) Stay a minute, Matthew.

RICH (*pointing*): *That's* one of his sources!

MORE: Of course; that's one of my servants.

RICH (*hurried, low voice again*): Signor Chapuys, the Imperial Ambassador——

MORE – Collects information too. That's one of his functions. (*He looks at* RICH *very gravely.*)

RICH (*voice cracking*): You look at me as though I were an enemy!

MORE (*puts out a hand to steady him*): Why, Richard, you're shaking.

RICH: I'm adrift. Help me.

MORE: How?

RICH: Employ me.

MORE: No.

RICH (*desperately*): Employ me!

MORE: No!

RICH (*moves swiftly to exit: turns there*): I would be steadfast!

MORE: Richard, you couldn't answer for yourself even so far as tonight.

    Exit RICH. *All watch him; the others turn to* MORE, *their faces alert.*

ROPER: Arrest him.

ALICE: Yes!

MORE: For what?

ALICE: He's dangerous!

ROPER: For libel; he's a spy.

ALICE: He is! Arrest him!

MARGARET: Father, that man's bad.

MORE: There is no law against that.

ROPER: There is! God's law!

MORE: Then God can arrest him.

ROPER: Sophistication upon sophistication!

MORE: No, sheer simplicity. The law, Roper, the law. I know what's legal not what's right. And I'll stick to what's legal.

ROPER: Then you set Man's law above God's!

MORE: No far below; but let me draw your attention to a

fact – I'm *not* God. The currents and eddies of right and wrong, which you find such plain-sailing, I can't navigate, I'm no voyager. But in the thickets of the law, oh there I'm a forester. I doubt if there's a man alive who could follow me there, thank God. . . . (*He says this to himself.*)

ALICE (*exasperated, pointing after* RICH): While you talk, he's gone!

MORE: And go he should if he was the devil himself until he broke the law!

ROPER: So now you'd give the Devil benefit of law!

MORE: Yes. What would you do? Cut a great road through the law to get after the Devil?

ROPER: I'd cut down every law in England to do that!

MORE (*roused and excited*): Oh? (*Advances on* ROPER.) And when the last law was down, and the Devil turned round on you – where would you hide, Roper, the laws all being flat? (*Leaves him.*) This country's planted thick with laws from coast to coast – Man's laws, not God's – and if you cut them down – and you're just the man to do it – d'you really think you could stand upright in the winds that would blow then? (*Quietly.*) Yes, I'd give the Devil benefit of law, for my own safety's sake.

ROPER: I have long suspected this; this is the golden calf; the law's your god.

MORE (*wearily*): Oh, Roper, you're a fool, God's my god. . . . (*Rather bitter.*) But I find him rather too (*very bitter*) subtle . . . I don't know where he is nor what he wants.

ROPER: My god wants service, to the end and unremitting; nothing else!

MORE (*dry*): Are you sure that's God? – He sounds like Moloch. But indeed it may be God—— And whoever hunts for me, Roper, God or Devil, will find me hiding in the thickets of the law! And I'll hide my daughter with me! Not hoist her up the mainmast of your seagoing principles! They put about too nimbly!

Exit MORE. *They all look after him.* MARGARET *touches* ROPER's *hand.*

MARGARET: Oh, that was harsh.

ROPER (*turning to her, serious*): What's happened here?

ALICE (*still with her back to them, her voice strained*): He can't abide a fool, that's all! Be off!

ROPER (*to* MARGARET): Hide you. Hide you from what?

ALICE (*turning, near to tears*): He said nothing about hiding me you noticed! I've got too fat to hide I suppose!

MARGARET: You know he meant us both.

ROPER: But from what?

ALICE: I don't know. I don't know if he knows. He's not said one simple, direct word to me since this divorce came up. It's not God who's gone subtle! It's him!

Enter MORE, *a little sheepish. Goes to* ROPER.

MORE (*kindly*): Roper, that was harsh: your principles are – (*can't resist sending him up*) excellent – the very best quality. (ROPER *bridles. Contrite.*) No truly now, your principles are fine. (*Indicating stairs, to all.*) Look, we must make a start on all that food.

MARGARET: Father, can't you be plain with us?

MORE (*looks quickly from daughter to wife. Takes* ALICE's *hand.*) I stand on the wrong side of no statute, and no common law. (*Takes* MEG's *hand too.*) I have not disobeyed my sovereign. I truly believe no man in England is safer than myself. And I want my supper. (*He starts them up the stairs and goes to* ROPER.) We shall need your assistance, Will. There's an excellent Burgundy – if your principles permit.

ROPER: They don't, sir.

MORE: Well, have some water in it.

ROPER: Just the water, sir.

MORE: My poor boy.

ALICE (*stopping at head of stairs, as one who will be answered.*) Why does Cromwell collect information about you?

MORE: I'm a prominent figure. Someone somewhere's collect-

ing information about Cromwell. Now no more shirking;
we must make a start. (*Shepherding* ROPER *up the stairs.*)
There's a stuffed swan if you please. (ALICE *and* MARGARET
exit above.) Will, I'd trust *you* with my life. But not your
principles. (*They mount the stairs.*) You see, we speak of being
anchored to our principles. But if the weather turns nasty
you up with an anchor and let it down where there's less
wind, and the fishing's better. And 'look' we say 'I'm
anchored!' (*Laughing, inviting* ROPER *to laugh with him.*) 'To
my principles!'

    Exit above, MORE *and* ROPER. *Enter* COMMON MAN *pull-
ing basket. From it he takes an Inn Sign which he hangs on to the
alcove. He inspects it.*

COMMON MAN: 'The Loyal Subject' . . . (*to audience*) a pub
(*takes from basket and puts on jacket, cap and napkin*). A publican.
(*Places two stools at the table, and mugs and a candle which he
lights.*) Oh, he's a deep one that Sir Thomas More. . . .
Deep. . . . It takes a lot of education to get a man as deep as
that. . . . (*Straight to audience.*) And a deep nature to begin
with too. (*Deadpan.*) The likes of me can hardly be *expected*
to follow the processes of a man like that. . . . (*Sly.*) Can we?
(*Inspects pub.*) Right, ready. (*Goes right.*) Ready, sir!

    Enter CROMWELL, *carrying bottle. Goes to alcove.*

CROMWELL: Is this a *good* place for a conspiracy, innkeeper?

PUBLICAN (*woodenly*): You asked for a private room, sir.

CROMWELL (*looking round*): Yes, I want one without too many
little dark corners.

PUBLICAN: I don't understand you, sir. Just the four corners
as you see.

CROMWELL (*sardonic*): You don't understand me.

PUBLICAN: That's right, sir.

CROMWELL: Do you know who I am?

PUBLICAN (*promptly*): No, sir.

CROMWELL: Don't be too tactful, innkeeper.

PUBLICAN: I don't understand, sir.

CROMWELL: When the likes of you *are* too tactful, the likes of me begin to wonder who's the fool.

PUBLICAN: I just don't understand you, sir.

CROMWELL (*puts back his head and laughs silently*): The master statesman of us all. 'I don't understand.' (*Looks at* PUBLICAN *almost with hatred.*) All right. Get out. (*Throws coin. Exit* PUBLICAN. CROMWELL *goes to exit opposite. Calling.*) Come on. (*Enter* RICH. *He glances at bottle in* CROMWELL'S *hand and remains cautiously by the exit.*) Yes, it may be that I am a little intoxicated. (*Leaves* RICH *standing.*) But not with alcohol, with success! And who has a strong head for success? None of us gets enough of it. Except Kings. And they're born drunk.

RICH: Success? What success?

CROMWELL: Guess.

RICH: Collector of Revenues for York.

CROMWELL (*amused*): You do keep your ear to the ground don't you? No. Better than that.

RICH: High Constable.

CROMWELL: Better than that.

RICH: Better than High Constable?

CROMWELL: Much better. Sir Thomas Paget is – retiring.

RICH: Secretary to the Council!

CROMWELL: 'Tis astonishing, isn't it?

RICH (*hastily*): Oh no – I mean – one sees, it's logical.

CROMWELL: No ceremony, no courtship. Be seated. (RICH *sits.*) As His Majesty would say. (RICH *laughs nervously and involuntarily glances round.*) Yes; see how I trust you.

RICH: Oh, I would never repeat or report a thing like that——

CROMWELL (*pouring wine*): What kind of thing would you repeat or report?

RICH: Well, nothing said in friendship – may I say 'friendship'?

CROMWELL: If you like. D'you believe that – that you would never repeat or report anything etcetera?

RICH: Why yes!

CROMWELL: No, but seriously.

RICH: Yes!

CROMWELL (*puts down bottle. Not sinister, but rather as a kindly teacher with a promising pupil*): Rich; seriously.

RICH (*pauses, then bitterly*): It would depend what I was offered.

CROMWELL: Don't say it just to please me.

RICH: It's true. It would depend what I was offered.

CROMWELL (*patting his arm*): Everyone knows it; not many people can say it.

RICH: There are *some* things one wouldn't do for anything. Surely.

CROMWELL: Mm – that idea's like these lifelines they have on the embankment: comforting, but you don't expect to have to use them. (*Briskly.*) Well, congratulations!

RICH (*suspicious*): On what?

CROMWELL: I think you'd make a good Collector of Revenues for York Diocese.

RICH (*gripping on to himself*): Is it in your gift?

CROMWELL: Effectively.

RICH (*conscious cynicism*): What do I have to do for it?

CROMWELL: Nothing. (*He lectures, pacing pedantically up and down.*) It isn't like that, Rich. There are no rules. With rewards and penalties – so much wickedness purchases so much worldly prospering—— (*He breaks off and stops, suddenly struck.*) Are you sure you're not religious?

RICH: Almost sure.

CROMWELL: Get sure. (*Resumes pacing.*) No, it's not like that, it's much more a matter of convenience, administrative convenience. The normal aim of administration is to keep steady this factor of convenience – and Sir Thomas would agree. Now normally when a man wants to change his woman, you let him if it's convenient and prevent him if it's not – normally indeed it's of so little importance that you leave it to the priests. But the constant factor is this element of convenience.

RICH: Whose convenience? (CROMWELL *stops.*)

CROMWELL: Oh ours. But everybody's too. (*Sets off again.*) However, in the present instance the man who wants to change his woman is our Sovereign Lord, Harry, by the Grace of God, the Eighth of that name. Which is a quaint way of saying that if he wants to change his woman he will. So *that* becomes the constant factor. And our job as administrators is to make it as convenient as we can. I say 'our' job, on the assumption that you'll take this post at York I've offered you?

RICH: Yes . . . yes, yes. (*But he seems gloomy.*)

CROMWELL (*sits. Sharply*): It's a bad sign when people are depressed by their own good fortune.

RICH (*defensive*): I'm not depressed!

CROMWELL: You look depressed.

RICH (*hastily buffooning*): I'm lamenting. I've lost my innocence.

CROMWELL: You lost that some time ago. If you've only just noticed, it can't have been very important to you.

RICH (*much struck*): That's true! Why that's true, it can't!

CROMWELL: We experience a sense of release do we, Master Rich? An unfamiliar freshness in the head, as of open air?

RICH (*takes wine*): Collector of Revenues isn't bad!

CROMWELL: Not bad for a start. (*He watches* RICH *drink.*) Now our present Lord Chancellor – *there's* an innocent man.

RICH (*puts down glass. Indulgently*): The odd thing is – he *is*.

CROMWELL (*looks at him with dislike*): Yes, I say he is. (*The light tone again.*) The trouble is, his innocence is tangled in this proposition that you can't change your woman without a divorce, and can't have a divorce unless the Pope says so. And although his present Holiness is – judged even by the most liberal standards – a strikingly corrupt old person, yet he still has this word 'Pope' attached to him. And from this quite meaningless circumstance I fear some degree of . . .

RICH (*pleased, waving his cup*): Administrative inconvenience.

CROMWELL (*nodding as to a pupil word perfect*): Just so. (*Dead-*

pan.) This goblet that he gave you, how much was it worth? (RICH *puts down cup, looks down. Quite gently.*) Come along, Rich, he gave you a silver goblet. How much did you get for it?

RICH: Fifty shillings.

CROMWELL: Could you take me to the shop?

RICH: Yes.

CROMWELL: Where did he get it? (*No reply.*) It was a gift from a litigant, a woman, wasn't it?

RICH: Yes.

CROMWELL: Which court? Chancery? (*Restrains* RICH *from filling his glass.*) No, don't get drunk. In which court was this litigant's case?

RICH: Court of Requests.

CROMWELL (*grunts, his face abstracted. Becoming aware of* RICH'S *regard he smiles*): There, that wasn't too painful was it?

RICH (*laughing a little and a little rueful*): No!

CROMWELL (*spreading his hands*): That's all there is. And you'll find it easier next time.

RICH (*looks up briefly, unhappily*): What application do they have, these titbits of information you collect?

CROMWELL: None at all, usually.

RICH (*stubbornly, not looking up*): But sometimes.

CROMWELL: Well, there *are* these men – you know – 'upright', 'steadfast', men who want themselves to be the constant factor in the situation. Which of course they can't be. The situation rolls forward in any case.

RICH (*the same*): So what happens?

CROMWELL (*not liking his tone, coldly*): If they've any sense they get out of its way.

RICH: What if they haven't any sense?

CROMWELL (*the same*): What none at all? Well, then they're only fit for Heaven. But Sir Thomas has plenty of sense; he could be frightened.

RICH (*looks up, his face nasty*): Don't forget he's an innocent, Master Cromwell.

CROMWELL: I think we'll finish there for tonight. (*Rising.*) After all, he *is* the Lord Chancellor. (*Going.*)

RICH: You wouldn't find him easy to frighten! (*Calls after him.*) You've mistaken your man this time! He doesn't know how to be frightened!

CROMWELL (*returning. RICH rises at his approach*): Doesn't know how to be frightened? Why, then he never put his hand in a candle. . . . Did he? (*And seizing RICH by the wrist he holds his hand in the candle flame.*)

RICH (*screeches and darts back, hugging his hand in his armpit, regarding CROMWELL with horror*): You enjoyed that! (*CROMWELL's downturned face is amazed. Triumphantly.*) You enjoyed it!

CURTAIN

ACT TWO

The scene is as for start of Act One. When the curtain rises the stage is in darkness save for a spot, front stage, in which stands the COMMON MAN. *He carries the book, a place marked by his finger, and wears his spectacles.*

COMMON MAN: The interval started early in the year 1530 and it's now the middle of May 1532. (*Explanatory.*) Two years. During that time a lot of water's flowed under the bridge and among the things that have come floating along on it is ... (*Reads.*) 'The Church of England, that finest flower of our Island genius for compromise; that system, peculiar to these shores, which deflects the torrents of religious passion down the canals of moderation.' That's very well put. (*Returns to book, approvingly.*) 'Typically, this great effect was achieved not by bloodshed but by simple Act of Parliament. Only an unhappy few were found to set themselves against the current of their times, and in so doing to court disaster. For we are dealing with an age less fastidious than our own. Imprisonment without trial, and even examination under torture, were common practice.'

Lights rise to show MORE, *seated, and* ROPER, *standing. Exit* COMMON MAN. ROPER *is dressed in black and wears a cross. He commences to walk up and down, watched by* MORE. *A pause.*

MORE: Must you wear those clothes, Will?

ROPER: Yes, I must.

MORE: Why?

ROPER: The time has come for decent men to declare their allegiance!

MORE: And what allegiance are those designed to express?

ROPER: My allegiance to the Church.

MORE: Well, you *look* like a Spaniard.

ROPER: All credit to Spain then!

MORE: You wouldn't last six months in Spain. You'd have been burned alive in Spain, during your heretic period.

ROPER: I suppose you have the right to remind me of it. (*Points accusingly*). That chain of office that *you* wear is a degradation!

MORE (*glances down at it*): I've told you. If the bishops in Convocation submitted this morning, I'll take it off. . . . It's no degradation. Great men have worn this.

ROPER: When d'you expect to hear from Canterbury?

MORE: About now. The Archbishop promised me an immediate message.

ROPER (*recommences pacing*): I don't see what difference Convocation can make. The Church is already a wing of the Palace is it not? The King is already its 'Supreme Head'! Is he not?

MORE: No.

ROPER (*is startled*): You are denying the Act of Supremacy!

MORE: No, I'm not; the Act states that the King——

ROPER: – is Supreme Head of the Church in England.

MORE: Supreme Head of the Church in England—— (*Underlining the words.*) 'so far as the law of God allows.' How far the law of God does allow it remains a matter of opinion, since the Act doesn't state it.

ROPER: A legal quibble.

MORE: Call it what you like, it's there, thank God.

ROPER: Very well: in your opinion how far does the law of God allow this?

MORE: I'll keep my opinion to myself, Will.

ROPER: Yes? I'll tell you mine——!

MORE: Don't! If your opinion's what I think it is, it's High Treason, Roper!

    Enter MARGARET *above, unseen.*

Will, you remember you've a wife now! And may have children!

MARGARET: Why must he remember that?

ROPER: To keep myself 'discreet'.

MARGARET (*smiling*): Then I'd rather you forgot it.

MORE (*unsmiling*): You are either idiots, or children.

Enter CHAPUYS, *above.*

CHAPUYS: Or saints, my lord! (*Very sonorous.*)

MARGARET: Oh, Father, Signor Chapuys has come to see you.

MORE (*rising*): Your Excellency.

CHAPUYS (*strikes pose with* MARGARET *and* ROPER): Or saints, my lord; or saints.

MORE (*grins maliciously at* ROPER): That's it of course – saints! Roper – turn your head a bit – yes, I think I do detect, a faint radiance. (*Reproachful.*) You should have told us, Will.

CHAPUYS: Come come, my lord; you too at this time are not free from some suspicion of saintliness.

MORE (*quietly*): I don't like the sound of that, Your Excellency. What do you require of *me*? What, Your Excellency?

CHAPUYS (*awkward beneath his sudden keen regard*): May I not come simply, to pay my respects to the English Socrates – as I see your angelic friend Erasmus calls you.

MORE (*wrinkles nose*): Yes, I'll think of something presently to call Erasmus. (*Checks.*) Socrates! I've no taste for hemlock, Your Excellency, if that's what you require.

CHAPUYS (*display of horror*): Heaven forbid!

MORE (*dryly*): Amen.

CHAPUYS (*spreads hands*): Must I require anything? (*Sonorous.*) After all, we are brothers in Christ, you and I!

MORE: A characteristic we share with the rest of humanity. You live in Cheapside, Signor? To make contact with a brother in Christ you have only to open your window and empty a chamberpot. There was no need to come to Chelsea. (CHAPUYS *titters nervously. Coldly.*) William. The Imperial Ambassador is here on business. Would you mind?

ROPER *and* MARGARET *going.*

CHAPUYS (*rising, unreal protestations*): Oh no! I protest!

MORE: He is clearly here on business.

CHAPUYS (*the same*): No; but really, I protest! (*It is no more than token: when* ROPER *and* MARGARET *reach head of stairs he calls:*) Dominus vobiscum filii mei!

ROPER (*pompous*): Et cum spiritu tuo, excellencis!

Exit ROPER *and* MARGARET.

CHAPUYS (*approaching* MORE, *thrillingly*): And how much longer shall we hear that holy language in these shores?

MORE (*alert, poker-faced*): 'Tisn't 'holy', Your Excellency; just old.

CHAPUYS *sits with the air of one coming to brass tacks*

CHAPUYS: My Lord, I cannot believe you will allow yourself to be associated with the recent actions of King Henry! In respect of Queen Catherine.

MORE: Subjects are associated with the actions of Kings willy-nilly.

CHAPUYS: The Lord Chancellor is not an ordinary subject. He bears responsibility (*he lets the word sink in;* MORE *shifts*) for what is done.

MORE (*agitation begins to show through*): Have you considered that what has been done badly, might have been done worse, with a different Chancellor.

CHAPUYS (*mounting confidence, as* MORE'S *attention is caught*): Believe me, Sir Thomas, your influence in these policies has been much searched for, and where it has been found it has been praised – *but* . . . There comes a point, does there not? . . .

MORE: Yes. (*Agitated.*) There does come such a point.

CHAPUYS: When the sufferings of one unfortunate lady swell to an open attack on the religion of an entire country that point has been passed. Beyond that point, Sir Thomas, one is not merely 'compromised', one is in truth corrupted.

MORE (*stares at him*): What do you want?

CHAPUYS: Rumour has it that if the Church in Convocation has submitted to the King, you will resign.

MORE (*looks down and regains composure*): I see. (*Suave.*) Supposing rumour to be right. Would you approve of that?

CHAPUYS: Approve, applaud, admire.

MORE (*still looking down*): Why?

CHAPUYS: Because it would show one man – and that man known to be temperate – unable to go further with this wickedness.

MORE (*the same*): And that man known to be Chancellor of England too.

CHAPUYS: Believe me, my lord, such a signal would be seen——

MORE (*the same*): 'Signal'?

CHAPUYS: Yes, my lord; it would be seen and understood.

MORE (*the same, and now positively silky*): By whom?

CHAPUYS: By half of your fellow countrymen! (*Now* MORE *looks up sharply*). Sir Thomas, I have just returned from Yorkshire and Northumberland, where I have made a tour.

MORE (*softly*): Have you indeed?

CHAPUYS: Things are very different there, my lord. There they are ready.

MORE: For what?

CHAPUYS: Resistance!

Enter ROPER, *above, excited.*

ROPER: Sir Thomas——! (MORE *looks up angrily*.) Excuse me, sir—— (*Indicates off.*) His Grace the Duke of Norfolk—— (MORE *and* CHAPUYS *rise.* ROPER *excitedly descends.*) It's all over, sir, they've——

Enter NORFOLK *above,* ALICE *and* MARGARET, *below.*

NORFOLK: One moment, Roper, I'll do this! Thomas—— (*Sees* CHAPUYS.) Oh. (*He stares at* CHAPUYS, *hostile.*)

CHAPUYS: I was on the point of leaving, Your Grace. Just a personal call. I have been trying . . . er to borrow a book – but without success – you're sure you have no copy, my

lord? Then I'll leave you. (*Bowing.*) Gentlemen, ladies.
(*Going, up stairs. Stops unseen as* ROPER *speaks.*)

ROPER: Sir Thomas——

NORFOLK: I'll do it, Roper! Convocation's knuckled under,
Thomas. They're to pay a fine of a hundred thousand pounds.
And . . . we've severed the connection with Rome.

MORE (*smiling bitterly*): 'The connection with Rome' is nice.
(*Bitter.*) 'The connection with Rome.' Did *anyone* resist?

NORFOLK: Bishop Fisher.

MORE: Lovely man. (NORFOLK *shrugs.*)

ROPER (*looking at* MORE): Your Grace, this is quite certain is it?

NORFOLK: Yes. (MORE *puts his hand to his chain.* CHAPUYS
exit. All turn.) Funny company, Thomas?

MORE: It's quite unintentional. He doesn't mean to be funny.
(*Fumbles with chain.*) Help me with this.

NORFOLK: Not I.

ROPER (*takes a step forward. Then, subdued*): Shall I, sir?

MORE: No thank you, Will. Alice?

ALICE: Hell's fire – God's blood and body *no*! Sun and moon,
Master More, you're taken for a wise man! Is this wisdom –
to betray your ability, abandon practice, forget your station
and your duty to your kin and behave like a printed book!

MORE (*listens gravely: then*): Margaret, will you?

MARGARET: If you want.

MORE: There's my clever girl. (*She takes it from his neck.*)

NORFOLK: Well, Thomas, why? Make me understand –
because I'll tell you now, from where I stand, this looks like
cowardice!

MORE (*excited and angry*): All right I will – this isn't 'Reforma-
tion'; this is war against the Church! . . . (*Indignant.*) Our
King, Norfolk, has declared war on the Pope – because the
Pope will not declare that our Queen is not his wife.

NORFOLK: And is she?

MORE (*cunning*): I'll answer that question for one person only,
the King. Aye, and that in private too.

NORFOLK (*contemptuous*): Man, you're cautious.

MORE: Yes, cautious. I'm not one of your hawks.

NORFOLK (*walks away and turns*): All right – we're at war with the Pope! The Pope's a Prince, isn't he?

MORE: He is.

NORFOLK: And a bad one?

MORE: Bad enough. But the theory is that he's also the Vicar of God, the descendant of St Peter, our only link with Christ.

NORFOLK (*sneer*): A tenuous link.

MORE: Oh, tenuous indeed.

NORFOLK (*to the others*): Does this make sense? (*No reply; they look at* MORE.) You'll forfeit all you've got – which includes the respect of your country – for a theory?

MORE (*hotly*): The Apostolic Succession of the Pope is—— (*Stops: interested.*) . . . Why, it's a theory yes; you can't see it; can't touch it; it's a theory. (*To* NORFOLK, *very rapid but calm.*) But what matters to me is not whether it's true or not but that I believe it to be true, or rather not that I *believe* it, but that *I* believe it . . . I trust I make myself obscure?

NORFOLK: Perfectly.

MORE: That's good. Obscurity's what I have need of now.

NORFOLK: Man, you're sick. This isn't Spain you know.

MORE (*looks at him: takes him aside: lowered voice*): Have I your word, that what we say here is between us and has no existence beyond these walls?

NORFOLK (*impatient*): Very well.

MORE (*almost whispering*): And if the King should command you to repeat what I have said?

NORFOLK: I should keep my word to you!

MORE: Then what has become of your oath of obedience to the King?

NORFOLK (*indignant*): You lay traps for me!

MORE (*now grown calm*): No, I show you the times.

NORFOLK: Why do you insult me with these lawyer's tricks?

MORE: Because I am afraid.

NORFOLK: And here's your answer. The King accepts your resignation very sadly; he is mindful of your goodness and past loyalty and in any matter concerning your honour and welfare he will be your good lord. So much for your fear.

MORE (*flatly*): You will convey my humble gratitude.

NORFOLK: I will. Good day, Alice (*Going.*) I'd rather deal with you than your husband.

MORE (*complete change of tone; briskly professional*): Oh, Howard! (*Goes to him.*) Signor Chapuys tells me he's just made a 'tour' of the North Country. He thinks we shall have trouble there. So do I.

NORFOLK (*stolid*): Yes? What kind of trouble?

MORE: The Church – the old Church, not the new Church – is, very strong up there. I'm serious, Howard, keep an eye on the Border, this next year; and bear in mind the Old Alliance.

NORFOLK (*looks at him*): We will. We do. . . . As for the Dago, Thomas, it'll perhaps relieve your mind to know that one of Secretary Cromwell's agents made the tour with him.

MORE: Oh. (*Flash of jealousy.*) Of course if Master Cromwell has matters in hand——

NORFOLK: – He has.

MORE: Yes, I can imagine.

NORFOLK: But thanks for the information. (*Going.*) It's good to know you still have . . . some vestige of patriotism.

MORE (*anger*): That's a remarkably stupid observation, Norfolk!

Exit NORFOLK.

ALICE: So there's an end of you. What will you do now – sit by the fire and make goslings in the ash?

MORE: Not at all, Alice, I expect I'll write a bit. (*He woos them with unhappy cheerfulness.*) I'll write, I'll read, I'll think. I think I'll learn to fish! I'll play with my grandchildren – when son Roper's done his duty. (*Eager.*) Alice, shall I teach you to read?

ALICE: No, by God!

MORE: . . . Son Roper, *you're* pleased with me I hope?

ROPER (*goes to him: moved*): Sir, you've made a noble gesture.

MORE (*blankly*): A gesture? (*Eager.*) It wasn't possible to continue, Will. I was not *able* to continue. I would have if I could! I make no gesture! (*Apprehensive, looks after NORFOLK.*) My God, I hope it's understood I make no gesture! (*Turns back to them.*) – Alice, you don't think I would do this to you for a gesture! *That's* a gesture! (*Thumbs his nose.*) *That's* a gesture! (*Jerks up two fingers.*) I'm no street acrobat to make gestures! I'm practical!

ROPER: You belittle yourself, sir, this was not practical; (*resonant*) this was moral!

MORE: Oh now I understand you, Will. Morality's *not* practical. Morality's a gesture. A complicated gesture learned from books – that's what you say, Alice, isn't it? . . . And you, Meg?

MARGARET: It *is*, for most of us, Father.

MORE: Oh no, if you're going to plead humility——! Oh, you're cruel. I have a cruel family.

ALICE: Yes, you can fit the cap on anyone you want, I know that well enough. If there's cruelty in this house, I know where to look for it.

MARGARET: No, Mother——!

ALICE: Oh, you'd walk on the bottom of the sea and think yourself a crab if he suggested it! (*To* ROPER.) And you! You'd dance him to the Tower—— You'd dance him to the block! Like David with a harp! Scattering hymn-books in his path! (*To* MORE.) Poor silly man, d'you think they'll *leave* you here to learn to fish?

MORE (*straight at her*): If we govern our tongues they will! . . . Look, I have a word to say about that. I have made no statement. I've resigned, that's *all*. On the King's Supremacy, the King's divorce which he'll now grant himself, the marriage he'll then make – have you heard me make a statement?

ALICE: No – and if I'm to lose my rank and fall to housekeeping I want to know the reason; so make a statement now.

MORE: No – (ALICE *exhibits indignation*) – Alice, it's a point of law! Accept it from me, Alice, that in silence is my safety under the law, but my silence must be absolute, it must extend to you.

ALICE: In short you don't trust us!

MORE (*impatient*): Look – (*advances on her*) I'm the Lord Chief Justice, I'm Cromwell, I'm the King's Head Jailer – and I take your hand (*does so*) and I clamp it on the Bible, on the Blessed Cross (*clamps her hand on his closed fist*) and I say: 'Woman, has your husband made a statement on these matters?' Now – on peril of your soul remember – what's your answer?

ALICE: No.

MORE: And so it must remain. (*He looks round at their grave faces.*) Oh, it's only a life-line, we shan't have to use it but it's comforting to have. No, no, when they find I'm silent they'll ask nothing better than to leave me silent; you'll see.

   Enter STEWARD.

STEWARD: Sir, the household's in the kitchen. They want to know what's happened.

MORE: Oh. Yes. We must speak to them. Alice, they'll mostly have to go, my dear. (*To* STEWARD.) But not before we've found them places.

ALICE: We can't find places for them all!

MORE: Yes, we can; yes, we can. Tell them so.

ALICE: God's death it comes on us quickly...

   Exit ALICE, MARGARET *and* ROPER.

MORE: What about you, Matthew? It'll be a smaller household now, and for you I'm afraid, a smaller wage. Will you stay?

STEWARD: Don't see how I could then, sir.

MORE: You're a single man.

STEWARD (*awkward*): Well, yes, sir, but I mean I've got my own——

MORE (*quickly*): Quite right, why should you? . . . I shall miss you, Matthew.

STEWARD (*man to man jocosity*): No-o-o. You never had much time for *me*, sir. You see through *me*, sir, I know that. (*He almost winks.*)

MORE (*gently insists*): I shall miss you, Matthew; I shall miss you.

Exit MORE. STEWARD *snatches off hat and hurls it to the floor.*

STEWARD: Now, damn me isn't that them all over! (*He broods, face downturned.*) Miss——? . . . He—— . . . Miss——? . . . *Miss* me? . . . What's *in* me for *him* to miss. . .? (*Suddenly he cries out like one who sees a danger at his very feet.*) WO-AH! (*Chuckling.*) We-e-eyup! (*To audience.*) I nearly fell for it. (*Walks away.*) 'Matthew, will you kindly take a cut in your wages?' 'No, Sir Thomas, I will not.' That's it and (*fiercely*) that's all of it! (*Falls to thought again. Resentfully.*) All right so he's down on his luck! I'm sorry. I don't mind saying that: I'm sorry! Bad luck! If I'd any good luck to spare he could have some. I wish we could *all* have good luck, *all* the time! I wish we had wings! I wish rainwater was beer! But it isn't! . . . And what with not having wings but walking – on two flat feet; and good luck and bad luck being just exactly even stevens; and rain being water – don't you complicate the job by putting things in me for me to miss! (*He takes off* STEWARD's *coat, picks up his hat: draws the curtain to alcove. Chuckling.*) I did you know. I nearly fell for it.

Exit COMMON MAN. NORFOLK *and* CROMWELL *enter to alcove.*

NORFOLK: But he makes no noise, Mr Secretary; he's silent, why not leave him silent?

CROMWELL (*patiently*): Not being a man of letters, Your Grace, you perhaps don't realise the extent of his reputation. This 'silence' of his is bellowing up and down Europe! Now may I recapitulate: He reported the Ambassador's conversation to you, informed on the Ambassador's tour of the North-country, warned against a possible rebellion there.

NORFOLK: He did!

CROMWELL: We may say then, that he showed himself hostile to the hopes of Spain.

NORFOLK: That's what I *say*!

CROMWELL (*patiently*): Bear with me, Your Grace. Now if he opposes Spain, he supports us. Well, surely that follows? (*Sarcastically*.) Or do you see some third alternative?

NORFOLK: No no, that's the line-up all right. And I may say Thomas More——

CROMWELL: Thomas More will line up on the right side.

NORFOLK: Yes! Crank he may be, traitor he is not.

CROMWELL (*spreading his hands*): And with a little pressure, he can be got to say so. And that's all we need – a brief declaration of his loyalty to the present administration.

NORFOLK: I still say let sleeping dogs lie.

CROMWELL (*heavily*): The King does not agree with you.

NORFOLK (*glances at him; flickers, but then rallies*): What kind of 'pressure' d'you think you can bring to bear?

CROMWELL: I have evidence that Sir Thomas, during the period of his judicature, accepted bribes.

NORFOLK (*incredulous*): What! Goddammit he was the only judge since Cato who *didn't* accept bribes! When was there last a Chancellor whose possessions after three years in office totalled one hundred pounds and a gold chain.

CROMWELL (*rings hand-bell and calls*): Richard! It is, as you imply, common practice, but a practice may be common and remain an offence; this offence could send a man to the Tower.

NORFOLK (*contemptuous*): I don't believe it.

    Enter RICH *and* A WOMAN. *He motions her to remain, and*

approaches the table, where CROMWELL *indicates a seat. He has acquired self-importance.*

CROMWELL: Ah, Richard. You know His Grace of course.

RICH (*respectful affability*): Indeed yes, we're *old* friends.

NORFOLK (*savage snub*): Used to look after my books or something, didn't you?

CROMWELL (*clicks his fingers at* WOMAN): Come here. This woman's name is Catherine Anger; she comes from Lincoln. And she put a case in the Court of Requests in—— (*Consults paper.*)

WOMAN: A property case, it was.

CROMWELL: Be quiet. A property case in the Court of Requests in April 1526.

WOMAN: And got a wicked false judgement!

CROMWELL: And got an impeccably correct judgement from our friend Sir Thomas.

WOMAN: No, sir, it was not!

CROMWELL: We're not concerned with the judgement but the gift you gave the judge. Tell this gentleman about that. The judgement for what it's worth was the right one.

WOMAN: No, sir! (CROMWELL *looks at her: she hastily addresses* NORFOLK.) I sent him a cup, sir; an Italian silver cup I bought in Lincoln for a hundred shillings.

NORFOLK: Did Sir Thomas accept this cup?

WOMAN: I sent it.

CROMWELL: He did accept it, we can corroborate that. You can go. (*She opens her mouth.*) Go!

Exit WOMAN.

NORFOLK (*scornful*): Is that your witness?

CROMWELL: No; by an odd coincidence this cup later came into the hands of Master Rich here.

NORFOLK: How?

RICH: He gave it to me.

NORFOLK (*brutal*): Can you corroborate that?

CROMWELL: I have a fellow outside who can; he was More's

steward at that time. Shall I call him?

NORFOLK: Don't bother, I know him. When did Thomas give you this thing?

RICH: I don't exactly remember.

NORFOLK: Well, make an effort. Wait! I can tell you! I can tell you – it was that Spring – it was that night we were there together. You had a cup with you when we left; was that it?

    RICH *looks to* CROMWELL *for guidance but gets none.*

RICH: It may have been.

NORFOLK: Did he often give you cups?

RICH: I don't suppose so, Your Grace.

NORFOLK: That was it then. (*New realisation.*) And it was April! The April of 26. The very month that cow first put her case before him! (*Triumphant.*) In other words the moment he knew it was a bribe, he got rid of it.

CROMWELL (*nodding judicially*): The facts will bear that interpretation I suppose.

NORFOLK: Oh, this is a horse that won't run, Master Secretary.

CROMWELL: Just a trial canter, Your Grace. We'll find something better.

NORFOLK (*between bullying and plea*): Look here, Cromwell, I want no part of this.

CROMWELL: You have no choice.

NORFOLK: What's that you say?

CROMWELL: The King particularly wishes you to be active in the matter.

NORFOLK (*winded*): He has not told me that.

CROMWELL (*politely*): Indeed? He told me.

NORFOLK: But *why*?

CROMWELL: We feel that, since you are known to have been a friend of More's, your participation will show that there is nothing in the nature of a 'persecution', but only the strict processes of law. As indeed you've just demonstrated. I'll tell the King of your loyalty to your friend. If you like, I'll tell him that you 'want no part of it', too.

NORFOLK (*furious*): Are you threatening me, Cromwell?

CROMWELL: My *dear* Norfolk. . . . This isn't Spain.

    NORFOLK *stares, turns abruptly and exit.* CROMWELL *turns a look of glacial coldness upon* RICH.

RICH: I'm sorry, Secretary, I'd forgotten he was there that night.

CROMWELL (*scrutinises him dispassionately, then*): You must try to remember these things.

RICH: Secretary, I'm sincerely——!

CROMWELL (*dismisses the topic with a wave and turns to look after* NORFOLK): Not such a fool as he looks, the Duke.

RICH (*Civil Service simper*): That would hardly be possible, Secretary.

CROMWELL (*straightening papers, briskly*): Sir Thomas is going to be a slippery fish, Richard; we need a net with a finer mesh.

RICH: Yes, Secretary?

CROMWELL: We'll weave one for him shall we, you and I?

RICH (*uncertain*): I'm only anxious to do what is correct, Secretary.

CROMWELL (*smiling at him*): Yes, Richard, I know. (*Straight-faced.*) You're absolutely right, it must be done by law. It's just a matter of finding the right law. Or making one. Bring my papers, will you?

    Exit CROMWELL. *Enter* STEWARD.

STEWARD: Could we have a word now, sir?

RICH: We don't require you after all, Matthew.

STEWARD: No, sir, but about . . .

RICH: Oh yes. . . . Well, I begin to need a steward, certainly; my household is expanding. . . . (*Sharply.*) But as I remember, Matthew, your attitude to me was sometimes – disrespectful! (*The last word is shrill.*)

STEWARD (*with humble dignity*): Oh. Oh, I must contradict you there, sir; that's your imagination. In those days, sir, you still had your way to make. And a gentleman in that position often imagines these things. Then when he's risen to his proper level, sir, he stops thinking about it. (*As one offering tangible proof.*) Well – I don't think you find people 'disrespectful' nowadays, do you, sir?

RICH: There may be something in that. Bring my papers. (*Going, turns at exit and anxiously scans* STEWARD'*s face for signs of impudence.*) I'll permit no breath of insolence!

STEWARD (*the very idea is shocking*): I should hope not, sir. (*Exit* RICH.) Oh, I can manage this one! He's just my size! (*Lighting changes so that the set looks drab and chilly.*) Sir Thomas More's again gone down a bit.

    Exit COMMON MAN.

    Enter, side, CHAPUYS *and* ATTENDANT, *cloaked. Above,* ALICE, *wearing big coarse apron over her dress.*

ALICE: My husband is coming down, Your Excellency.

CHAPUYS: Thank you, madam.

ALICE: And I beg you to be gone before he does!

CHAPUYS (*patiently*): Madam, I have a Royal Commission to perform.

ALICE: Aye. You said so. (*Exit* ALICE.)

CHAPUYS: For sheer barbarity, commend me to a good-hearted Englishwoman of a certain class. . . . (*Wraps cloak about him.*)

ATTENDANT: It's very cold, Excellency.

CHAPUYS: I remember when these rooms were warm enough.

ATTENDANT (*looking about*): 'Thus it is to incur the enmity of a Prince.'

CHAPUYS: – A heretic Prince. (*Looking about.*) Yes, Sir Thomas is a good man.

ATTENDANT: Yes, Excellency, I like Sir Thomas very much.

CHAPUYS: Carefully, carefully.

ATTENDANT: It's uncomfortable dealing with him, isn't it?

CHAPUYS: Goodness presents its own difficulties. Attend and learn now.

ATTENDANT: Excellency?

CHAPUYS: Well?

ATTENDANT: Excellency, is he really *for* us?

CHAPUYS (*testy*): He's opposed to Cromwell. He's shown that, I think?

ATTENDANT: Yes, Excellency, but——

CHAPUYS: If he's opposed to Cromwell, he's for us. There's no third alternative.

ATTENDANT: I suppose not, Excellency.

CHAPUYS: I wish your mother had chosen some other career for you; you've no political sense whatever. Sh!

Enter MORE. *His clothes match the atmosphere of the room and he moves rather more deliberately than before.*

MORE (*descending*): Is this another 'personal' visit, Chapuys, or is it official?

CHAPUYS: It falls between the two, Sir Thomas.

MORE (*reaching the bottom of stairs*): Official then.

CHAPUYS: No, I have a personal letter for you.

MORE: From whom?

CHAPUYS: From King Charles! (MORE *puts hands behind back.*) You will take it?

MORE: I will not lay a finger on it.

CHAPUYS: It is in no way an affair of State. It expresses my master's admiration for the stand which you and Bishop Fisher of Rochester have taken over the so-called divorce of Queen Catherine.

MORE: I have taken no stand!

CHAPUYS: But your views, Sir Thomas, are well known——

MORE: My views are much guessed at. (*Irritably.*) Oh come, sir, could you undertake to convince (*grimly*) King Harry that this letter is 'in no way an affair of State'?

CHAPUYS: My dear Sir Thomas, I have taken extreme precautions. I came here very much incognito. (*Self-indulgent chuckle.*) Very nearly in disguise.

MORE: You misunderstand me. It is not a matter of your precautions but my duty; which would be to take this letter immediately to the King.

CHAPUYS (*flabbergasted*): But, Sir Thomas, your views——

MORE: – Are well known you say. It seems my loyalty is less so.
   Enter MARGARET *bearing before her a huge bundle of bracken.*

MARGARET: Look, Father! (*Dumps it.*) Will's getting more.

MORE: Oh, well done! (*Not whimsy; they're cold and their interest
   in fuel is serious.*) Is it dry? (*Feels it expertly.*) Oh it *is*. (*Sees*
   CHAPUYS *staring; laughs.*) It's bracken, Your Excellency.
   We burn it. (*Enter* ALICE.) Alice, look at this. (*The bracken.*)

ALICE (*eyeing* CHAPUYS): Aye.

MORE (*crossing to* CHAPUYS): May I——? (*Takes letter to*
   ALICE *and* MARGARET.) This is a letter from King Charles;
   I want you to see it's not been opened. I have declined it.
   You see the seal has not been broken? (*Returning it to*
   CHAPUYS.) I wish I could ask you to stay, Your Excellency
   – the bracken fire is a luxury.

CHAPUYS (*cold smile*): One I must forego. (*Aside to* ATTEN-
   DANT.) Come. (*Crosses to exit, pauses.*) May I say I am sure
   my master's admiration will not be diminished. (*Bows.*)

MORE: I am gratified. (*Bows, women curtsey.*)

CHAPUYS (*aside to* ATTENDANT): The man's utterly unreliable!
   Exit CHAPUYS *and* ATTENDANT.

ALICE (*after a little silence kicks the bracken*): 'Luxury'! (*She sits
   wearily on the bundle.*)

MORE: Well, it's a luxury while it lasts. . . . There's not much
   sport in it for you, is there? . . . (*She neither answers nor looks
   at him from the depths of her fatigue. After a moment's hesitation
   he braces himself.*) Alice, the money from the Bishops. I
   wish – oh heaven how I wish I could take it! But I can't.

ALICE (*as one who has ceased to expect anything*): I didn't think
   you would.

MORE (*reproachful*): Alice, there *are* reasons.

ALICE: We couldn't come so deep into your confidence as to
   know these reasons why a man in poverty can't take four
   thousand pounds?

MORE (*gently but very firm*): Alice, this isn't poverty.

ALICE: D'you know what we shall eat tonight?

MORE (*trying for a smile*): Yes, parsnips.

ALICE: Yes, parsnips and stinking mutton! (*Straight at him.*) For a knight's lady!

MORE (*pleading*): But at the worst, we could be beggars, and still keep company, and be merry together!

ALICE (*bitterly*): Merry!

MORE (*sternly*): Aye, merry!

MARGARET (*her arm about her mother's waist*): I think you should take that money.

MORE: Oh, don't you see? (*Sits by them.*) If I'm paid by the Church for my writings——

ALICE: – This had nothing to do with your writings! This was charity pure and simple! Collected from the clergy high and low!

MORE: It would *appear* as payment.

ALICE: You're not a man who deals in appearances!

MORE (*fervent*): Oh, am I not though. . . . (*Calmly.*) If the King takes this matter any further, with me or with the Church, it will be very bad, if I even appear to have been in the pay of the Church.

ALICE (*sharply*): Bad?

MORE: If you will have it, dangerous. (*He gets up.*)

MARGARET: But you don't write against the King.

MORE: I write! And that's enough in times like these!

ALICE: You said there *was* no danger!

MORE: I don't think there is! And I don't want there to be!
     Enter ROPER *carrying sickle.*

ROPER (*steadily*): There's a gentleman here from Hampton Court. You are to go before Secretary Cromwell. To answer certain charges. (ALICE *and* MARGARET, *appalled, turn to* MORE.)

MORE (*after a silence, rubs his nose*): Well, that's all right. We expected that. (*Not very convincing.*) When?

ROPER: Now. (ALICE *exhibits distress*.)

MORE: That means nothing, Alice; that's just technique. . . . Well, I suppose 'now' means now.

Lighting change commences, darkness gathering on the others, leaving MORE *isolated in the light, out of which he answers them in the shadows.*

MARGARET: Can I come with you?

MORE: Why? No. I'll be back for dinner. I'll bring Cromwell to dinner, shall I? It'd serve him right.

MARGARET: Oh, Father, don't be witty!

MORE: Why not? Wit's what's in question.

ROPER (*quietly*): While we are witty, the Devil may enter us unawares.

MORE: He's not the Devil, son Roper, he's a lawyer! And my case is watertight!

ALICE: They say he's a very nimble lawyer.

MORE: What, Cromwell? Pooh, he's a pragmatist – and that's the only resemblance he has to the Devil, son Roper; a pragmatist, the merest plumber.

Exit ALICE, MARGARET, ROPER, *in darkness.*

Lights come up. Enter CROMWELL, *bustling, carrying file of papers.*

CROMWELL: I'm sorry to invite you here at such short notice, Sir Thomas; good of you to come. (*Draws back curtain from alcove, revealing* RICH *seated at table, with writing materials.*) Will you take a seat? I think you know Master Rich?

MORE: Indeed yes, we're old friends. That's a nice gown you have, Richard.

CROMWELL: Master Rich will make a record of our conversation.

MORE: Good of you to tell me, Master Secretary.

CROMWELL (*laughs appreciatively. Then*): Believe me, Sir Thomas – no, that's asking too much – but let me tell you all the same, you have no more sincere admirer than myself.

(RICH *begins to scribble.*) Not yet, Rich, not yet. (*Invites* MORE *to join him in laughing at* RICH.)

MORE: If I might hear the charges?

CROMWELL: Charges?

MORE: I understand there are certain charges.

CROMWELL: Some ambiguities of behaviour I should like to clarify – hardly 'charges'.

MORE: Make a note of that will you, Master Rich? There are no charges.

CROMWELL (*laughing and shaking head*): Sir Thomas, Sir Thomas. . . . You know it amazes me that you, who were once so effective *in* the world, and are now so *much* retired from it, should be opposing yourself to the whole movement of the times? (*He ends on a note of interrogation.*)

MORE (*nods*): It amazes me too.

CROMWELL (*picks up and drops paper. Sadly*): The King is not pleased with you.

MORE: I am grieved.

CROMWELL: Yet do you know that even now, if you could bring yourself to agree with the Universities, the Bishops, and the Parliament of this realm, there is no honour which the King would be likely to deny you?

MORE (*stonily*): I am well acquainted with His Grace's generosity.

CROMWELL (*coldly*): Very well. (*Consults paper.*) You have heard of the so-called 'Holy Maid of Kent' – who was executed for prophesying against the King?

MORE: Yes; I knew the poor woman.

CROMWELL (*quick*): You sympathise with her?

MORE: She was ignorant and misguided; she was a bit mad I think. And she has paid for her folly. Naturally I sympathise with her.

CROMWELL (*grunts*): You admit meeting her. You met her – and yet you did not warn His Majesty of her treason. How was that?

MORE: She spoke no treason. Our conversation was not political.

CROMWELL: My dear More, the woman was notorious! Do you expect me to believe that?

MORE: Happily there were witnesses.

CROMWELL: You wrote a letter to her?

MORE: Yes, I wrote advising her to abstain from meddling with the affairs of Princes and the State. I have a copy of this letter – also witnessed.

CROMWELL: You have been cautious.

MORE: I like to keep my affairs regular.

CROMWELL: Sir Thomas, there is a more serious charge——

MORE: Charge?

CROMWELL: For want of a better word. In the May of 1526 the King published a book, (*he permits himself a little smile*) a theological work. It was called *A Defence of the Seven Sacraments*.

MORE: Yes. (*Bitterly.*) For which he was named 'Defender of the Faith', by His Holiness the Pope.

CROMWELL: – By the Bishop of Rome. Or do you insist on 'Pope'?

MORE: No, 'Bishop of Rome' if you like. It doesn't alter his authority.

CROMWELL: Thank you, you come to the point very readily; what *is* that authority? As regards the Church in other parts of Europe; (*approaching*) for example, the Church in England. What exactly *is* the Bishop of Rome's authority?

MORE: You will find it very ably set out and defended, Master Secretary, in the King's book.

CROMWELL: The book published under the King's name would be more accurate. You wrote that book.

MORE: – I wrote no part of it.

CROMWELL: – I do not mean you actually held the pen.

MORE: – I merely answered to the best of my ability certain

questions on canon law which His Majesty put to me. As I was bound to do.

CROMWELL: – Do you deny that you *instigated* it?

MORE: – It was from first to last the King's own project. This is trivial, Master Cromwell.

CROMWELL: I should not think so if I were in your place.

MORE: Only two people know the truth of the matter. Myself and the King. And, whatever he may have said to you, he will not give evidence to support this accusation.

CROMWELL: Why not?

MORE: Because evidence is given on oath, and he will not perjure himself. If you don't know that, you don't yet know him. (CROMWELL *looks at him viciously*.)

CROMWELL (*goes apart, formally*): Sir Thomas More, is there anything you wish to say to me concerning the King's marriage with Queen Anne?

MORE (*very still*): I understood I was not to be asked that again.

CROMWELL: Evidently you understood wrongly. These charges——

MORE (*anger breaking through*): They are terrors for children, Mr Secretary, not for me!

CROMWELL: Then know that the King commands me to charge you in his name with great ingratitude! And to tell you that there never was nor never could be so villainous a servant nor so traitorous a subject as yourself!

MORE: So I am brought here at last.

CROMWELL: Brought? You brought yourself to where you stand now.

MORE: Yes. Still, in another sense I was brought.

CROMWELL (*indifferent*): Oh yes. (*Official.*) You may go home now. For the present. (*Exit* MORE.) I don't like him so well as I did. There's a man who raises the gale and won't come out of harbour.

Scene change commences here, i.e., rear of stage becoming water patterned.

RICH (*covert jeer*): Do you still think you can frighten him?

CROMWELL: No, he's misusing his intelligence.

RICH: What will you do now, then?

CROMWELL (*as to an importunate child*): Oh, be quiet, Rich. . . . We'll do whatever's necessary. The King's a man of conscience and he wants either Sir Thomas More to bless his marriage or Sir Thomas More destroyed. Either will do.

RICH (*shakily*): They seem odd alternatives, Secretary.

CROMWELL: Do they? That's because you're not a man of conscience. If the King destroys a man, that's proof to the King that it must have been a bad man, the kind of man a man of conscience *ought* to destroy – and of course a bad man's blessing's not worth having. So either will do.

RICH (*subdued*): I see.

CROMWELL: Oh, there's no going back, Rich. I find we've made ourselves the keepers of this conscience. And it's ravenous.

   Exit CROMWELL *and* RICH.

   Enter MORE.

MORE (*calling*): Boat! . . . Boat! . . . (*To himself.*) Oh, come along, it's not as bad as that. . . . (*Calls.*) Boat!

   Enter NORFOLK. *He stops.*

(*Pleased.*) Howard! . . . I can't get home. They won't bring me a boat.

NORFOLK: Do you blame them?

MORE: Is it as bad as that?

NORFOLK: It's every bit as bad as that!

MORE (*gravely*): Then it's good of you to be seen with me.

NORFOLK (*looking back, off*): I followed you.

MORE (*surprised*): Were *you* followed?

NORFOLK: Probably. (*Facing him.*) So listen to what I have to say: You're behaving like a fool. You're behaving like a crank. You're not behaving like a gentleman—— All right, that means nothing to you; but what about your friends?

MORE: What about them?

NORFOLK: Goddammit, you're dangerous to know!

MORE: Then don't know me.

NORFOLK: There's something further. . . . You must have realised by now there's a . . . policy, with regard to you. (MORE *nods*.) The King is using me in it.

MORE: That's clever. That's Cromwell. . . . You're between the upper and the nether millstones then.

NORFOLK: I am!

MORE: Howard, you must cease to know me.

NORFOLK: I do know you! I wish I didn't but I do!

MORE: I mean as a friend.

NORFOLK: You *are* my friend!

MORE: I can't relieve you of your obedience to the King, Howard. You must relieve yourself of our friendship. No one's safe now, and you have a son.

NORFOLK: You might as well advise a man to change the colour of his hair! I'm fond of you, and there it is! You're fond of me, and there it is!

MORE: What's to be done then?

NORFOLK (*with deep appeal*): Give in.

MORE (*gently*): I can't give in, Howard – (*smile*) you might as well advise a man to change the colour of his eyes. I can't. Our friendship's more mutable than *that*.

NORFOLK: Oh, that's immutable is it? The one fixed point in a world of changing friendships is that Thomas More will not give in!

MORE (*urgent to explain*): To me it *has* to be, for that's myself! Affection goes as deep in me as you I think, but only God is love right through, Howard; and *that's* my *self*.

NORFOLK: And who are you? Goddammit, man, it's disproportionate! *We're* supposed to be the arrogant ones, the proud, splenetic ones – and we've all given in! Why must you stand out? (*Quiet and quick.*) You'll break my heart.

MORE (*moved*): We'll do it now, Howard: part, as friends, and meet as strangers. (*He attempts to take* NORFOLK'S *hand.*)

NORFOLK (*throwing it off*): Daft, Thomas! Why d'you want to take your friendship from me? For friendship's sake! You say we'll meet as strangers and every word you've said confirms our friendship!

MORE (*takes a last affectionate look at him*): Oh, that can be remedied. (*Walks away, turns: in a tone of deliberate insult.*) Norfolk, you're a fool.

NORFOLK (*starts: then smiles and folds his arms*): *You* can't place a quarrel; you haven't the style.

MORE: Hear me out. You and your class have 'given in' – as you rightly call it – because the religion of this country means nothing to you one way or the other.

NORFOLK: Well, that's a foolish saying for a start; the nobility of England has always been——

MORE: The nobility of England, my lord, would have snored through the Sermon on the Mount. But you'll labour like Thomas Aquinas over a rat-dog's pedigree. Now what's the name of those distorted creatures you're all breeding at the moment?

NORFOLK (*steadily, but roused towards anger by* MORE'S *tone*): An artificial quarrel's not a quarrel.

MORE: Don't deceive yourself, my lord, we've had a quarrel since the day we met, our friendship was but sloth.

NORFOLK: You can be cruel when you've a mind to be; but I've always known that.

MORE: What's the name of those dogs? Marsh mastiffs? Bog beagles?

NORFOLK: Water spaniels!

MORE: And what would you do with a water spaniel that was afraid of water? You'd hang it! Well, as a spaniel is to water, so is a man to his own self. I will not give in because I oppose it – *I* do – not my pride, not my spleen, nor any other of my appetites but *I* do – *I*! (*He goes up to him and feels him up and down like an animal.* MARGARET'S *voice is heard, well off, call-*

ing her father. MORE'S *attention is irresistibly caught by this; but he turns back determinedly to* NORFOLK.) Is there no single sinew in the midst of this that serves no appetite of Norfolk's but is, just, Norfolk? There is! Give *that* some exercise, my lord!

MARGARET (*off, nearer*): Father?

NORFOLK (*breathing hard*): Thomas. . . .

MORE: Because as you stand, you'll go before your Maker in a very ill condition!

Enter MARGARET, *below; she stops, amazed at them.*

NORFOLK: Now steady, Thomas. . . .

MORE: And he'll have to think that somewhere back along your pedigree – a bitch got over the wall!

NORFOLK *lashes out at him; he ducks and winces. Exit* NORFOLK.

MARGARET: Father! (*As he straightens up.*) Father, what was that?

MORE: That was Norfolk. (*Looks after him wistfully.*)

Enter ROPER.

ROPER (*excited, almost gleeful*): Do you know, sir? Have you heard? (MORE *still looking off, unanswering. To* MARGARET.) Have you told him?

MARGARET (*gently*): We've been looking for you, Father. (MORE *the same.*)

ROPER: There's to be a new Act through Parliament, sir!

MORE (*half-turning, half attending*): Act?

ROPER: Yes, sir – about the Marriage!

MORE (*indifferent*): Oh. (*Turning back again.*)

ROPER *and* MARGARET *look at one another.*

MARGARET (*puts hand on his arm*): Father, by this Act, they're going to administer an oath.

MORE (*instantaneous attention*): An oath! (*Looks from one to other.*) On what compulsion?

ROPER: It's expected to be treason!

MORE (*very still*): What is the oath?

ROPER (*puzzled*): It's about the Marriage, sir.

MORE: But what is the wording?

ROPER: We don't need to know the (*contemptuous*) wording –
we know what it will mean!

MORE: It will mean what the words say! An oath is *made* of
words! It may be possible to take it. Or avoid it. Have we
a copy of the Bill? (*To* MARGARET.)

MARGARET: There's one coming out from the City.

MORE: Then let's get home and look at it. Oh, I've no boat
(*He looks off again after* NORFOLK.)

MARGARET (*gently*): What happened, Father?

MORE: I spoke, slightingly, of water spaniels. Let's get home.
(*He turns and sees* ROPER *excited and truculent.*) Now listen,
Will. And, Meg, you know I know you well, you listen too.
God made the *angels* to show him splendour – as he made
animals for innocence and plants for their simplicity. But
Man he made to serve him wittily, in the tangle of his mind!
If he suffers us to fall to such a case that there is no escaping,
then we may stand to our tackle as best we can, and yes,
Will, then we may clamour like champions . . . if we have
the spittle for it. And no doubt it delights God to see
splendour where he only looked for complexity. But it's
God's part, not our own, to bring ourselves to that ex-
tremity! Our natural business lies in escaping – so let's get
home and study this Bill.

Exit MORE, ROPER *and* MARGARET.

Enter COMMON MAN, *dragging basket. The rear of the stage
remains water-lit in moonlight. Iron grills now descend to cover
all the apertures. Also, a rack, which remains suspended, and a
cage which is lowered to the floor. While this takes place the
COMMON MAN arranges three chairs behind a table. Then he
turns and watches the completion of the transformation.*

COMMON MAN (*aggrieved*): *Now* look! . . . I don't suppose
anyone enjoyed it any more than he did. Well, not much
more. (*Takes from basket and dons coat and hat.*) Jailer! (*Shrugs.*)

It's a job. The pay scale being what it is they have to take a rather common type of man into the prison service. But it's a job like any other job. Bit nearer the knuckle than most perhaps.

Enter right, CROMWELL, NORFOLK, CRANMER, *who sit, and* RICH, *who stands behind them. Enter left,* MORE, *who enters the cage and lies down.*

They'd let him out if they could but for various reasons they can't. (*Twirling keys.*) I'd let him out if I could but I can't. Not without taking up residence in there myself. And he's in there already, so what'd be the point? You know the old adage? 'Better a live rat than a dead lion,' and that's about it.

An envelope descends swiftly before him. He opens it and reads: 'With reference to the old adage: Thomas Cromwell was found guilty of High Treason and executed on 28 July 1540. Norfolk was found guilty of High Treason and should have been executed on 27 January 1547 but on the night of 26 January, the King died of syphilis and wasn't able to sign the warrant. Thomas Cranmer.' (*Jerking thumb.*) That's the other one – 'was burned alive on 21 March 1556.' (*He is about to conclude but sees a postscript.*) Oh. 'Richard Rich became a Knight and Solicitor-General, a Baron and Lord Chancellor, and died in his bed.' So did I. And so, I hope (*pushing off basket*) will all of you.

He goes to MORE *and rouses him. Heavy bell strikes one.*

MORE (*rousing*): What, again?

JAILER: Sorry, sir.

MORE(*flops back*): What time is it?

JAILER: Just struck one, sir.

MORE: Oh, this is iniquitous!

JAILER (*anxious*): Sir.

MORE (*sitting up*): All right. (*Putting on slippers.*) Who's there?

JAILER: The Secretary, the Duke, and the Archbishop.

MORE: I'm flattered. (*Stands. Claps hand to hip.*) Ooh! (*Preceded by* JAILER *limps across stage right: he has aged and is pale, but his manner though wary, is relaxed: while that of the Commission is bored, tense, and jumpy.*)

NORFOLK (*looks at him*): A chair for the prisoner. (*While JAILER brings a chair and MORE sits in it, NORFOLK rattles off*): This is the Seventh Commission to enquire into the case of Sir Thomas More, appointed by His Majesty's Council. Have you anything to say?

MORE: No. (*To JAILER.*) Thank you.

NORFOLK (*sitting back*): Mr Secretary.

CROMWELL: Sir Thomas – (*breaks off*) – do the witnesses attend?

RICH: Mr Secretary.

JAILER: Sir.

CROMWELL (*to JAILER*): Nearer! (*He advances a bit.*) Come where you can hear! (*JAILER takes up stance by RICH. To MORE.*) Sir Thomas, you have seen this document before?

MORE: Many times.

CROMWELL: It is the Act of Succession. These are the names of those who have sworn to it.

MORE: I have, as you say, seen it before.

CROMWELL: Will you swear to it?

MORE: No.

NORFOLK: Thomas, we must know plainly——

CROMWELL (*throws down document*): Your Grace, *please*!

NORFOLK: Master Cromwell! (*They regard one another in hatred.*)

CROMWELL: I beg Your Grace's pardon. (*Sighing, rests head in hands.*)

NORFOLK: Thomas, we must know plainly whether you recognise the offspring of Queen Anne as heirs to His Majesty.

MORE: The King in Parliament tells me that they are. Of course I recognise them.

NORFOLK: Will you swear that you do?

MORE: Yes.

NORFOLK: Then why won't you swear to the Act?

CROMWELL (*impatient*): Because there is more than that *in* the Act.

NORFOLK: Is that it?

MORE (*after a pause*): Yes.

NORFOLK: Then we must find out what it is in the Act that he objects to!

CROMWELL: Brilliant. (NORFOLK *rounds on him.*)

CRANMER (*hastily*): Your Grace—— May I try?

NORFOLK: Certainly. I've no pretension to be an expert, in police work.

During next speech CROMWELL *straightens up and folds arms resignedly.*

CRANMER (*clears throat fussily*): Sir Thomas, it states in the preamble that the King's former marriage, to the Lady Catherine, was unlawful, she being previously his brother's wife and the – er – 'Pope' having no authority to sanction it. (*Gently.*) Is that what you deny? (*No reply.*) Is that what you dispute? (*No reply.*) Is that what you are not sure of? (*No reply.*)

NORFOLK: Thomas, you insult the King and His Council in the person of the Lord Archbishop!

MORE: I insult no one. I will not take the oath. I will not tell you why I will not.

NORFOLK: Then your reasons must be treasonable!

MORE: Not 'must be'; may be.

NORFOLK: It's a fair assumption!

MORE: The law requires more than an assumption; the law requires a fact. (CROMWELL *looks at him and away again.*)

CRANMER: I cannot judge your legal standing in the case; but until I know the *ground* of your objections, I can only guess your spiritual standing too.

MORE (*is for a second furiously affronted; then humour overtakes him*): If you're willing to guess at that, Your Grace, it should be a small matter to guess my objections.

CROMWELL (*quickly*): You do have objections to the Act?

NORFOLK (*happily*): Well, we know *that*, Cromwell!

MORE: You don't, my lord. You may *suppose* I have objections. All you *know* is that I will not swear to it. From sheer delight to give you trouble it might be.

NORFOLK: Is it material why you won't?

MORE: It's most material. For refusing to swear my goods are forfeit and I am condemned to life imprisonment. You cannot lawfully harm me further. But if you were right in supposing I had reasons for refusing and right again in supposing my reasons to be treasonable, the law would let you cut my head off.

NORFOLK (*he has followed with some difficulty*): Oh yes.

CROMWELL (*admiring murmur*): Oh, well done, Sir Thomas. I've been trying to make that clear to His Grace for some time.

NORFOLK (*hardly responds to the insult; his face is gloomy and disgusted*): Oh, confound all this. . . . (*With real dignity.*) I'm not a scholar, as Master Cromwell never tires of pointing out, and frankly I don't know whether the marriage was lawful or not. But damn it, Thomas, look at those names. . . . You know those men! Can't you do what I did, and come with us, for fellowship?

MORE (*moved*): And when we stand before God, and you are sent to Paradise for doing according to your conscience, and I am damned for not doing according to mine, will you come with me, for fellowship?

CRANMER: So those of us whose names are there are damned. Sir Thomas?

MORE: I don't know, Your Grace. I have no window to look into another man's conscience. I condemn no one.

CRANMER: Then the matter is capable of question?

MORE: Certainly.

CRANMER: But that you owe obedience to your King is not

capable of question. So weigh a doubt against a certainty –
and sign.

MORE: Some men think the Earth is round, others think it flat;
it is a matter capable of question. But if it is flat, will the
King's command make it round? And if it is round, will the
King's command flatten it? No, I will not sign.

CROMWELL (*leaping up, with ceremonial indignation*): Then you
have more regard to your own doubt than you have to his
command!

MORE: For myself, I have no doubt.

CROMWELL: No doubt of what?

MORE: No doubt of my grounds for refusing this oath.
Grounds I will tell to the King alone, and which you, Mr
Secretary, will not trick out of me.

NORFOLK: Thomas——

MORE: Oh, gentlemen, can't I go to bed?

CROMWELL: You don't seem to appreciate the seriousness of
your position.

MORE: I defy anyone to live in that cell for a year and not
appreciate the seriousness of his position.

CROMWELL: Yet the State has harsher punishments.

MORE: You threaten like a dockside bully.

CROMWELL: How should I threaten?

MORE: Like a Minister of State, with justice!

CROMWELL: Oh, justice is what you're threatened with.

MORE: Then I'm not threatened.

NORFOLK: Master Secretary, I think the prisoner may retire as
he requests. Unless you, my lord——?

CRANMER (*pettish*): No, I see no purpose in prolonging the
interview.

NORFOLK: Then good night, Thomas.

MORE (*hesitates*): Might I have one or two more books?

CROMWELL: You have books?

MORE: Yes.

CROMWELL: I didn't know; you shouldn't have.

MORE (*turns to go: pauses. Desperately*): May I see my family?

CROMWELL: No! (MORE *returns to cell*.) Jailer!

JAILER: Sir!

CROMWELL: Have you ever heard the prisoner speak of the King's divorce, or the King's Supremacy of the Church, or the King's marriage?

JAILER: No, sir, not a word.

CROMWELL: If he does, you will of course report it to the Lieutenant.

JAILER: Of course, sir.

CROMWELL: You will swear an oath to that effect.

JAILER (*cheerfully*): Certainly, sir!

CROMWELL: Archbishop?

CRANMER (*laying cross of vestment on table*): Place your left hand on this and raise your right hand – take your hat off—— Now say after me: I swear by my immortal soul – (JAILER *overlapping, repeats the oath with him*) that I will report truly anything said by Sir Thomas More against the King the Council or the State of the Realm. So help me God. Amen.

JAILER (*overlapping*): So help me God. Amen.

CROMWELL: And there's fifty guineas in it if you do.

JAILER (*looks at him gravely*): Yes, sir. (*And goes*.)

CRANMER (*hastily*): That's not to tempt you into perjury, my man!

JAILER: No, sir! (*At exit pauses; to audience*.) Fifty guineas isn't tempting; fifty guineas is alarming. If he'd left it at swearing. . . . But fifty—— That's serious money. If it's worth that much now it's worth my neck presently. (*Decision*.) I want no part of it. They can sort it out between them. I feel my deafness coming on.

    Exit JAILER. *The Commission rises*.

CROMWELL: Rich!

RICH: Secretary?

CROMWELL: Tomorrow morning, remove the prisoner's books.

NORFOLK: Is that necessary?

CROMWELL (*suppressed exasperation*): Norfolk. With regards this case, the King is becoming impatient.

NORFOLK: Aye, with you.

CROMWELL: With all of us. (*He walks over to the rack.*) You know the King's impatience, how commodious it is!

> NORFOLK *and* CRANMER *exit.* CROMWELL *is brooding over the instrument of torture.*

RICH: Secretary!

CROMWELL (*abstracted*): Yes . . . ?

RICH: Sir Redvers Llewellyn has retired.

CROMWELL (*not listening*): Mm . . . ?

RICH (*goes to other end of rack and faces him. Some indignation*): The Attorney-General for Wales. His post is vacant. You said I might approach you.

CROMWELL (*contemptuous impatience*): Oh, not *now*. . . . (*Broods.*) He must submit, the alternatives are bad. While More's alive the King's conscience breaks into fresh stinking flowers every time he gets from bed. And if I bring about More's death – I plant my own, I think. There's no other good solution! He must submit! (*He whirls the windlass of the rack, producing a startling clatter from the ratchet. They look at each other. He turns it again slowly, shakes his head and lets go.*) No; the King will not permit it. (*Walks away.*) We have to find some gentler way.

> *The scene change commences as he says this and exit* RICH *and* CROMWELL. *From night it becomes morning, cold grey light from off the grey water. And enter* JAILER *and* MARGARET.

JAILER: Wake up, Sir Thomas! Your family's here!

MORE (*starting up. A great cry*): Margaret! What's this? You can visit me? (*Thrusts arms through cage.*) Meg. Meg. (*She goes to him. Then horrified.*) For God's sake, Meg, they've not put *you* in here?

JAILER (*reassuring*): No-o-o, sir. Just a visit; a short one.

MORE (*excited*): Jailer, jailer, let me out of this.

JAILER (*stolid*): Yes, sir. I'm allowed to let you out.

MORE: Thank you. (*Goes to door of cage, gabbling while* JAILER *unlocks it.*) Thank you, thank you. (*Comes out. He and she regard each other; then she drops into a curtsey.*)

MARGARET: Good morning, Father.

MORE (*ecstatic, wraps her to him*): Oh, good morning—— Good morning. (*Enter* ALICE, *supported by* WILL. *She, like* MORE, *has aged and is poorly dressed.*) Good morning, Alice. Good morning, Will.

　　ROPER *is staring at the rack in horror.* ALICE *approaches* MORE *and peers at him technically.*

ALICE (*almost accusatory*): Husband, how do you do?

MORE (*smiling over* MARGARET): As well as need be, Alice. Very happy now. Will?

ROPER: This is an awful place!

MORE: Except it's keeping me from you, my dears, it's not so bad. Remarkably like any other place.

ALICE (*looks up critically*): It drips!

MORE: Yes. Too near the river. (ALICE *goes apart and sits, her face bitter.*)

MARGARET (*disengages from him, takes basket from her mother*): We've brought you some things. (*Shows him. There is constraint between them.*) Some cheese. . . .

MORE: Cheese.

MARGARET: And a custard. . . .

MORE: A custard!

MARGARET: And, these other things. . . . (*She doesn't look at him.*)

ROPER: And a bottle of wine. (*Offering it.*)

MORE: Oh. (*Mischievous.*) Is it good, son Roper?

ROPER: I don't know, sir.

MORE (*looks at them, puzzled*): Well.

ROPER: Sir, come out! Swear to the Act! Take the oath and come out!

MORE: Is this why they let you come?

ROPER: Yes . . . Meg's under oath to persuade you.

MORE (*coldly*): That was silly, Meg. How did you come to do that?

MARGARET: I wanted to!

MORE: You want me to swear to the Act of Succession?

MARGARET: 'God more regards the thoughts of the heart than the words of the mouth' or so you've always told me.

MORE: Yes.

MARGARET: Then say the words of the oath and in your heart think otherwise.

MORE: What is an oath then but words we say to God?

MARGARET: That's very neat.

MORE: Do you mean it isn't true?

MARGARET: No, it's true.

MORE: Then it's a poor argument to call it 'neat', Meg. When a man takes an oath, Meg, he's holding his own self in his own hands. Like water (*cups hands*) and if he opens his fingers *then* – he needn't hope to find himself again. Some men aren't capable of this, but I'd be loathe to think your father one of them.

MARGARET: So should I. . . .

MORE: Then——

MARGARET: There's something else I've been thinking.

MORE: Oh, Meg!

MARGARET: In any state that was half good, you would be raised up high, not here, for what you've done already.

MORE: All right.

MARGARET: It's not your fault the State's three-quarters bad.

MORE: No.

MARGARET: Then if you elect to suffer for it, you elect yourself a hero.

MORE: That's very neat. But look now . . . If we lived in a State where virtue was profitable, common sense would make us good, and greed would make us saintly. And we'd live like animals or angels in the happy land that *needs* no heroes. But since in fact we see that avarice, anger, envy, pride, sloth, lust and stupidity commonly profit far beyond humility, chastity, fortitude, justice and thought, and have to choose, to be human at all . . . why then perhaps we *must* stand fast a little – even at the risk of being heroes.

MARGARET (*emotional*): But in reason! Haven't you done as much as God can reasonably *want*?

MORE: Well . . . finally . . . it isn't a matter of reason; finally it's a matter of love.

ALICE (*hostile*): You're content then, to be shut up here with mice and rats when you might be home with us!

MORE (*flinching*): Content? If they'd open a crack that wide (*between finger and thumb*) I'd be through it. (*To* MARGARET.) Well, has Eve run out of apples?

MARGARET: I've not yet told you what the house is like, without you.

MORE: Don't, Meg.

MARGARET: What we do in the evenings, now that you're not there.

MORE: Meg, have done!

MARGARET: We sit in the dark because we've no candles. And we've no talk because we're wondering what they're doing to you here.

MORE: The King's more merciful than you. He doesn't use the rack.

    Enter JAILER.

JAILER: Two minutes to go, sir. I thought you'd like to know.

MORE: Two minutes!

JAILER: Till seven o'clock, sir. Sorry. Two minutes.

    Exit JAILER.

MORE: Jailer——! (*Seizes* ROPER *by the arm.*) Will – go to him, talk to him, keep him occupied—— (*Propelling him after* JAILER.)

ROPER: How, sir?

MORE: Anyhow! – Have you got any money?

ROPER (*eager*): Yes!

MORE: No, don't try and bribe him! Let him play for it; he's got a pair of dice. And talk to him, you understand! And take this (*the wine*) – and mind you share it – do it properly, Will! (ROPER *nods vigorously and exit.*) Now listen, you must leave the country. All of you must leave the country.

MARGARET: And leave you here?

MORE: It makes no difference, Meg; they won't let you see me again. (*Breathlessly, a prepared speech under pressure.*) You must all go on the same day, but not on the same boat; different boats from different ports——

MARGARET: After the trial, then.

MORE: There'll be no trial, they have no case. Do this for me I beseech you?

MARGARET: Yes.

MORE: Alice? (*She turns her back.*) Alice, I command it!

ALICE (*harshly*): Right!

MORE (*looks into basket*): Oh, this is splendid; I know who packed this.

ALICE (*harshly*): I packed it.

MORE: Yes. (*Eats a morsel.*) You still make superlative custard, Alice.

ALICE: Do I?

MORE: That's a nice dress you have on.

ALICE: It's my cooking dress.

MORE: It's very nice anyway. Nice colour.

ALICE (*turns. Quietly*): By God, you think very little of me. (*Mounting bitterness.*) I know I'm a fool. But I'm no such fool as at this time to be lamenting for my dresses! Or to relish complimenting on my custard!

MORE (*regarding her with frozen attention. He nods once or twice*): I am well rebuked. (*Holds out his hands.*) Al——!

ALICE: No! (*She remains where she is, glaring at him.*)

MORE (*he is in great fear of her*): I am faint when I think of the worst that they may do to me. But worse than that would be to go, with you not understanding why I go.

ALICE: I don't!

MORE (*just hanging on to his self-possession*): Alice, if you can tell me that you understand, I think I can make a good death, if I have to.

ALICE: Your death's no 'good' to me!

MORE: Alice, you must tell me that you understand!

ALICE: I don't! (*She throws it straight at his head.*) I don't believe this had to happen.

MORE (*his face is drawn*): If you say that, Alice, I don't see how I'm to face it.

ALICE: It's the truth!

MORE (*gasping*): You're an honest woman.

ALICE: Much good may it do me! I'll tell you what I'm afraid of; that when you've gone, I shall hate you for it.

MORE (*turns from her: his face working*): Well, you mustn't, Alice, that's all. (*Swiftly she crosses the stage to him; he turns and they clasp each other fiercely*). You mustn't, you——

ALICE (*covers his mouth with her hand*): S-s-sh. . . . As for understanding, I understand you're the best man that I ever met or am likely to; and if you go – well God knows why I suppose – though as God's my witness God's kept deadly quiet about it! And if anyone wants my opinion of the King and his Council they've only to ask for it!

MORE: Why, it's a lion I married! A lion! A lion! (*He breaks away from her his face shining.*) Get them to take half this to Bishop Fisher – they've got him in the upper gallery——

ALICE: It's for you, not Bishop Fisher!

MORE: Now do as I ask—— (*Breaks off a piece of the custard and eats it.*) Oh, it's good, it's very, very good. (*He puts his face in his hands;* ALICE *and* MARGARET *comfort him;* ROPER *and* JAILER *erupt on to the stage above, wrangling fiercely.*)

JAILER: It's no good, sir! I know what you're up to! And it can't be done!

ROPER: Another minute, man!

JAILER (*to* MORE *descending*): Sorry, sir, time's up!

ROPER (*gripping his shoulder from behind*): For pity's sake—!

JAILER (*shaking him off*): Now don't do that, sir! Sir Thomas, the ladies will have to go now!

MORE: You said seven o'clock!

JAILER: It's seven now. You must understand my position, sir.

MORE: But one more minute!

MARGARET: Only a little while – give us a little while!

JAILER (*reproving*): Now, Miss, you don't want to get me into trouble.

ALICE: Do as you're told. Be off at once!

The first stroke of seven is heard on a heavy, deliberate bell, which continues, reducing what follows to a babble.

JAILER (*taking* MARGARET *firmly by the upper arm*): Now come along, Miss; you'll get your father into trouble as well as me. (ROPER *descends and grabs him.*) Are you obstructing me, sir? (MARGARET *embraces* MORE, *and dashes up the stairs and exit, followed by* ROPER. *Taking* ALICE *gingerly by the arm.*) Now, my lady, no trouble!

ALICE (*throwing him off as she rises*): *Don't* put your muddy hand on me!

JAILER: Am I to call the guard then? Then come on!

ALICE, facing him, puts foot on bottom stair and so retreats before him, backwards.

MORE: For God's sake, man, we're saying good-bye!

JAILER: You don't know what you're asking, sir. You don't know how you're watched.

ALICE: Filthy, stinking, gutter-bred turnkey!

JAILER: Call me what you like, ma'am; you've got to go.

ALICE: I'll see you suffer for this!

JAILER: You're doing your husband no good!

MORE: Alice, good-bye, my love!

On this, the last stroke of the seven sounds. ALICE *raises her hand, turns, and with considerable dignity, exit.* JAILER *stops at head of stairs and addresses* MORE, *who, still crouching,* **turns** *from him, facing audience.*

JAILER (*reasonably*): You understand my position, sir, there's nothing I can do; I'm a plain simple man and just want to keep out of trouble.

MORE (*cries out passionately*): Oh, Sweet Jesus! These plain, simple, men!

Immediately: (1) *Music, portentous and heraldic.*

(2) *Bars, rack and cage flown swiftly upwards.*

(3) *Lighting change from cold grey to warm yellow, re-creating a warm interior.*

(4) *Several narrow panels, scarlet and bearing the monogram 'HR VIII' in gold are lowered. Also an enormous Royal Coat-of-Arms which hangs above the table stage right.*

(5) *The* JAILER, *doffing costume comes down the stairs and:*

(A) *Places a chair for the Accused, helps* MORE *to it, and gives him a scroll which he studies.*

(B) *Fetches from the wings his prop basket, and produces:* (I) *A large hour-glass and papers which he places on table, stage right.* (II) *Twelve folding stools which he arranges in two rows of six each. While he is still doing this, and just before the panels and Coat-of-Arms have finished their descent, enter* CROMWELL. *He ringingly addresses the audience (while the* COMMON MAN *is still bustling about his chores) as soon as the music ends, which it does at this point, on a fanfare.*

CROMWELL (*indicating descending props*):

What Englishman can behold without Awe.
The Canvas and the Rigging of the Law!
(*Brief fanfare.*)
Forbidden here the galley-master's whip—
Hearts of Oak, in the Law's Great Ship!
(*Brief fanfare.*)

(*To* COMMON MAN *who is tiptoeing discreetly off stage.*) Where are you going?

COMMON MAN: I've finished here, sir.

Above the two rows of stools the COMMON MAN *has suspended from two wires, supported by two pairs of sticks, two rows of hats for the presumed occupants. Seven are plain grey hats, four are those worn by the* STEWARD, BOATMAN, INNKEEPER *and* JAILER. *And the last is another of the plain grey ones. The basket remains on stage, clearly visible.*

CROMWELL: You're the Foreman of the Jury.

COMMON MAN: Oh no, sir.

CROMWELL: You are John Dauncey. A general dealer?

COMMON MAN (*gloomy*): Yes, sir?

CROMWELL (*resuming his rhetorical stance*): Foreman of the Jury. Does the cap fit?

COMMON MAN *puts on the grey hat. It fits.*

COMMON MAN: Yes, sir.

CROMWELL (*resuming rhetorical stance*):

So, now we'll apply the good, plain sailor's art,

And fix these quicksands on the Law's plain chart!

Renewed, more prolonged fanfare, during which enter CRANMER *and* NORFOLK, *who stand behind the table stage right. On their entry* MORE *and* FOREMAN *rise. So soon as fanfare is finished* NORFOLK *speaks.*

NORFOLK (*takes refuge behind a rigorously official manner*): Sir Thomas More, you are called before us here at the Hall of Westminster to answer charge of High Treason. Nevertheless, and though you have heinously offended the King's Majesty, we hope if you will even now forthink and repent of your obstinate opinions, you may still taste his gracious pardon.

MORE: My lords, I thank you. Howbeit I make my petition to Almighty God that he will keep me in this, my honest mind to the last hour that I shall live. . . . As for the matters you may charge me with, I fear, from my present weakness, that

neither my wit nor my memory will serve to make sufficient
answers. . . . I should be glad to sit down.

NORFOLK: Be seated. Master Secretary Cromwell, have you
the charge?

CROMWELL: I have, my lord.

NORFOLK: Then read the charge.

CROMWELL (*approaching* MORE, *behind him, with papers; informally*): It is the same charge, Sir Thomas, that was brought
against Bishop Fisher. . . . (*As one who catches himself up
punctiliously.*) The *late* Bishop Fisher I should have said.

MORE (*tonelessly*): 'Late'?

CROMWELL: Bishop Fisher was executed this morning.

   MORE's *face expresses violent shock, then grief; he turns his
   head away from* CROMWELL *who is observing him clinically.*

NORFOLK: Master Secretary, read the charge!

CROMWELL (*formal*): That you did conspire traitorously and
maliciously to deny and deprive our liege lord Henry of his
undoubted certain title, Supreme Head of the Church in
England.

MORE (*surprise, shock, and indignation*): But I have never denied
this title!

CROMWELL: You refused the oath tendered to you at the
Tower and elsewhere——

MORE (*the same*): Silence is not denial. And for my silence I
am punished, with imprisonment. Why have I been called
again? (*At this point he is sensing that the trial has been in some
way rigged.*)

NORFOLK: On a charge of High Treason, Sir Thomas.

CROMWELL: For which the punishment is *not* imprisonment.

MORE: Death . . . comes for us all, my lords. Yes, even for
Kings he comes, to whom amidst all their Royalty and brute
strength he will neither kneel nor make them any reverence
nor pleasantly desire them to come forth, but roughly grasp
them by the very breast and rattle them until they be stark
dead! So causing their bodies to be buried in a pit and send-

ing *them* to a judgement . . . whereof at their death their success is uncertain.

CROMWELL: Treason enough here!

NORFOLK: The death of Kings is not in question, Sir Thomas,

MORE: Nor mine, I trust, until I'm proven guilty.

NORFOLK (*leaning forward urgently*): Your life lies in your own hand, Thomas, as it always has.

MORE (*absorbs this*): For our own deaths, my lord, yours and mine, dare we for shame desire to enter the Kingdom with ease, when Our Lord Himself entered with so much pain?

And now he faces CROMWELL *his eyes sparkling with suspicion.*

CROMWELL: Now, Sir Thomas, you stand upon your silence.

MORE: I do.

CROMWELL: But, Gentlemen of the Jury, there are many kinds of silence. Consider first the silence of a man when he is dead. Let us say we go into the room where he is lying; and let us say it is in the dead of night – there's nothing like darkness for sharpening the ear; and we listen. What do we hear? Silence. What does it betoken, this silence? Nothing. This is silence, pure and simple. But consider another case. Suppose I were to draw a dagger from my sleeve and make to kill the prisoner with it, and suppose their lordships there, instead of crying out for me to stop or crying out for help to stop me, maintained their silence. That *would* betoken! It would betoken a willingness that I should do it, and under the law they would be guilty with me. So silence can, according to circumstances, speak. Consider, now, the circumstances of the prisoner's silence. The oath was put to good and faithful subjects up and down the country and they had declared His Grace's Title to be just and good. And when it came to the prisoner he refused. He calls this silence. Yet is there a man in this court, is there a man in this country, who does not *know* Sir Thomas More's opinion of this title? Of course not! But how can that be? Because this silence be-

tokened – nay this silence *was* – not silence at all, but most
eloquent denial.

MORE (*with some of the academic's impatience for a shoddy line of
reasoning*): Not so, Mr Secretary, the maxim is 'qui tacet
consentire'. (*Turns to* COMMON MAN.) The maxim of the
law is: (*very carefully*) 'Silence Gives Consent'. If therefore,
you wish to construe what my silence 'betokened', you must
construe that I consented, not that I denied.

CROMWELL: Is that what the world in fact construes from it?
Do you pretend that is what you *wish* the world to construe
from it?

MORE: The world must construe according to its wits. This
Court must construe according to the law.

CROMWELL: I put it to the Court that the prisoner is pervert-
ing the law – making smoky what should be a clear light to
discover to the Court his own wrongdoing! (CROMWELL'S
official indignation is slipping into genuine anger and MORE
responds.)

MORE: The law is not a 'light' for you or any man to see by;
the law is not an instrument of any kind. (*To the* FOREMAN.)
The law is a causeway upon which so long as he keeps to it a
citizen may walk safely. (*Earnestly addressing him.*) In matters
of conscience——

CROMWELL (*bitterly smiling*): The conscience, the conscience...

MORE (*turning*): The word is not familiar to you?

CROMWELL: By God, too familiar! I am very used to hear it
in the mouths of criminals!

MORE: I am used to hear bad men misuse the name of God, yet
God exists. (*Turning back.*) In matters of conscience, the loyal
subject is more bounden to be loyal *to* his conscience than
to any other thing.

CROMWELL (*breathing hard: straight at* MORE): – And so provide
a noble motive for his frivolous self-conceit!

MORE (*earnestly*): It is not so, Master Cromwell – very and pure
necessity for respect of my own soul.

CROMWELL: – Your own self you mean!

MORE: Yes, a man's soul is his self!

CROMWELL (*thrusts his face into* MORE'S. *They hate each other and each other's standpoint*): A miserable thing, whatever you call it, that lives like a bat in a Sunday School! A shrill incessant pedagogue about its own salvation – but nothing to say of your place in the State! Under the King! In a great native country!

MORE (*not untouched*): Can I help my King by giving him lies when he asks for truth? Will you help England by populating her with liars?

CROMWELL (*backs away. His face stiff with malevolence*): My lords, I wish to call (*raises voice*) Sir Richard Rich!

Enter RICH. *He is now splendidly official, in dress and bearing; even* NORFOLK *is a bit impressed.*

Sir Richard (*indicating* CRANMER).

CRANMER (*proffering Bible*): I do solemnly swear . . .

RICH: I do solemnly swear that the evidence I shall give before the Court shall be the truth, the whole truth, and nothing but the truth.

CRANMER (*discreetly*): So help me God, Sir Richard.

RICH: So help me God.

NORFOLK: Take your stand there, Sir Richard.

CROMWELL: Now, Rich, on 12 March, you were at the Tower?

RICH: I was.

CROMWELL: With what purpose?

RICH: I was sent to carry away the prisoner's books.

CROMWELL: Did you talk with the prisoner?

RICH: Yes.

CROMWELL: Did you talk about the King's Supremacy of the Church?

RICH: Yes.

CROMWELL: What did you say?

RICH: I said to him: 'Supposing there was an Act of Parliament to say that I, Richard Rich, were to be King, would not you, Master More, take me for King?' 'That I would,' he said, 'for then you would be King.'

CROMWELL: Yes?

RICH: Then he said——

NORFOLK (*sharply*): The prisoner?

RICH: Yes, my lord. 'But I will put you a higher case,' he said. 'How if there were an Act of Parliament to say that God should not be God?'

MORE: This is true; and then you said——

NORFOLK: Silence! Continue.

RICH: I said 'Ah, but I will put you a middle case. Parliament has made our King Head of the Church. Why will you not accept him?'

NORFOLK (*strung up*): Well?

RICH: Then he said Parliament had no power to do it.

NORFOLK: Repeat the prisoner's words!

RICH: He said 'Parliament has not the competence.' Or words to that effect.

CROMWELL: He denied the title?

RICH: He did.

All look to MORE *but he looks to* RICH.

MORE: In good faith, Rich, I am sorrier for your perjury than my peril.

NORFOLK: Do you deny this?

MORE: Yes! My lords, if I were a man who heeded not the taking of an oath, you know well I need not to be here. Now I will take an oath! If what Master Rich has said is true, then I pray I may never see God in the face! Which I would not say were it otherwise for anything on earth.

CROMWELL (*to* FOREMAN, *calmly*, *technical*): That is not evidence.

MORE: Is it probable – is it probable – that after so long a silence, on this, the very point so urgently sought of me, I should open my mind to such a man as that?

CROMWELL (*to* RICH): Do you wish to modify your testimony?

RICH: No, Secretary.

MORE: There were two other men! Southwell and Palmer!

CROMWELL: Unhappily, Sir Richard Southwell and Master Palmer are both in Ireland on the King's business. (MORE *gestures helplessly.*) It has no bearing. I have their deposition here in which the Court will see they state that being busy with the prisoner's books they did not hear what was said. (*Hands deposition to* FOREMAN *who examines it with much seriousness.*)

MORE: If I had really said this is it not obvious he would instantly have called these men to witness?

CROMWELL: Sir Richard, have you anything to add?

RICH: Nothing, Mr Secretary.

NORFOLK: Sir Thomas?

MORE (*looking at* FOREMAN): To what purpose? I am a dead man. (*To* CROMWELL.) You have your desire of me. What you have hunted me for is not my actions, but the thoughts of my heart. It is a long road you have opened. For first men will disclaim their hearts and presently they will have no hearts. God help the people whose Statesmen walk your road.

NORFOLK: Then the witness may withdraw.

RICH *crosses stage, watched by* MORE.

MORE: I *have* one question to ask the witness. (RICH *stops.*) That's a chain of office you are wearing. (*Reluctantly* RICH *faces him.*) May I see it? (NORFOLK *motions him to approach.* MORE *examines the medallion.*) The red dragon. (*To* CROMWELL.) What's this?

CROMWELL: Sir Richard is appointed Attorney-General for Wales.

MORE (*looking into* RICH'S *face: with pain and amusement*): For Wales? Why, Richard, it profits a man nothing to give his soul for the whole world.... But for Wales——!

Exit RICH, *stiff faced, but infrangibly dignified.*

CROMWELL: Now I must ask the Court's indulgence! I have a message for the prisoner from the King: (*urgent*) Sir Thomas, I am empowered to tell you that even now——

MORE: No no, It cannot be.

CROMWELL: The case rests! (NORFOLK *is staring at* MORE.) My lord!

NORFOLK: The Jury will retire and consider the evidence.

CROMWELL: Considering the evidence it shouldn't be necessary for them to retire. (*Standing over* FOREMAN.) Is it necessary?

FOREMAN *shakes his head.*

NORFOLK: Then is the prisoner guilty or not guilty?

FOREMAN: Guilty, my lord!

NORFOLK (*leaping to his feet; all rise save* MORE): Prisoner at the bar, you have been found guilty of High Treason. The sentence of the Court——

MORE: My lord!

NORFOLK *breaks off.* MORE *has a sly smile. From this point to end of play his manner is of one who has fulfilled all his obligations and will now consult no interests but his own.*

My lord, when *I* was practising the law, the manner was to ask the prisoner *before* pronouncing sentence, if he had anything to say.

NORFOLK (*flummoxed*): Have you anything to say?

MORE: Yes. (*He rises: all others sit.*) To avoid this I have taken every path my winding wits would find. Now that the court has determined to condemn me, God knoweth how, I will discharge my mind . . . concerning my indictment and the King's title. The indictment is grounded in an Act of Parliament which is directly repugnant to the Law of God. The King in Parliament cannot bestow the Supremacy of the Church because it is a Spiritual Supremacy! And more to this the immunity of the Church is promised both in Magna Carta and the King's own Coronation Oath!

CROMWELL: Now we plainly see that you *are* malicious!

MORE: Not so, Mr Secretary! (*He pauses, and launches, very quietly, ruminatively, into his final stock-taking.*) I am the King's true subject, and pray for him and all the realm . . . I do none harm, I say none harm, I think none harm. And if this be not enough to keep a man alive, in good faith I long not to live . . . I have, since I came into prison, been several times in such a case that I thought to die within the hour, and I thank Our Lord I was never sorry for it, but rather sorry when it passed. And therefore, my poor body is at the King's pleasure. Would God my death might do him some good. . . . (*With a great flash of scorn and anger.*) Nevertheless, it is not for the Supremacy that you have sought my blood – but because I would not bend to the marriage!

Immediately scene change commences, while NORFOLK *reads the sentence.*

NORFOLK: Prisoner at the bar, you have been found guilty on the charge of High Treason. The sentence of the Court is that you shall be taken from this Court to the Tower, thence to the place of execution, and there your head shall be stricken from your body, and may God have mercy on your soul!

The scene change is as follows:

(I) *The trappings of justice are flown upwards.*

(II) *The lights are dimmed save for three areas: spots, left and right front, and the arch at the head of the stairs which begins to show blue sky.*

(III) *Through this arch – where the axe and the block are silhouetted against a light of steadily increasing brilliance – comes the murmuration of a large crowd, formalised almost into a chant and mounting, so that* NORFOLK *has to shout the end of his speech.*

In addition to the noise of the crowd and the flying machinery there is stage activity: FOREMAN *doffs cap, as* COMMON MAN *removes the prisoner's chair and then goes to the spot, left.*

CRANMER *also goes to spot, left.*

MORE *goes to spot, right.*

> WOMAN *enters, up right, and goes to spot, left.*
>
> NORFOLK *remains where he is.*
>
> *When these movements are complete – they are made naturally, technically –* CROMWELL *goes and stands in the light streaming down the stairs. He beckons the* COMMON MAN *who leaves spot, left, and joins him.* CROMWELL *points to the head of the stairs.* COMMON MAN *shakes his head and indicates in mime that he has no costume. He drags basket into the light and again indicates that there is no costume in it.* CROMWELL *takes a small black mask from his sleeve and offers it to him. The* COMMON MAN *puts it on, thus, in his black tights, becoming the traditional headsman. He ascends the stairs, straddles his legs and picks up the axe, silhouetted against the bright sky. At once the crowd falls silent.*
>
> *Exit* CROMWELL, *dragging basket.*
>
> NORFOLK *joins* MORE *in spot, right.*

NORFOLK : I can come no further, Thomas. (*Proffering goblet.*) Here, drink this.

MORE: My master had easel and gall, not wine, given him to drink. Let me be going.

MARGARET: Father! (*She runs to him in the spot from right and flings herself upon him.*) Father! Father, Father, Father, Father!

MORE: Have patience, Margaret, and trouble not thyself. Death comes for us all; even at our birth (*he holds her head and looks down at it for a moment in recollection*) – even at our birth, death does but stand aside a little. It is the law of nature, and the will of God. (*He disengages from her. Dispassionately.*) You have long known the secrets of my heart.

WOMAN: Sir Thomas! (*He stops.*) Remember me, Sir Thomas? When you were Chancellor, you gave a false judgement against me. Remember that now.

MORE: Woman, you see how I am occupied. (*With sudden decision goes to her in spot, left. Crisply.*) I remember your matter well, and if I had to give sentence now I assure you I should not alter it. You have no injury; so go your ways;

and content yourself; and trouble me not! (*He walks swiftly to the stairs. Then stops, realising that* CRANMER, *carrying his Bible, has followed him. Quite kindly.*) I beseech Your Grace, go back.

Offended, CRANMER *does so. The lighting is now complete, i.e., darkness save for three areas of light, the one at head of stairs now dazzlingly brilliant. When* MORE *gets to head of stairs by the* HEADSMAN *there is a single shout from the crowd. He turns to* HEADSMAN.

Friend, be not afraid of your office. You send me to God.

CRANMER (*envious rather than waspish*): You're very sure of that, Sir Thomas.

MORE (*takes off his hat, revealing the grey disordered hair*): He will not refuse one who is so blithe to go to him. (*Kneeling.*)

Immediately, harsh roar of kettledrums and total blackout at head of stairs. While the drums roar, WOMAN *backs into* CRANMER *and exit together.* NORFOLK *assists* MARGARET *from the stage, which is now 'occupied' only by the two spots left and right front. The drums cease.*

HEADSMAN (*from the darkness*): Behold – the head – of a traitor!

Enter into spots left and right, CROMWELL *and* CHAPUYS. *They stop on seeing one another, arrested in postures of frozen hostility while the light spreads plainly over the stage, which is empty save for themselves.*

Then simultaneously they stalk forward, crossing mid-stage with heads high and averted. But as they approach their exits they pause, hesitate, and slowly turn. Thoughtfully they stroll back towards one another. CROMWELL *raises his head and essays a smile.* CHAPUYS *responds. They link arms and approach the stairs. As they go we hear that they are chuckling. There is nothing sinister or malignant in the sound; rather it is the self-mocking, self-indulgent, rather rueful laughter of men who know what the world is and how to be comfortable in it. As they go,* THE CURTAIN FALLS.

ALTERNATIVE ENDING

In the London production of this play at the Globe Theatre the play ended as follows:

Instead of the CROMWELL *and* CHAPUYS *entrance after the* HEADSMAN'S *line* 'Behold – the head – of a traitor!', *the* COMMON MAN *came to the centre stage, having taken off his mask as the executioner, and said:*

'I'm breathing. . . . Are you breathing too? . . . It's nice isn't it? It isn't difficult to keep alive friends . . . just don't make trouble – or if you must make trouble, make the sort of trouble that's expected. Well, I don't need to tell you that. Good night. If we should bump into one another, recognise me.'

(*Exits*)

CURTAIN

The Tiger and the Horse

*The Tygers of wrath are wiser
than the horses of instruction*
—Blake

THE TIGER AND THE HORSE *was first presented in London at the Queen's Theatre on 24 August 1960 by H. M. Tennent Ltd and Frith Banbury Ltd, with the following cast:*

JACK DEAN	Michael Redgrave
GWENDOLINE DEAN	Catherine Lacey
MARY DEAN	Jennifer Wright
STELLA DEAN	Vanessa Redgrave
LOUIS FLAX	Alan Dobie
SIR HUGO SLATE	Kynaston Reeves

The play directed by
FRITH BANBURY

Settings by
SAM LOCK

ACT ONE

Early morning, high summer. The present year.

JACK DEAN's *study: a Georgian room with tall windows in deep white recesses which almost reach the floor. Most of the wall space is occupied from floor to ceiling by books on white shelves. One panel of the wall is similarly taken up by astronomical photographs, one very large. Conspicuously placed is a splendid Holbein of two adults and a row of children. Beyond the windows are lawns, weeping willows, college buildings. In the room is a large table with books, papers, files. Other furniture as necessary. Two tall white doors Left and Right.*

STELLA *stands front stage, facing audience, her head bent, immobilised by intense thought.*

STELLA *is about twenty-two years old. The daughter of academic parents, she is intellectually and morally advanced, untried emotionally. She has the candour and generosity of an even younger person, but can also be awkwardly didactic, unseasonably serious. She had assumed most people to be nicer than herself and is just finding that the reverse is true. She is more alarmed by than proud of this, and anxious to do right. She wears a summer dress disfigured with a diamanté brooch. Her shoes are outdoor, her hair untidy. But in her rare moments of repose, face and figure are cast into lines of downright nobility.*

Enter through window, with a jump, MRS DEAN. *She is about fifty-four years old. She became a blue-stocking in the decade of the flapper. She wears gardening gloves, brown sweater, brown skirt with large pockets, and sandals.*

Her movements are healthy and vigorous; she is the nut-brown maid. But a mass of meaningless lines runs about her face, her large

215

clear eyes are frightened, and her manner is altogether too sensible to be true.

STELLA: Mummy!

MRS DEAN: What?

STELLA: You frightened me.

MRS DEAN: Sorry. What is that?

STELLA: Daddy's birthday present. (*Takes book out of envelope and hands it to her mother.*) D'you think he'll mind?

MRS DEAN: Oh! He may *like* it. Or he may not. He won't *mind* in either case. (*Hands the book back, and starts looking about.*)

STELLA: He'll like it—if he reads it. (*Amused and admiring*) Did you jump the flower bed?

MRS DEAN: Certainly. When I was your age, I could high hurdle a hundred yards in twelve seconds.

STELLA: I wish I'd seen you. Daddy says: Other women run like rabbits; you ran like a deer.

MRS DEAN (*arrested*): Did he say that?

STELLA: I run like a camel. (*This is dreamy rather than bitter; she is leaning on the window frame in the hot sunshine.*)

MRS DEAN (*not comforting, crisp*): It's not a very serious accomplishment. My father encouraged me. (*She is again looking round*) He felt I was in danger of neglecting the body; (*without either condemnation or approval, as a fact*) himself he hardly knew he had a body.

STELLA: You say how marvellous your father was, but as you describe him he sounds a bit offputting.

MRS DEAN (*as before*): He had a radiant mind. (*She pauses in her search to glance dryly at* STELLA.) *You* would have liked him. (*But* STELLA *goes on dreaming and* MRS DEAN *goes on searching.*)

STELLA: Isn't it a heavenly morning?

MRS DEAN: Yes, dear.

STELLA: It's good to be alive, isn't it?

MRS DEAN: Yes, dear.

STELLA: What are you looking for?

MRS DEAN: For some reason, I left my secateurs in here.

STELLA: They're here.

MRS DEAN (*sternly*): I'm cutting down the ramblers from the loggia. (*She takes the secateurs.*)

STELLA: Oh why?

MRS DEAN: They're diseased.

STELLA: What a pity.

MRS DEAN: Yes. McGredy's Lemon Tower, a lovely plant. They'll have to come down though; they're dying. I think I overfed them.

STELLA: No, they probably got a bug.

MRS DEAN: Yes, I ought to have sprayed them.

STELLA: Don't get upset about it.

MRS DEAN: Oh, it's nothing to get upset about. I know that.

STELLA: Have you got a present for Daddy?

MRS DEAN: Of course.

STELLA (*smiling*): It's not a pipe, is it?

MRS DEAN (*irritable. Goes to window*): No, it is not a pipe. The standards look well, don't they? (*Anxiously*) The whole garden doesn't look too bad . . .?

STELLA: Oh, Mummy! (*Persuasive*) It's one of the sights of— (*waves her hand.*)

MRS DEAN (*eagerly*): Of what?

STELLA: Of the college! The whole University come to that!

MRS DEAN (*still cool*): It is creative. It's a very minor form of course, but it is creative. (*Looks out of window.*)

STELLA (*with false enthusiasm*): Creative. I should just think so!

MRS DEAN: Why do you adopt that tone towards me?

STELLA: What tone?

MRS DEAN: (*sits on window sill*): As though you were being kind to the poor.

STELLA: Sorry. I suppose it's because I'm young and cocky.

MRS DEAN: A disingenuous remark if ever I heard one. You're not cocky. (*Slips to the ground.*) Is Louis coming?

STELLA (*crosses to her mother and kneels by her*): No, I expect I'll go over to Trinity. Mummy, do you like him?

MRS DEAN: If I knew him I imagine I should like him very much. (*She prepares to clear the lobelias again.*) Do you? (*And exit with a flying leap. She has left the secateurs.*)

STELLA (*leans out of the window and looks after her*): Well, of course! . . .

Enter MARY, *by door left.*

What a heavenly morning, Mary!

MARY *is about twenty-six years old. Her features are regular, her figure tall and thin, and on this basis she has created, with the usual aids, an image of the very smart woman. Her hair is unequivocally bleached, and dressed to accentuate a neat, small skull. The principal feature of her face is the perfection of its make-up. She wears a summer dress and her skirt is of the correct tightness. Her shoes are light on spidery heels. Her movements are brittly sexual, brisk but constricted. She is on the market, but no whore—indeed her flawless social acceptability is the guide star of her life, and only passion.*

MARY: Not bad.

STELLA: It's heavenly.

MARY: Are you trying to sell it?

STELLA: It just makes me feel good. How's life?

MARY: Jolly good. I can't think why you don't try it.

STELLA (*pause. Not indignant, humiliated*): That's a lousy crack. (*Pause.*) Going out?

MARY: Mhm . . .

STELLA: Who with?

MARY: Nobody you know. (*She can't resist communicating it, so compensates by extreme offhandedness.*) He's a Squadron Leader.

STELLA: What happened to Brian?

MARY: Oh, he's around.

STELLA: But he's still a Flight Lieutenant.

MARY (*sees* STELLA'S *parcel and picks it up*): Oh my God . . . The birthday! Lend me a couple of quid will you?

STELLA: Yes O.K.— Sure.

MARY: Can you make it three?

STELLA: All right. (*Takes pound notes from pocket and hands them to* MARY.)

  Enter MRS DEAN, *she goes straight up to small table by window for the secateurs.*

MRS DEAN: I left my secateurs again. I am reluctant to use them on my ramblers, I suppose . . . (*Moves to go, then stops.*) Have you seen your father this morning?

STELLA: No.

MARY: Yes, I saw him just now.

MRS DEAN (*eager*): Where is he?

MARY: He was going into the Chancery Gardens.

MRS DEAN: Ah. He must have gone to see Hugo. (*Lightly*) Was he wearing his flower?

MARY (*she treats her mother with a sort of empty patience*): I didn't notice, dear.

MRS DEAN: Oh, you would surely have noticed? A rose? A large white rose; Virgin Queen.

MARY: I don't think he was then.

MRS DEAN (*her face falls*): Oh. (*Sensibly*) The Chancery Gardens?

MARY: Yes, dear.

MRS DEAN: He will have gone to see Hugo. (*Exit down left leaving door open.*)

  STELLA *stands looking at door where her mother has gone out then turns to* MARY.

STELLA: How's life? Oh, I've said that, haven't I?

MARY (*offhandedly serious*): You'd better get busy, Stella.

STELLA: Busy? What at?

MARY: Anything better than nothing. Why don't you study? You're good at that.

STELLA: I don't want to study, thank you.

MARY: Get married then. (*As* STELLA *doesn't reply.*) You could always marry Louis.

STELLA: Oh yes, any time. Only thing is, he hasn't asked me.

MARY: Well, make him.

STELLA: Wish I could.

MARY (*coming to life*): Really? (STELLA *nods.*) Then don't wear this . . . (*removing brooch*) with this. (*Plucks at dress.*) Don't wear those shoes with anything. Take that belt off and—comb your hair . . .

STELLA (*pulling away from her. Testy but not ungrateful*): It isn't that, it isn't that. (*But she obeys the instructions.*)

MARY: You'd be surprised. Why d'you hoist your bosom up here? (*Indicates her own collar-bone.*) It's impossible.

STELLA: He likes it.

MARY: He's got terrible taste for a poet.

STELLA: He says its working-class taste. He's very sincere . . . isn't he?

MARY: Oh, Louis's all right.

    Enter LOUIS, *quietly, right. He stops in the doorway.*

    (*Not sure if he heard or not, a shade embarrassed.*) Hello, Louis. (LOUIS *nods and remains still.*) Well, I'll nip out and get something. (*Gets hand-bag from desk and crosses to door.*) Thanks darling. (*About to go*) Oh, d'you know if mother's got anything?

STELLA: Yes, she has.

MARY: She say what it was?

STELLA: It's not a pipe.

MARY: Good. (*Looks at* LOUIS *still standing.*) Why don't you invite him in?

    Exit MARY.

    LOUIS *is about thirty. He is thin; his movements are those of a physically poor specimen with much nervous energy; vigorous but without rhythm. He has a large head and a thin, big-*

jointed body. His face is seamed and expressive; big, commanding nose, wide over-mobile mouth, brilliant eyes—an excess of feature to charm and repel, carrying the impac of active, obtrusive, undeniable intellect. His clothes reveal a determination not to be slovenly; a sports coat, good but a bit tight, flannel trousers, clean but kneed and a bit short, collar and tie a bit tight and stringy. The cast of his features is sad and somewhat wasted, but his persona demands some degree of mockery.

LOUIS: Am I under discussion?

STELLA (a bit breathless): No, I just asked if you weren't very sincere.

LOUIS: Oh. (Smiling) You feel the need of a second opinion, do you?

STELLA: Not now.

LOUIS (closing door, jerks head after MARY): And how is the toast of Bomber Command? I hear she's been promoted.

STELLA: Mm? Oh yes, Squadron Leader. What are you doing here?

LOUIS: That's a silly question. (Advances upon her.)

STELLA (sits at desk. Hurriedly): I—I've got Daddy's birthday present. (She holds before her the parcel.)

LOUIS (pausing): Oh?

STELLA: D'you know what it is?

LOUIS: Yes, it's a book. (Takes book. Comes on again and kisses her.) See? Nothing to be alarmed about. (Gives book back.)

STELLA: I wasn't alarmed.

LOUIS: Yes you were. (Looks at her sharply and moves away.) You always are.

STELLA: I never know what you're going to do.

LOUIS: Oh, you don't know the half of it—The News of the World pays me a retaining fee. (He advances upon her, knees bent, arms held above his head, fingers crooked; she flinches slightly; reaching her he takes her head by the fingertips

*and kisses her with elaborate chastity on the forehead.
Satirically*) There. How's that?

STELLA (*defiant*): Nice. (*Defensive*) There's more than one way
of kissing, Louis.

LOUIS: And you like that way.

STELLA: Sometimes.

LOUIS: Where's your dad?

STELLA: I don't know. Do you want him?

LOUIS: Aye, that's what I came for—I've brought the
petition—what's the matter?

STELLA: Nothing.

LOUIS: Then stop looking like Little Orphan Annie.

STELLA: I'm not looking like Little Orphan Annie. You said
you'd come to see me.

LOUIS (*remonstrative*): Bloody hell, Stella . . .

STELLA: No, but you *said* you had. The fact is that you came
to get Daddy's signature to the petition!

LOUIS: Well, it's important to get his signature on the
petition!

STELLA: I don't mind what you came for, but you said you'd
come to see me and the fact is——

LOUIS: Oh, the facts, yes let's get at the facts. You sound like
your ruddy father.

STELLA: There'd be nothing wrong with that either!

LOUIS: Nothing at all, except I don't happen to be (*deep
breath for effort, and even so the words are somewhat held back*)
in love with your father.

STELLA (*gently, happily*): What?

LOUIS (*getting out cigarettes*): Your father hasn't got such nice
legs as you. Fag?

STELLA: Are my legs nice?

LOUIS (*cold and quick*): How should I know? The bits I've seen
are all right.

STELLA (*she looks down, ashamed*): Louis . . . don't you *ever*
want that kind of kiss?

LOUIS: No. Well, yes—it's a nice kind of kiss for after.

STELLA (*small-voiced*): After?

LOUIS: Yes.

STELLA: Oh.

LOUIS: But it's a bit pre-Raphaelite before. And you *want* it before, don't you? In fact, you want it instead. (*Pause.*) We've had this conversation once or twice, haven't we?

STELLA: Yes. (*Throws her head back in her chair.*) Oh, Louis, I'm— (*Rocks her head from side to side. Distressed*) I'm— I'm—

LOUIS (*quickly, comforting*): You're a bit inhibited, that's all. (*Looking round the room*) 'Tisn't to be wondered at. (*Earnest*) You'll have to break out of this family, honey, you'll have to.

STELLA: It so happens I like this family. And what's more so do you.

LOUIS: I can afford to; I'm not in it.

STELLA: For heaven's sake; they're not monsters.

LOUIS: No, they're upper-class academics. Aw, look, this 'sticking up for Mummy and Daddy'—it's plain irresponsible. He's a marvellous bloke—was a marvellous bloke—

STELLA: He still is—

LOUIS: Mm—well, in a way . . . But forty years ago he had genius. (*She looks at him surprised.*) Yeh, you don't get made an F.R.S. before you're thirty without genius. Now all he does is write these lousy philosophy books.

STELLA: They're marvellous books. (*This is stubborn rather than convinced.*)

LOUIS: They're beautifully written, *lousy* books: 'Don't commit yourself! Examine your umbilicus! Breathe deeply; turn round in slow circles and quietly, quietly, disappear up your own imagination' . . . He's dangerous, he's off the ground—oh yes he is; when your father walks

across the quad you can see light under his boots. That's
why your mother's off her head.

STELLA (*scornful*): 'Off her head'—really, Louis—

LOUIS: O.K. have it your way. (*Crosses to window.*) What
was that about a pipe?

STELLA: Well . . . last year and the year before she gave
Daddy a pipe for his birthday.

LOUIS: So?

STELLA: He hasn't smoked since before I was born. (*He raises
eyebrows.*) —Well all that means is she's got a bad memory—
she forgot!

LOUIS: No, it means more than that . . . sounds like a distress
signal. Perhaps she liked him better when he did smoke
a pipe. (*Turns from window, a new tack*) You know he's
going to be the new Vice-Chancellor?

STELLA (*attentive*): We know he may be.

LOUIS: Well the grape vine says that Tyldesley turned it down
last night. And if Tyldesley's turned it down, it's your dad.
(*Soupçon of a sneer*) Nice for him, eh?

STELLA: Nice for us. If it's true. He wouldn't give it two
thoughts, Louis. He's not ambitious.

LOUIS: Don't you believe it, honey. That's the top of the
tree. And you don't get there by levitation.

STELLA: Oh really, Louis!

LOUIS: O.K. I don't want to talk about your family.

STELLA (*haughty*): Then please let's not.

LOUIS: Oh ho, 'then please let's not. Young man, that's my
ball and chain you're messing about with. Kindly replace
it.'

STELLA: You know it all, don't you. (*This is not a sneer but a
grumble. There is a pause.*)

LOUIS: Another row.

STELLA: My fault.

LOUIS: Oh I don't see that. (*Rises.*)

STELLA: No, you do know a lot. I know that.

LOUIS (*going to her and squatting*): Have a bit of courage, darling, commit yourself . . . that's all, a bit of courage. (*Puts his hand on her knee.*)

STELLA: It can't be as simple as getting into bed with someone, Louis— Life can't be as simple as that.

LOUIS: It isn't. But you've got the rest of it. You're civilised. You've got enough money. You're politically educated— there's a bit of an undertow there but on the whole you're politically educated.

STELLA: Isn't there anything else?

LOUIS (*quietly*): Yes, there's this bit you're missing.

STELLA: In a hotel somewhere?

LOUIS (*uncomfortable*): I expect so.

STELLA: It feels wrong, Louis.

LOUIS: Well of course it does; that's how inhibitions work.

STELLA: What if I had a baby?

LOUIS (*he doesn't want to go into technicalities—but—brushing it aside*): No, no.

STELLA: You can't be a hundred per cent certain though, can you?

LOUIS: Practically. (*Irritable*) I'll do all that—

STELLA (*muttering*): It's messy.

LOUIS: What?

STELLA: It's messy!

LOUIS (*shrugs*): That's life. (*She looks at him. He gently beats the arm of her chair.*) That—is—life.

STELLA (*frightened of him*): But it feels so wrong it would spoil it. (*Begins to gabble*) It wouldn't be any fun, it wouldn't be any pleasure, it wouldn't be . . . (*Looks down*) You don't want me to do it—therapeutically; like a medicine?

LOUIS: No, I don't . . . Well done, Stella. Now you're in a complete circle, aren't you?

Enter MRS DEAN *and* SIR HUGO SLATE *down left.* STELLA *crosses to desk.*

MRS DEAN: Mary—oh. Mary saw him going into the Chancery Gardens, Hugo.

　　HUGO *crosses to arm-chair.* MRS DEAN *is by the door.*

SLATE: But I've just left the Chancery.

STELLA: Perhaps he used the Master's Gate, Sir Hugo.

SLATE (*clicks his fingers*): That's it! ... I've come to see him and he's gone to see me. Well, they'll tell him I'm here. I'll wait.

　　SIR HUGO SLATE *is an old man with a bright manner; the academic life is no mere enthusiasm with him, but his only possible element, and hence he has found his way among college affairs with an innocent felicity beyond more powerful intellects—he himself being not merely intellectual but intellectually pixilated. He wears a light brown suit.*

SLATE: Good morning, Mr Flax.

LOUIS: Good morning, sir.

SLATE: I understand that your petition is not meeting with much success?

LOUIS: Not much, Vice-Chancellor.

SLATE: Splendid. Not even among your own contemporaries, they tell me. Why is that do you suppose?

LOUIS: I think they don't want to offend their seniors, a lot of them.

SLATE: They would like to sign it in principle but fear it would be disapproved of by persons like myself, and so damage their careers.

LOUIS: Yes.

SLATE: Better and better; I'm agreeably surprised.

MRS DEAN (*like a hound scenting a fox*): A petition? What is it about?

SLATE (*pantomimes an effort of memory*): Let me see . . . Gas warfare, is it? . . . The abolition of the crossbow?

LOUIS: It's a petition for unconditional nuclear disarmament, Mrs Dean.

MRS DEAN: Unconditional?

LOUIS: Absolute. The whole thing got rid of.

MRS DEAN: Good.

LOUIS: It's for Members of the University. It's going round all the Universities this year.

MRS DEAN (*she is nodding happily*): Good. Good. (*To* SLATE) Oh, Hugo, surely it is a devilish waste of human ingenuity?

SLATE: Er—to which are you referring—the bomb or the petition?

MRS DEAN: Can you laugh? (*Her tone has a note of envy, but she is still rapt.*)

   SLATE *turns determinedly to* STELLA.

SLATE: Stella—

MRS DEAN: And that is merely the high peak, the show place, of the wickedness that's in us . . . There are the refugees too. People starving everywhere; among them, small children.

SLATE (*looms at her sharply and away*): Mm. Oh the world's a sad spectacle beyond doubt; always has been. (*Determined, to* STELLA) You're not extending your studies I understand, Stella: How has that come about? Does the academic life not appeal? It should.

MRS DEAN: Of course one knows one is not *personally* responsible; one has *done* nothing . . .

SLATE (*his eyes flick round but he does not move. To* STELLA): It should, you know.

STELLA: There doesn't seem to be anything I want to go on studying.

SLATE: That's not an insuperable obstacle. We should be able to do—

MRS DEAN (*crosses to* LOUIS): I'll certainly sign the petition, Louis.

   LOUIS *takes out petition.*

SLATE: No . . . Well, may I ask why?

MRS DEAN: Largely, it is the unborn. (*He looks at her. Impatiently*) The unborn. Radioactivity stimulates mutation;

and the chances are astronomically against a mutation being favourable.

SLATE (*interested*): Ah biology! Your subject of course!

MRS DEAN: In other words it produces monsters. Babies that are monsters. I shall certainly sign the petition.

SLATE: You can't.

MRS DEAN (*dignified*): I can, Hugo.

SLATE: No you can't— Has Jack said nothing to you?

MRS DEAN (*puzzled*): About what?

SLATE: I see. (*Irritable*) Where is the man?

MRS DEAN: I agree with the petition. I think the thing *should* be abolished . . . Not that my signature carries much weight.

SLATE: Well, the petition's not a matter of any urgency; Mr Flax can leave it and you can decide what to do when you've talked about it with Jack. (*Significantly, to* LOUIS) You'll *leave* your petition, won't you, Mr Flax? (*He is urging him from the room.*)

LOUIS (*taking, not liking, the point*): Yes, that's all right. (*Places it on table; goes to door. Parting shot*) I'd be proud to have your signature, Mrs Dean.

    SLATE *is irritated.*

MRS DEAN: Thank you, Louis.

STELLA: Are you going, Louis?

LOUIS: No, I'll be around.

    Exit LOUIS. STELLA *looks after him.*

STELLA: Shall I go and see if I can *find* Daddy?

SLATE (*grateful*): That would be excellent. (*He holds door open for her and smiles approvingly as she goes out.* SLATE *closes door. Impressively*) Gwendoline, your husband is to be the new Vice-Chancellor.

MRS DEAN: Oh yes, he did tell me that.

SLATE (*wryly*): It's an office to which I myself attach a certain importance. Don't you?

MRS DEAN: You've been a very good Vice-Chancellor, Hugo.

SLATE: Perhaps that is what I meant. (*Crosses to desk.*) But I don't think I should sign this, you see.

MRS DEAN: What about Professor Vanbrugh?

SLATE: For Vice-Chancellor? Too old, most of us think.

MRS DEAN: And Tyldesley?

SLATE: Doesn't want it. No, Jack's the man. (*Waves the petition.*) And this thing's bound to get publicity, Gwen.

MRS DEAN: The more the better!

SLATE: Not for Jack. Not right at the beginning of his term. Now come along, be practical. It's not the thing itself, it's the people you'd be associated with—that group at Angels and Martyrs. At any rate will you postpone it?

MRS DEAN (*makes up her mind*): Very well. Though the motivation seems somewhat unworthy.

SLATE: Thank you. (*Turns to face right, sees picture on wall.*) Ah, the Master's Holbein. You know, I've coveted this college for that picture. Beautiful, isn't it?

MRS DEAN: Very beautiful.

SLATE: Nine—ten—eleven. Eleven children. An extraordinary man, your founder.

MRS DEAN: There were two more born later, but they died. (*Moves above table to picture.*) Four of these died too: this one, and this one, and this one, and this one. I think he's a hunchback poor little fellow. But Jack says not.

SLATE: Really? It's difficult to tell.

MRS DEAN: Yes. We ought to have it cleaned.

SLATE: No, don't do that. I love that ancient patina. Tell me, Gwen, is Jack working? I don't mean his, what can we say, his philosophic work? One knows about that, of course. I mean is he doing any of the old stuff?

MRS DEAN (*surprised*): Astronomy?

SLATE: Yes. Original work.

MRS DEAN (*flatly*): No. (*Sits at desk.*) No, he was in his fortieth year when I met him and he turned to philosophy then.

SLATE: I just wondered.

MRS DEAN: He was writing his last paper on Agamemnon. He's done no astronomy since.

SLATE: Agamemnon was adequate by all accounts.

MRS DEAN (*proudly, a little reprovingly*): The most important discovery in its field since Hirschveldt, Hugo.

SLATE (*peering at the photograph*): Oh more than adequate for one man's life. (*Turning away from it*) And it leaves him free for (*indicating the Master's study and the college through the windows in a single gesture*) this. He's entirely the man for the job, Gwen, entirely. Tranquillising, restraining, sobering, Perfectly immune to even the subtlest corruption, for the simple reason that no one would know what to bribe him with—don't you agree? So far as his desires are concerned, he remains what he always was—a tower of silence.

MRS DEAN: Oh yes, he'll do it.

SLATE: Marvellously; he'll do it marvellously. (*Speaks seriously*) You see, Gwen—your Mr Flax (*picks up petition*) it reminds me uncomfortably of the thirties, when, as you remember, the younger dons talked like election agents, and the undergraduates to all appearances regarded their time up here as an extended leave from the Spanish Civil War. They're getting agitated again. And when they get like that it isn't enough to be phlegmatic—Vanbrugh's phlegmatic—it simply makes them feel superior. And it isn't enough to laugh at them—as I do—because that makes them feel superior too. Indeed there are few things that don't. But not Jack. He has this extraordinary knack for isolating agitation, denying it sustenance, starving it out. In Jack's presence the morally indignant man is made to feel—mm—like one who turns up to a formal ball in fancy dress.

MRS DEAN: Oh yes, he'll do it.

SLATE: Marvellously. So you see . . . (*He wags the petition at her.*)

MRS DEAN: If it would do Jack harm, I won't sign it, of course.

SLATE: I think it might. The name's what people see; not the Mrs or Mr. (*Puts petition on desk. Looks at his watch.*) I saw Mary in the High—she's become very decorative.

MRS DEAN: Yes. But she has no ability.

SLATE: She seemed to be exercising considerable ability in the High this morning.

MRS DEAN (*smiles politely*): I failed to pass on to her any ability.

SLATE: Did you? Then you must take credit for her—mmm—formal qualities.

MRS DEAN: She has that from her aunts.

SLATE: And where are you going to delegate the credit for Stella? Marked ability there, I fancy.

MRS DEAN: Yes, but she has no discipline. I've been a bad influence.

SLATE: In what way, Gwen?

MRS DEAN: I don't know. (*Rises and moves to picture again.*)

SLATE: Gwendoline, you must not indulge this . . . appetite for responsibility.

Enter DEAN *from upstage right.* SLATE *rises.*

DEAN *is about thirteen years older than his wife. His manner is formal to the point of elegance. His clothes too are formal and almost rakishly well cut. His habitual expression is one of polite, humorous interest—to imply a state of unshakable detachment in himself; but the fundamental cast of feature beneath the expression is stern and with that shade almost of bitterness engendered by intellectual stoicism in a temperament by nature rich and sanguine. Physically too he is still impressive. When he is truly engaged he drops the don and gentleman and becomes still and almost threateningly attentive. He is a formidable, magnanimous and accomplished man, with a stratum of conceit.*

DEAN: Good morning, Vice-Chancellor. I received your note and stepped across to the Chancery. Is it certain?

SLATE: Perfectly. Congratulations.

DEAN: Thank you. I'm very pleased about it.

SLATE (*this is evidently something that can't be taken for granted*): You are?

DEAN: Oh yes. Ridiculously so.

MRS DEAN: Good morning, Jack. Many happy returns of the day. You're wearing it.

DEAN: Mm? Oh—I am indeed. One day in every year Hugo—*which* day I can never remember—I wake to find my wife has been into my room and left beside my bed this gentle reminder of mortality. It's my birthday. Thank you, dear, how are you?

MRS DEAN: I'm very well, dear. There's been a tragedy in the garden though.

DEAN (*to* SLATE): I'm not altogether happy about Vanbrugh.

SLATE: Vanbrugh's seventy-five.

DEAN: Well seventy-five's no age. (*To* MRS DEAN) A tragedy in the garden?

MRS DEAN: Yes. The chrysanthemums—

DEAN: Oh, the chrysanthemums. One visualised an open air performance of *Hamlet*. What about Tyldesley? Is he quite sure he doesn't want it?

SLATE: He not only doesn't want this. Between ourselves he's giving up Gabriels at the end of the year.

DEAN: He is? Why?

SLATE: If you will believe me, he's going to Birmingham.

DEAN: I see. He must be on to something important.

SLATE: Let us hope so.

DEAN (*sees* MRS DEAN *move to door*): Oh, are you going, dear? (*Holds door for her.*) What happened to the chrysanthemums?

MRS DEAN: I don't know. I must have . . . they're all dying anyway.

DEAN: Can't you plant some more?

MRS DEAN: Not now. If it had happened a month ago . . . (*Sensible*) I'll think of something. It'll spoil the autumn show I'm afraid.

DEAN: Nonsense! You'll think of something. It'll look splendid!

Exit MRS DEAN.

SLATE (*rather hesitantly, broaching what he feels to be a rather delicate subject*): A garden can be a . . . great thing, can't it?

DEAN (*briskly*): Oh yes, she's a keen gardener. (*Crosses to window.*) So Tyldesley's going to Birmingham?

SLATE: Yes. They have something there, atom smasher, crystal crusher, something. Do you envy him, Jack?

DEAN: No, I don't envy him, Hugo. The desire is dead in me. (*This is said as a claim, not as an admission.*)

SLATE: I'm not sure I believe you.

DEAN (*mildly*): Why not?

SLATE: Well. (*Approaching the astro-photographs*) I'm a scissors-and-paste man myself, a barren stock. But I've often thought that if anything could frighten me into giving birth to an idea, it would be . . . this. 'The eternal silence of those infinite spaces terrifies me.' That, at any rate, I have in common with Pascal.

DEAN: Oh well, Pascal; does a bottle of water terrify you? You've got the same phenomenon there, silence and space. Now how to be a good Vice-Chancellor, there's something I do want to know. I haven't thanked you. It's a job I shall enjoy.

SLATE: We shall enjoy watching you. (*Smiling in anticipatory admiration*) What policy have you in mind?

DEAN (*as though this were a very novel suggestion*): Policy?

SLATE (*laughs silently*): Of course. No policy at all. Excellent.

(*Rubs his hands.*) I foresee great things. Alas for Mr Flax and his petition. He left it for you.

DEAN: So I see. (*Sits right of desk. Reads, quite sympathetically*) 'We, the undersigned, being Members of the University ...'

SLATE (*alarmed*): You won't sign it?

DEAN: Good heavens no.

SLATE (*delighted*): Good heavens no. Just so. The tone is one of gentle surprise. (*Grave*) Ah, by the way—Gwendoline rather wanted to sign it.

DEAN: Did she?

SLATE: Yes. (*Lightly*) I hadn't realised she had become so . . . eccentric, Jack. (*Looks covertly at him.*)

DEAN: She's always been 'eccentric'. (*He uses the word to convey his contempt for those who thus apply it.*) The purest hearted creature I ever met. (*This is not said reminiscently but factually, to explain the impression of eccentricity. Glances at signatures with mild interest.*) Then why hasn't she signed it?

SLATE: I urged upon her that it would be tactless.

DEAN: If that prevented her, she can't have wanted to very badly. She comes of a tactless family.

SLATE: I effected a postponement merely . . . (*Gravely*) It would be very tactless, Jack . . . I've said your election is certain, but there's a lot of time between now and then. It can always become *un*certain.

DEAN (*seriously*): Yes, clearly.

SLATE: I think she could be dissuaded quite easily.

DEAN: Oh no! I'm not going to start persuading and dissuading, Hugo. If I can't have it without that, without (*distastefully*) opinion and bullying, then I can't have it at all.

SLATE: May *I* then? I'd like to assure myself before I go, Jack?

DEAN (*calmly*): If you want to. (SLATE *rises rather defiantly.*) Gwendoline's not as eccentric as her parents. Did you know that family? Balliol folk. Her father in the evening of his days subsisted almost entirely upon oats. (*Enter* STELLA *and* LOUIS.) Yes, come in. Where's your mother, Stella?

STELLA: She's having a bonfire at the back.

SLATE: The oat man! Was that Gwendoline's father? (*He moves towards door down left. Turns to* DEAN.) He was a saint, wasn't he?

DEAN: No, don't say that. I am reputed to resemble him. (*Passes* SLATE *towards door, and they exit together.*) Yes, he used to bake these little biscuits. Staying with him was quite a penance . . . (*They have gone.*)

LOUIS: Gossip. I must hear the rest of that. (*To table.*) He hasn't signed it. She won't now either. Don't know why I bother.

STELLA: You're fishing. (*He looks up and smiles at her.*) You bother because when *you* believe in a thing, you *believe* in it.

LOUIS: Is that good?

STELLA: It's terrific. (*The smile leaves his face and they look at one another gravely. She steps forward hesitantly.*) Look, Louis—

LOUIS: No, I don't want to talk about that any more. Let's drop it for a bit. Hell, Stella, I don't want to *nag* you into it!

STELLA: You're not nagging, darling. You *know* about these things. I don't.

LOUIS (*slightly worked up excitement*): Look, all I know is perfectly obvious; there's something very unhealthy about necking and petting and . . . (*again he has difficulty*) . . . being in love, and not . . . (*gestures helplessly*) taking it to its natural conclusion.

STELLA: Says Freud.

LOUIS: It's common knowledge, honey. But now let's let it rest a bit (*Sits.*) I can't take much more of this.

STELLA (*alarmed*): What d'you mean? Louis, what are you thinking?

LOUIS: All right then—I'm thinking that next week-end I'm going to be in town. And I'm thinking that you could be in town too. There's a bloke there will lend us his flat —he's a good bloke, you'd like him—and it's a nice flat. Not a hotel.

STELLA: I see.

LOUIS (*rises*): Yes, and I'm thinking that if you won't do it, we'd better turn the whole thing in. I can't take it, Stella— I don't want to take it.

STELLA (*shakily*): This is what they call a proposition?

LOUIS: This is what they call blackmail I think.

STELLA: Jeepers, you're unscrupulous!

LOUIS: I don't believe it . . . we've been marking time so long we've worn a damn great pit in the ground.

STELLA: Are you absolutely serious about this?

LOUIS (*at door, warningly*): Here's your dad. (*Sotto*) Yes, I am.

STELLA (*urgent, sotto*): I love you.

LOUIS (*sotto*): I know.

   Enter DEAN. *He sits at his table. He is perfectly unaware of the obvious tension between them.*

DEAN: Now, Stella, my birthday present if you please.

   She hands it to him; he begins to unwrap it.

STELLA (*rather miserably*): Many happy returns.

DEAN (*looks at her*): Thank you. Oh! It's a book. (*Opens parcel, sits right of desk. Holds up book.*) Ha! Is this from both of you?

LOUIS (*uncomprehending*): No?

DEAN: I have here 'Silver Poets of the Renaissance in Spain' translated, and with an Introduction by, one Louis Flax.

LOUIS (*surprised and pleased. Reaches out and touches* STELLA. *They stare at one another.*): Oh! Stella . . . Well, that's another one and six.

DEAN: Is that all you get?

LOUIS (*sly*): Adequate, for poets, I should have thought, Master.

DEAN (*looks up from book, smiles briefly*): The payment for works of mathematical astronomy is not exactly prodigal. (*Looks at book.*) 1950 . . . You must have been very young. You've not published anything since?

LOUIS: No.

STELLA (*defensively*): You'll publish your thesis won't you?

LOUIS (*quick glance at DEAN*): When it's finished.

DEAN: It might be finished more quickly if you expended less time on— (*picks up petition*) these other activities.

LOUIS: Yes, it would be finished more quickly.

DEAN: It might be better too—I mean even better than it's expected to be.

LOUIS: No, it wouldn't be better, Master; it might have better footnotes but it wouldn't be—

DEAN: Wouldn't be what? Ah—it wouldn't be 'rooted in reality' would it? 'Rooted in reality' . . . Well that's your concern, my dear fellow. Here you are. (*Returns petition, which* LOUIS *gloomily accepts.*)

STELLA (*rallying to* LOUIS *almost protectively*): Then do you think they *should* go on dropping bombs?

DEAN: How could I possibly know? The diplomatic and military considerations must be grotesquely complicated. I haven't the facts, Stella.

STELLA: 'Leave it to the experts'. That's typical, isn't it, Louis?

   LOUIS *shakes his head and frowns at her.*

DEAN: Ah, that note of indignation. Louis, suppose you did secure—let us say—75 per cent of the signatures you would wish for? And sent your petition to the Prime Minister. Do you suppose it would cause him to alter his policy? The facts now.

LOUIS: No.

STELLA: No?

LOUIS: Probably not.

STELLA: Then . . . what's the good of it?

DEAN (*to* LOUIS): I see some force in the question. You know, Louis, refined down to fact this talk of roots in reality looks suspiciously like— (*He searches for the word.*)

LOUIS: Poetry.

DEAN: You said it, not me.

LOUIS (*tentatively*): Is there any point in my asking Mrs Dean?

DEAN: I much doubt it. The VC has been talking to her.

LOUIS (*hesitant*): You don't mind if I try?

DEAN (*flash of irritation*): Of course I don't mind if you try!

LOUIS (*abashed*): Sorry, Master; I thought you might not want me to.

DEAN (*almost angry*): Good heavens, why shouldn't I want you to? I have never brought any kind of pressure to bear on my wife, Mr Flax!

LOUIS (*awkward*): No . . . well I'll try then. (*Going to door down left.*)

DEAN (*looks at his hand, seeking a way down from the undignified eminence of his anger. As* LOUIS *reaches the door he raises his head. Gaily*): I shall look forward to reading your book.

LOUIS (*solemnly*): I feel I should warn you, Master; much of it is in poetry.

DEAN (*innocently*): But I have nothing against poetry, Mr Flax; poetry is . . . mm . . . charming mm . . .

LOUIS (*smiling, despite himself*): Decorative—

DEAN: —Decorative certainly—delightful—all those things.

LOUIS: You won't find much charming in some of those.

DEAN (*glancing into book with affected bewilderment*): Then what on earth shall I find in them?

LOUIS (*happily*): Facts, Master, facts.

　　　He nods. Exit LOUIS. STELLA *looks after him, anxious.*

DEAN: I beg leave to doubt that. (*Sits on desk. He reads, rather satirically*) 'Shall I admit I do not love thee much . . .' (*His attention is taken. Puts down the book.*) Yes, well I must read it. (*But he goes on reading.*)

STELLA: Daddy, can I ask you a question?

DEAN: If it's the sort of question that needs a preface, I'd much rather you didn't.

STELLA: Why wouldn't you sign Louis' petition?

DEAN (*leaving book*): Oh, Stella, must we?

STELLA: It wasn't because if you did sign it, some of the Masters mightn't vote for you?

DEAN (*lightly*): That would certainly be a very *good* reason for not signing it.

STELLA: Why—is it so important to be Vice-Chancellor?

DEAN (*mock puzzlement*): Important? No, it isn't a bit important. Should it be? (*The more earnest she gets the lighter he takes her.*)

STELLA (*softly*): I hate it when you talk like this.

DEAN (*unwillingly forced to take her seriously. Looks at her*): You seem agitated. Have you something on your mind, Stella?

STELLA (*she would like to tell him what is on her mind but can't*): It's just this way you won't let anything be important.

DEAN (*her vehemence releases him; he walks up and down, very High Table*): Won't *let*? My dear! I have no permissive authority over the importance of things. If they're important to you, then to you they're important. Anyone's at liberty to cram significance into his life till it swells up and bursts if he wants to. It needn't affect you if I myself prefer—a rather low importance content.

STELLA: You've done important things all your life! (*He stops pacing, astonished.*) When you were young anyway. Measuring planets, weighing stars.

DEAN: Oh! (*Recommences pacing.*) No, no, Stella, the facts. I weighed one star—

STELLA: Two stars—

DEAN: It was one double star. In that galaxy. (*He takes up a lecturer's stance by the photograph.*) There are—let us say— a hundred million observable galaxies and in that particular galaxy about a hundred million stars. One of which I weighed. And what happened to it then?

STELLA (*rather sulkily*): It exploded.

DEAN: Exactly.

STELLA: But that was important! (*Rises.*) That's how the world was made! The world and the planets!

DEAN: Oh yes, precisely. (*Despite himself, he is moved by memories of his work.*)

STELLA: They made you an F.R.S. for it anyway. Don't tell me *that* wasn't important.

DEAN (*crosses behind desk to window*): No, that did have a certain importance at the time. I wanted to get married.

STELLA (*surprised*): You didn't know Mummy when you did Agamemnon.

DEAN: Oh this was long before I met Mummy.

STELLA (*a little shocked*): And you wanted to marry whoever she was?

DEAN (*comfortably*): No—o. (*As one in honesty compelled to admit*) I certainly thought I did. I was very young when I did Agamemnon, you know.

STELLA: Yes. (*Curious*) And she turned you down?

DEAN: No, she accepted me. And then at the last minute she married a merchant seaman. (*This still puzzles him.*)

STELLA (*frowning sympathetically*): That can't have been much fun.

DEAN: Oh 'twas a lucky escape. 'Twould have been disastrous . . . (*Cross to right of desk.*) The Fates sent me, by way of compensation, the Senior Fellowship at Queens. Her marriage to the merchant seaman turned out not too badly, I was told. My rooms at Queens were those of John James Pugh, the seventeenth century cartographer— (STELLA *sits left of desk.*) My neighbour there was Richard

Weller—by head and shoulders the most brilliant of our set; he became President of the Royal Society . . . From Queens I came straight here as Master—the youngest master this college ever had—that was the year I married Mummy . . . she was that rarest combination, a scholar, and to my mind a beauty. And now, it seems, I am to be Vice-Chancellor. Ripeness is all. (*Going towards door up right.*)

STELLA: Daddy! (*Rises.*) What d'you think of Louis?

DEAN (*unwillingly stops. Ruefully*): Yes, I thought there was something nearer home than Agamemnon.

STELLA: What d'you think of him?

DEAN (*the whole of what follows is more or less distasteful to him*): He's an excellent linguist obviously. And he's remarkably well read.

STELLA: He does know a lot, doesn't he?

DEAN: Yes. What we used to call 'a man of ideas'.

STELLA: That's a crack, isn't it?

DEAN (*persuasive smile*): Well, there's something about Louis that invites cracks—petitions and committees you know—

STELLA: He isn't really like that. (*Picks up book from table.*) You read these poems—

DEAN (*politely*): Oh yes, I mustn't forget that— (*Crosses to her above desk.*)

STELLA: You read them, Daddy.

DEAN (*gently mocking her warmth*): Good, are they?

STELLA (*with this speech we see she loves Louis*): Oh yes.

DEAN (*politely*): Well I shall certainly read them.

STELLA: Some of them are magnificent.

DEAN (*politely, wishes to draw away, but she unconsciously grips the book*): Good.

STELLA: That one you started by Juan Ferril y Garba—you liked that, didn't you?—'Shall I Admit'.

DEAN: Oh I hardly—

STELLA: Yes—'Shall I admit I do not love thee much'—
that one—

DEAN: Oh yes. (*rather snappish.*) Professor Justino says they're
very *free* translations?

STELLA: What does *he* know about it?

DEAN: Professor Justino? They think well of his Spanish in
Madrid.

STELLA: Well I think Louis's a bit of a genius.

DEAN (*murmurs*): I might have guessed he'd be *something*
transcendent.

STELLA: You don't like him, do you?

DEAN: Oh, Stella, these fantastic questions—you'll hurt
yourself.

STELLA: I think perhaps I need hurting.

DEAN (*alert*): What rubbish is this?

STELLA: Well there *are* these questions aren't there about
Louis and me, (*defiant*) and about the H-Bomb—

DEAN (*angered, rather harsh*): No, there are not these questions.
(*Rises, points accusingly to her forehead*) Except in there!
They're not out here anyway, are they? (*He looks about.*)
If they are, show them to me—where are they? They're
in there, just in there. They have none of this 'reality'
you're so attached to. (*More gently*) Out here, it's not so
splendidly tragic as it is in there; there's nothing tragic,
magnificent, out here. But it's much easier than it is in
there. I do wish you'd come out.

STELLA (*she sits and holds her head*): There's a question all
right. Unless I've got a tumour on the brain!

DEAN (*violently disapproving*): Paugh!

STELLA (*looks up, not hostile. Speculative*): Haven't you got a
question? D'you know exactly what kind of person you are?

DEAN: Oh. 'What kind of person am I?' That's not a question,
it's a request for reassurance. All these transcendent
questions boil down to that. A man asks: 'What lies beyond
the stars?'—and what he really means is: 'Do you like me?'

(*A note of winding up*) Well you're a *nice* person, (*crosses to her*) Stella, and I *do* like you. (*She does not respond.*) Isn't that enough? Do you want to be magnificent?

STELLA: I wouldn't mind being magnificent. But I reckon I'd settle for being really nice.

DEAN: Good. Can we leave it there then? (*She shakes her head. He is impatient*) Well I'm afraid I must leave it there. (*He would like to escape but her bent head prevents him. Impatient*) What is it, Stella?

STELLA (*looks up: hastily cheerful*): Nothing. Only I'm not the kind of person who's very happy.

DEAN (*irritated smile*): What nonsense, dear. Of *course* you're happy. (*Enter* MARY. *With her father she exhibits a poised gaiety that is very restful to him and he is patently relieved to see her.*) Mary, my dear!

MARY: Are we giving presents yet?

DEAN: I've had Stella's.

MARY: Many happy returns then. (*Giving him package.*)

DEAN: Oh. Another book.

MARY (*scornfully reassuring*): No-o-o.

STELLA: What's wrong with a book?

MARY (*a little tinkling laugh of protest*): Nothing, darling!

DEAN (*unwrapping*): It *is* a book. Oh, it's a— (*He doesn't know.*)

MARY: It's a visitors' book.

DEAN: A very handsome one.

MARY: You ought to have had one years ago.

DEAN: Yes, I suppose I ought. Thank you. (*Not knowing what to make of it.*) Now who would have thought of a visitors' book?

STELLA: Mary.

MARY (*reasonable: her attitude to* STELLA *in her father's presence is almost subservient*): It would be silly not to have one next year, darling.

DEAN (*taking her point*): So it would. We shall probably collect some remarkable names in it. Thank you, Mary.

(STELLA *crosses to window.*) I'll keep it in the hall. And all visitors of consequence must be constrained to sign their names in it.

MARY: Why not kick off with Sir Hugo?

DEAN: Is he still here?

MARY: With Mummy in the garden. Arguing about Louis' petition.

DEAN (*amused by the project*): Very well, Hugo Slate shall be our first victim.

    Exit DEAN. MARY *ceases to be sweet and takes out a hand-mirror.*

STELLA: Louis there?

MARY: What? Yes, Louis's there.

STELLA: Mary, I want to ask you something. (*No response.*) Do you think people should sleep together?

MARY (*icy*): I *beg* your pardon.

STELLA: All right, skip it.

MARY (*after a pause*): *You* shouldn't.

STELLA: Why?

MARY: You shouldn't, that's all.

STELLA: You do, don't you?

MARY: If I did, do you think I'd tell *you*?

STELLA (*she is back at school; little sister again: a bit hurt*): Why— I wouldn't tell, Mary.

MARY: You are just about as green as you could be, aren't you? (*Pause. Curiosity and scornful amusement break through. Incredulous*) Do you *want* to?

STELLA: Not much.

MARY: Anyone in mind?

STELLA (*a little shocked at the alternative*): Oh *yes*!

MARY (*incredulous*): Louis?

STELLA: Yes.

MARY: Crikey!

STELLA (*fiercely and distressed*): You leave Louis and me alone!

MARY: With pleasure. (*Goes back to her face.*)

STELLA: I could use a bit of help, Mary.

MARY (*mildly*): I've told you. Don't do it.

STELLA: Why not? (*Eager and warm*) I—I think you're right; but why?

MARY: You want to marry him, don't you?

STELLA: Yes.

MARY: Make him wait then.

STELLA: I think that's foul.

MARY (*quiet but very angry*): You get on my nerves, Stella. I wouldn't mind betting you get on Louis' nerves. Do you?

> *Enter* DEAN *and* SLATE, *talking.*

SLATE (*excited*): Mr Flax is a dangerous man!

> STELLA *and* MARY *look up interested.* MARY *rises. Throughout the ensuing exchange* STELLA *looks at her feet, while* MARY *smiles maliciously.*

DEAN (*deprecating*): Dangerous?

SLATE: I use the word advisedly. He's an indiscriminate moralist. Gwendoline is a moralist herself and has little resistance to these massive doses of rectitude which Mr Flax shoots into people so freely. If you'll permit me, Jack, you shouldn't have sent him out; he'll upset her—*has* upset her. (DEAN *is annoyed, smiles coldly.*) Yes all right—he's upset *me*— (*Sinks into a chair.*) And I may be thought to be more or less immune to rectitude, coming as I do of ecclesiastical stock.

> DEAN *declines to be amused.*

DEAN: You're quite out of breath.

SLATE: Little wonder. He scatters imperatives with the irresponsible vigour of an agricultural machine. Seriously, Jack, do you think he's fit company for her?

DEAN (*annoyed, partly on* STELLA'*s behalf, partly on grounds of principle*): I think, Hugo, that one must not too lightly interfere with folk.

SLATE (*sees* STELLA *embarrassed*): Oh. Quite so. (*Sees how very cold is* DEAN'*s smile. Put down*) Quite so. Er— (*Brightly*) What about this volume I am to inaugurate?

DEAN: Here you are, Hugo.

SLATE (*sits down at the table, puts on spectacles*): What a splendid object. (*He opens it; feels the paper; caresses the pages.*) Beautiful paper. Am I really to deface it with my signature? (*Dipping pen*) Not that I shan't enjoy it—nice black ink. How a virgin exercise book brings out the barbarian in one. (*He writes.*) Did I tell you Richard has been posted to the vicinity?

DEAN: Your wife told me. Very satisfactory for you.

SLATE: Yes; we see too little of him. He is to command Number 32 Squadron—they're out at that place beyond Granting, you know—barely a stone's throw.

DEAN: Good. I'm delighted.

SLATE: It is fortunate, isn't it? In the common sequence of events we can't have many years left in which to renew our acquaintance with him.

DEAN: What? Nonsense, Hugo.

SLATE (*mild*): Oh well, we can't live for ever. (*Finishes writing.*) There. Heavens, how unambiguous it looks.
    DEAN *blots book.*

MARY: 32 Squadron? That's Jupiters isn't it, Sir Hugo?

SLATE (*pleased*): That's it. He is seemingly something of an authority on high-altitude bombardment. He's coming in a month's time, from the Air Force Staff College.

DEAN: Do all these young heroes one sees about undertake that kind of study?

SLATE (*proudly*): Indeed they don't. Staff College is the *pons asinorum* to Higher Command. He's a Wing Commander. (*Smiling*) We're inordinately proud of him, as you see.

MARY: Will you stay for a drink, Sir Hugo? (*The others look at her, surprised.*) It's your birthday, Daddy, I think we ought to have a drink. You will stay, won't you?

SLATE: In that case, thank you. Only for a minute, I fear.

MARY: I'll fix something, while we wait for Mummy. (LOUIS *enters*.) Is Mummy coming, Louis?

LOUIS: Mrs Dean's burning some plants; she'll be along immediately.

Exit MARY.

DEAN: Stella gave me this, Vice-Chancellor. (*Hands book to* SLATE.)

SLATE: Oh?

DEAN: Mr Flax's translations.

SLATE (*with deliberate insincerity*): Oh how interesting. (*Puts book on desk.*)

LOUIS *is a little abashed by this overt hostility.*

STELLA (*gently*): I haven't put an inscription. (*Takes the book from desk. He looks at her.*) I must write something.

SLATE: I've not so much as offered my felicitations, Jack. I do so now.

LOUIS: Yes, happy returns, Master.

DEAN (*to* SLATE): Thank you. (*To* LOUIS) Thank you. (*Little pause.*) Really one would imagine there was something to celebrate.

STELLA: There's your birthday.

DEAN: Yes, and what's a birthday? . . . The Earth, since I was born has completed a quite arbitrary number of its customary revolutions round the Sun. No consequences follow; no improvement in the climate is to be expected. What then do we celebrate?

STELLA *has put into his hands the inscribed book. He now looks at it.*

. . . Why you silly girl! You've put sixty-four. I'm not sixty-four.

STELLA (*surprised*): You are.

DEAN: I'm sixty-four *next* year.

STELLA: No, Daddy, you're sixty-four to-day.

DEAN: I'm sixty-three to-day.

STELLA: No you're not; you're—

DEAN: Well, really—

They both stop.

STELLA (*weakening*): I'm sure you're sixty-four to-day.

DEAN: Very well dear; sixty-four will suit me admirably.

STELLA: Weren't you sixty-three last year?

DEAN: Certainly, if that would be more convenient.

STELLA (*downcast: regards her inscription*): Oh Lord. Wouldn't you just know I'd do something like that.

DEAN (*kindly*): It could hardly be less important my dear. (*Impish*) What does this reveal, Mr Flax, an unconscious desire to impel me towards the grave? (*He puts his hand on* STELLA*'s shoulder to take away any sting.*)

LOUIS (*irritated by* STELLA*'s easy capitulation*): Depends which of you's right, Master, doesn't it?

STELLA: No, I think I remember now.

Enter MARY.

MARY: Everything ready.

DEAN (*dropping hand*): Splendid. (*Preparing to go*) Your sister is circulating a vile rumour that I am sixty-four.

MARY: You are sixty-four.

DEAN: Sixty-three, surely?

MARY (*flatly*): No, darling, sixty-four.

DEAN *is abstracted. Enter* MRS DEAN. *She holds the petition.*

MRS DEAN (*pleasantly*): Jack, I should dearly love a decision about this. I should like to sign it—

DEAN (*coming to. Pleasantly*): Then sign it.

SLATE *twitches in his chair. She glances at him.*

MRS DEAN: But what are *your* wishes?

DEAN: My wishes are that you should do whatever you want.

MRS DEAN (*brightly*): But you must *have* a preference.

DEAN: None at all.

MRS DEAN: You see, there is this question of mutations. That seems to me to constitute an extension of our own wickedness into the future—

DEAN (*soothing*): Oh clearly you must sign it. You want to.

MRS DEAN: But Hugo says it will jeopardise your election. Do you think it will?

DEAN (*reproving*): You know as much about university politics as I do, my dear.

MRS DEAN (*seeing an opening here*): Oh no, I'm out of touch. Do tell me your opinion. (*Cunning*) I mean, I might not act on it; I just want to know.

DEAN: Ah, but I'm afraid you *would* act on it.

MRS DEAN: I *should* like to do your desire in the matter.

DEAN: No—I'm particularly anxious to avoid this kind of thing.

MRS DEAN: But I *want* to do what you desire, Jack.

DEAN: No, no.

MRS DEAN (*like a prisoner, humbly*): If you would tell me your desire, I'd be so grateful.

DEAN (*embarrassed*): Gwendoline, this is nonsense! (*With kindly impatience*) Sign it. Yes, yes, sign it. I should like you to. (*And drops pen in ink.*)

MRS DEAN (*to the others*): He is always so—just.

DEAN: Just? What on earth do you mean? Come along, sign it! (*Holds pen out to her.*)

MRS DEAN (*giving petition to* LOUIS): I'm sorry, Louis.

LOUIS: That's all right, Mrs Dean. One signature on one petition isn't going to make all that difference.

MRS DEAN (*looks at him as though this were an entirely novel idea*): No, of course it's not! (*Shakes her head as though to clear it.*) I'm so glad you said that! One loses one's sense of proportion! (*She, and everybody are relieved.*)

SLATE: Oh excellent! Excellent! (*A cheerful bustle commences.*)

DEAN: We were about to drink my health, Gwendoline.

MRS DEAN (*pleased*): Oh! That's nice. And Louis.

LOUIS: Thank you very much.

MRS DEAN (*claps her hands together*): Oh! Jack, your birthday present. (*She produces a small package, exactly the right size and shape for containing a pipe.*) It slipped my mind.

DEAN: Oh thank you. (*He takes it. She lingers. He smiles, puzzled.*) What—?

MRS DEAN: I was going to give you a kiss.

DEAN: Oh. (*She kisses him on the forehead exactly as Louis had demonstrated to Stella.*) Well now, what is it? (*There is tension and exchange of quick glances among the others as* DEAN *opens it.*) Splendid. A propelling pencil!

MRS DEAN: And pen.

DEAN: So there is. What a good idea. I can never find anything to write with. I shall wear them in here. (*Opens jacket.*) Good heavens, Gwendoline, is this gold?

> MARY *takes* SLATE *to door and they exit.*

MRS DEAN: It's my own money. I wanted to. (MRS DEAN *moves towards door. In doorway she turns.*) There was a lovely calabash pipe in Barton's; it quite made me wish you still smoked. (*Exit* MRS DEAN.)

DEAN (*following, calls cheerfully*): You did buy me a pipe last year! (*Exits.*)

> LOUIS *and* STELLA *are left.*

STELLA: Louis.

LOUIS (*stopping but not turning*): Yes?

STELLA: I will spend the week-end with you.

LOUIS (*turning, delighted*): You will?

STELLA: Mmm, you're right. We ought to.

LOUIS (*smiles helplessly*): Oh-h-h!

STELLA (*seriously apologetic*): I don't know that I'm looking forward to it specially.

LOUIS (*hurriedly reassuring. Crosses to her*): O.K. O.K. Look— we'll just go . . . and have a really fine week-end . . . and see what happens.

STELLA (*grateful*): Yes.

LOUIS: No more talk. We'll just go. We'll have a—oh a stupendous week-end, Stella. And see what happens.

STELLA (*nods smiling*): Yes.

LOUIS: No more talk till then.

STELLA: No.

LOUIS: Come on then— (*Holds out hand to her. Moves to door.*) Oh, just a bit. (*Looks about.*) The petition— (*Crosses to desk.*)

STELLA: Louis—when Mummy was in the garden talking about atomic deformities—did you notice?

LOUIS (*he didn't*): Yeah?

STELLA: She was in a kind of ecstasy!

LOUIS (*looking about for the petition*): Yes, that's quite an imagination she's got there.

STELLA (*a bit exasperated*): But, Louis, what I'm saying is, I think you're right about Mummy.

LOUIS (*complacent*): Oh, I tell you, she's— (*seeing her face, breaks off.*) Hey, wait a minute, Stella. When I say she's off her head, I don't mean she needs asylum.

STELLA: Didn't you?

LOUIS (*reassuring*): No-o-oo. (*Turning away*) Be easier for her if she did. (*Looking about again, indifferent*) There are thousands of people like that. (*There is a chilling lack of compassion,* STELLA *looks at his back.*)

STELLA: Louis.

LOUIS: Yes?

STELLA: Do you love me?

LOUIS (*turns, irritated; then a painful smile*): Sure I do.

STELLA: Do what?

LOUIS: What you said. (*Clears throat, hand before mouth, holding back the word.*) Love you. Where is the ruddy thing? (*Sees her face.*) Oh, don't *worry* about her, Stella. As a matter of fact it's quite a common thing, a fear of monstrosity.

STELLA (*it isn't her mother who is worrying her*): Is it?

LOUIS: Sure. (*Looking about*) For example, *all* women have this fear that their kids, when they're born, you know, won't be quite right.

STELLA: Do they? Why?

LOUIS: Well, everybody's got a suspicion that he's (*bangs his stomach gently*) bad inside.

STELLA (*thoughtfully*): Oh yes . . .

LOUIS (*finding the petition*): Ah. Here it is.

STELLA: Gosh, Louis.

LOUIS: What?

STELLA: You do *know* a lot.

LOUIS: Yes, sometimes I surprise myself. (*He starts to embrace her.*)

MRS DEAN (*off*): Louis!

    They move to door as

CURTAIN

ACT TWO

The garden of JACK DEAN's *residence. September. Evening. Late sunshine.*

Overhead foliage and garden furniture as required.

STELLA *is seated at a garden table on a garden chair. She wears sandals and a spotted print dress. She is reading a book and taking notes.*

DEAN *stands watching her. He is wearing the trousers and waistcoat of a dark suit, stiff white collar and rich purple tie, and a neat alpaca jacket.*

DEAN: That book's not up-to-date, you know.

STELLA: I know.

DEAN (*concealed irritation*): Can you follow it?

STELLA (*does not look up, goes on making notes*): Why not?

DEAN: It's reckoned difficult. Can you follow the maths?

STELLA: Yes, with an effort.

DEAN: The book's not up-to-date, though.

STELLA: No, but it's the last astronomy book you wrote. (*Turns back to title page.*) 1929. (*She still doesn't look up.*)

DEAN (*absorbs this, eyebrows raised rather coldly, then*): Why so defensive?

STELLA (*stops taking notes; does not look up*): You're attacking me.

DEAN: Nonsense.

STELLA: Could I see that— (*She shifts the book round to face him, open at a photograph. He moves forward and looks at it.*) Could I see that with your telescope?

DEAN (*comfortably*): There's no lens in it.

STELLA: No. The little one.

253

DEAN: Oh that. That's no good; it's just for star-gazing.

STELLA: That's all I'm doing.   Could I?

DEAN: Yes, you could see that. (*Looks up at sky.*) I rather think it's going to be cloudy.

STELLA: Looks all right to me.

DEAN: What d'you want to see that for?

STELLA: It looks pretty.

DEAN: Yes. Not as pretty as a sixpenny Catherine Wheel.

STELLA (*turning book back to herself*): Bigger though.

DEAN: Oh yes, there are a lot of noughts involved.

STELLA: Don't worry about it, Daddy, it just interests me.

DEAN (*easy humour*): Don't worry? My dear I'm not worried. (*Calls off*) Oh. Hugo!

SLATE (*off*): Hello there.

MARY (*off*): Hello!

    Enter MARY *and* SLATE. SLATE *wears a light cashmere suit and carries a panama.* MARY *wears a garden party dress, gloves, stockings, formal shoes.*

DEAN: Did you go up?

SLATE: I did. I went up in a de Havilland—?

MARY: 'Jackal.' (*To* STELLA) Hello, Titch.

SLATE: De Havilland 'Jackal'—the very latest thing. King's Lynn and back in about ten minutes. (*He is excited. He draws breath to speak.*)

DEAN (*smiling*): Tell us about it.

SLATE: That is my intention. (*Commences his set piece.*) My most vivid impression is of personal discomfort. One is swaddled in straps and secured to a thing like an apple-barrel. This is an ejector-seat and allegedly contains a parachute. The pilot—my son in this case—then operates the levers and one is whisked into the atmosphere like a falling stone—only upwards, of course. There is also (*flutters his fingers in front of his face*) a species of rubber tea-cosy the purpose of which eluded me throughout. The noise is not loud but curiously unfriendly, and the whole accompanied by a gentle shaking motion, (*he holds hands before him and imitates the motion of shaking something down into a sock*) well calculated to unhinge. (*Sits.*) Not for any consideration would I repeat the experience. But experience it undoubtedly is. The interior of those machines is of a complexity— (*He gestures helplessly.*) They live in a different world, Jack.

STELLA: Did you *get* a weather report?

SLATE: *Culpa mea.* I quite forgot, Stella. But if it's anything to go by, they are flying to-night, aren't they?

MARY: Dicky isn't. He's taking me to a dance at the 'Warming Pan'.

SLATE (*pleased, looks at* DEAN): Oh yes. Well. (*Picks up his hat. Sighs.*) Have you that stuff from the Board, Jack?

DEAN: Yes—(*takes folders from table to* SLATE) and the Holbein's back—beautifully restored—all sorts of things have turned up in it—Gwendoline's quite right by the way, that child is a hunchback—come and look. And do you know they value it at forty thousand pounds?

SLATE: Hmph. Rather a responsibility. One or two good men coming up to Trinity this year, I'm told. Ah me, they'll be here in a fortnight. Where I wonder did we get the idea that a university necessitates undergraduates?

DEAN: From the assumption that there is no Life without Pain.

SLATE: Ah the Puritans. Very probably. (*They move off together.*) Why no dahlias this year?

DEAN: It's getting too much for Gwen. (*Exit* DEAN *and* SLATE. *Off*) We shall *have* to get a gardener.

MARY: She has slipped a bit, hasn't she?

STELLA: Yes.

MARY: It might be a good idea to get Louis Flax off her back.

STELLA: He's not on her back.

MARY: She's far too interested in the ugly side of life as it is. Without him filling her up with his (*disgustedly*) politics.

STELLA: It's not his fault—It's Mummy—she pesters him; he doesn't want her to, Mary—honestly—he *says* it's bad for her!

MARY: Well get him off her back anyway. He's enough to drive anyone— (*she breaks off.*) Get him off her back.

STELLA (*quietly*): I've told you, he's not on her back . . . (*A note of regret*) He's not on anybody's back . . .

MARY (*looks at her, interested*): He's a dead-beat lately, did you know that? (*No answer.*) What's the matter with him?

STELLA (*rising, distressed*): Look, Louis's having a pretty tough time!

MARY: He's a liability. (*Sharply curious*) What sort of tough time?

STELLA (*faltering*): Oh . . . Personally . . .

MARY: Stella. (*Goes to her.*) Stella, are you?

STELLA: Am I what?

MARY: Stella! Are you?

STELLA: Am I what?

MARY (*quietly*): You're pregnant, aren't you?

STELLA: No! . . . Yes.

MARY: Oh you *fool*! . . . Oh you *fool*!

STELLA: Thank you very much; very helpful. (*Her face puckers.*) Yes, I am, I am, and I don't know what to do! (*Weeps.*)

MARY (*not unkindly*): Come on now, Stella, that's no good.

STELLA (*holding her middle*): It grows! It grows!

MARY: Oh you poor little twerp. (*Briefly, comforting*) Come on.

STELLA: It grows!

MARY: Come on. You've got to think.

STELLA (*stops weeping*): What is there to think about? (*She shrugs helplessly, but looks at her sister.*)

MARY (*incredulous*): Have you done nothing at all?

STELLA: What is there to do, Mary?

MARY (*looks at her and considers; then*): It *is* Louis, I suppose?

STELLA (*softly*): Of course it's Louis.

MARY (*sharply*): What does *he* say?

STELLA: He says we ought to get married.

MARY: Well what's the delay, then?

STELLA: I don't know really . . . (*Fearful*) Do you think people *ought* to get married like that?

MARY (*this is pain as well as anger; she walks away while STELLA watches her apprehensively*): Oh sister, am I fed up with oughtn't and ought! (*As one who has made up her mind.*) You've got no choice. (*Less hard*) Well what is the alternative? (*Gently*) 'Go away somewhere,' Titch, and have (*gently*) a bastard? (*No answer. Calmly*) Does anyone else know?

STELLA: No.

MARY (*calmly*): It hasn't occurred to you this affects anyone else.

STELLA (*distressed*): Yes it has!

MARY (*calmly*): No it hasn't. Have you thought about Daddy and the election?

STELLA (*distressed*): Yes I have!

MARY (*calmly*): Have you thought about me and . . . Richard? (*Finishes with a gesture.*)

STELLA (*distressed*): Yes I have!

MARY (*distressed too*): Not everyone takes this sort of thing as lightly as you do!

STELLA: Lightly! (*And she tugs at her hair.*) Lightly? (*She is vulnerable to any suggestion.*)

MARY (*alarmed*): All right. (*She rearranges STELLA's hair.*) All right. But you do pick your moments. My God, you pick your moments . . . (*Encouraging*) Still. If that's what Louis says? (*Comforting humour*) It's a very popular way of getting married. (*No response; she sits left of table. Hardens off*) But get it done. You tell Daddy, Stella, and you get it done. Tell him to-day; otherwise I shall.

LOUIS (*off*): It's not the methods that are important, Mrs Dean, it's the morals attached to them.

MRS DEAN (*enters*): Even so, even so, ought one not to recruit help wherever one can find it?

LOUIS (*patient*): I don't think so, Mrs Dean.

MRS DEAN: You don't.

LOUIS (*patient*): No, Mrs Dean.

MRS DEAN: I see. I mean the Bolshevists—over at Angels and Martyrs. If as you say they are dedicated and industrious—isn't that the most important thing about them?

  LOUIS *is dressed approximately as before.* MRS DEAN *wears a plain, faded cotton frock, a trifle short, and with an uneven hemline, ankle socks and sandals, one of which is undone; a pair of earrings and a necklace, circa* 1925. *She carries one magnificent rose.*

LOUIS: I don't think so, Mrs Dean.

MRS DEAN: For practical purposes?

LOUIS (*a shade impatient*): For practical purposes, they're a set of unprincipled bastards, Mrs Dean. That's the most important thing about them.

MRS DEAN: Oh-ho-ho-ho- I see, yes . . . (LOUIS *crosses down stage slightly,* MRS DEAN *follows*) you will persevere with the petition, won't you, Louis?

LOUIS: Yes, I will. (*To* STELLA) Hello. (*To* MARY) Hello.

MRS DEAN (*fading*): Because I do think it is so important that somebody should persevere. (*Coming back strongly*) There was an extremely cogent article in the *New Statesman and Na*—

LOUIS: Yes I saw it.

MRS DEAN (*woeful*): Did you see that dreadful, (*her voice quavers and she begins to pull the rose to pieces*) dreadful report from Naples?

LOUIS: Yes.

MRS DEAN: About the beggars.

LOUIS: Yes.

MRS DEAN: Look what I've done to your flower.

LOUIS: It doesn't matter.

MRS DEAN (*quite mildly*): That's dreadful; I love flowers. What a heavenly evening!

STELLA: It is, isn't it?

MRS DEAN: Yes, one would never think . . .

Exit MRS DEAN. *No one speaks.*

LOUIS: It's nothing to do with me, Mary.

MARY: This maniac obsession with politics is nothing to do with you?

LOUIS: She's not interested in politics, Mary; she's unhappy. (*Turns towards her, interested in his own exposition.*) The politics is just a substitute; it's a projection—

MARY (*rising*): Keep it, Louis, keep it. (*He stares at her.*) Stella has something to say to you. (*Exit* MARY.)

STELLA: She knows, Louis.

LOUIS: Oh . . . Did you *tell* her?

STELLA: No. She saw.

LOUIS (*grimaces*): Pt! Like that is it?

STELLA: I told you it would be, Louis.

LOUIS (*too cheerfully*): Well, 'name the day' then! (*This is half interrogative.*)

STELLA: Yes!

LOUIS (*drops on one knee, takes her hand*): My dear Miss Dean, you cannot be unaware—

STELLA (*withdraws her hand*): No don't, Louis.

LOUIS: Sorry. (*Gets up, wanders to above table and looks at book.*) Can you follow this stuff?

STELLA: Just about.

LOUIS: 'Mrs Flax.' How does it sound?

STELLA: Sounds fine to me. How does it sound to you?

LOUIS: Fine.

STELLA: Louis—

LOUIS: —Will she tell your dad?

STELLA: No, I'm going to tell him. I shall have to, Louis.

LOUIS: That's all right, I'm not afraid of your dad; (*sits on back of chair by table*) this is nothing to do with your dad; this is to do with us, no-one else. What were you going to say?

STELLA: Er—

LOUIS: You were going to say something.

STELLA: Was I, oh yes—

LOUIS: You don't seem terribly festive.

STELLA: What about?

LOUIS: Gettin' wed.

STELLA: Am I getting wed?

LOUIS (*laughs uncomfortably*): What d'you mean?

STELLA: I've not been asked.

LOUIS (*bit too loud*): What, do you want it in so many words? (*Remorseful*) Oh, I'm sorry, Stella, of course you do. (*Bit too loud*) Well that's easily done! (*Pause.*)

STELLA: All right then, do it.

LOUIS (*pause, giggles*): I can't think how to say it!

STELLA (*tremulous*): How about 'Will you marry me?'

LOUIS: Yeh, Will you— (*Sits on chair. Clears his throat.*) Stella, will you ma— (*He is interrupted by a fit of coughing. Indignantly*) I've swallowed a bloody gnat!

STELLA: Try again.

LOUIS: I did—honestly—I swallowed a— (STELLA *suddenly puts her face into her hands.*)

LOUIS (*goes to her*): Oh Jesus, Stella. Will you marry me?

STELLA: No, of course I won't.

LOUIS: Why not? I asked you didn't I?

STELLA: Yes, you made it, boy.

LOUIS (*very controlled*): Will you marry me?

STELLA (*admiring*): Bravo!

LOUIS (*temper rising*): Will you marry me?

STELLA: And again! Ladies and Gentlemen, Mr Louis Flax, the aerial psychopoet, will now dive three hundred feet from the high mind into a wet flannel.

LOUIS (*his voice shaking, stands over her*): You're a bloody fool, Stella.

STELLA (*looks up at him suddenly sober*): Oh, Louis, I *want* to.

LOUIS: Well do then! (*Tremulous*) Three times I've asked you.

STELLA: Yes, but you— (*Desperately flings arms round his legs.*) Then I will, Louis! I will marry you, please.

LOUIS: Well then.

STELLA: Yes. Yes.

LOUIS: All right then . . . (*Pause.*) Well let's see, what now?
  STELLA *against his legs, inaudible, mumbles.*

  Mm? Oh. Let go of my ruddy legs then.

  She does so; he squats to bring their faces level; but she goes to kiss him on the mouth, he to kiss her forehead, and they fumble.

STELLA (*giggles*): Oh. S-Sorry.

LOUIS: No, I was going to—

STELLA: I was— (*They manage an awkward kiss.*) Oh, I'm glad about this.

LOUIS (*lying*): Me too. (*Sits on ground.*)

STELLA: We shall have to get a house—or a flat more likely. What d'you think?

LOUIS: I don't mind.

STELLA: There are some nice houses towards Granting— might get one by the river.

LOUIS: Yes, that's a good idea.

STELLA: Oh, wait a bit though; it's like an air-raid out there . . . They'd wake the baby. (*She smiles shyly.*) LOUIS *takes a deep shuddering breath and is silent. She looks at him. With quiet dread.*) What's the matter, Louis?

LOUIS: Nothing— I'll get round to it. (*Catches himself up*) I mean, big experience for a young lad.

STELLA: Yes.

LOUIS: Fair mess I made of it too; I wasn't exactly the demon lover just now. (*No answer.*) Was I?

STELLA: Don't talk about it.

    A pause.

LOUIS: No, that was pretty insulting really though. (*His voice is falsely serious, falsely dispassionate. She doesn't answer.*) I want to apologise.

STELLA: Louis, *I don't care!*

LOUIS (*quickly*): Well, that's what matters. (*Rises, crosses up-stage. But he can't keep away from it.*) I might have done better than that though.

STELLA: Why? Was it such an effort? Oh yes it was, wasn't it— (*From this point in the play she is at the mercy of the Furies of Integrity and Truth.*)

LOUIS (*turns to* STELLA): I didn't say that! I'm just saying—

STELLA: I know what you're saying, Louis.

LOUIS: What d'you mean? I don't know what you mean. I just—

STELLA: O.K.! . . . O.K., *I'll* ask *you* the big question.

LOUIS (*uneasy*): What big question?

STELLA: It's wonderful how stupid you can make yourself. I want to know, Louis, if you would be marrying me if it wasn't for the baby.

LOUIS: Oh that's a *silly* question!

STELLA: Well let's hear the silly answer. Would you?

LOUIS: Oh, Stella, who can say?

STELLA: You.

LOUIS (*throughout this speech he paces jerkily about while she sits, motionless. He clings desperately to the forms of logic while the emotion of which he is ashamed forces through*): No I can't, no one can. I mean, if the circumstances weren't what the circumstances are, then for one thing I wouldn't be me and you wouldn't be you. You pregnant are a different person from you not pregnant. I mean you as you are now are a person I've asked to marry me—a person I *want* to marry me . . . It may be because—well no not *because*—but one of the things about you at the moment happens to be that you— (STELLA *is silent. He recommences with fresh funds of reasonableness but descends quickly into distress.*) What I mean is, I've asked you to and therefore I must want you to. Otherwise why should I have asked you? A person does what he wants to do. It's a proof that he wants to do it that he did it. That's inescapable, it's a matter of definition. I can't pretend— it's not to be expected—that I'm entirely, just *happy* now, because— Oh hell! Let's leave it!

STELLA: We've left it, Louis.

LOUIS: Oh Jesus, was there anything lower, was there ever anything lower? . . . than a left-wing, bloodless, gutless, cerebral, creep!

STELLA: So; we're not getting married, are we?

LOUIS: I don't know! I don't know!

STELLA: Well I do. We're not.

Enter SLATE. *They do not see him. He carries a tripod.*

SLATE: Does this go here?

After a moment of horror LOUIS *and* STELLA *escape. Left and Right, respectively, but enter* MARY.

MARY: Hello, Louis. (*She registers* STELLA'*s flight and his expression. Sharply*) Where is Stella?

LOUIS *attempts to escape but enter* MRS DEAN *carrying a paper.*

MRS DEAN (*sing-song*): Lou-ouis!

He stops.

LOUIS: Not just now, Mrs Dean. (*Sets off again.*)

MRS DEAN (*following*): But, Louis— (*her tone is hurt and bewildered. He stops. She joins him.*) There is a very cogent article here I thought you might like to see. It's about the effects of radio-activity upon reproductive tissues.

LOUIS: I have seen it, Mrs Dean.

MRS DEAN (*disappointed*): Oh.

LOUIS: For God's sake, I *told* you I had!

Enter DEAN *with barrel of telescope which he fits on to tripod.* SLATE *is indignant.*

MRS DEAN: I thought, you see, if you could show that to people—you could probably get some printed—if you show *that* to people when you ask them to sign the petition—

LOUIS: Rot the petition. If you're so keen on the petition—why don't you sign it?

DEAN (*quietly*): Mr Flax, will you recollect whom you are speaking to.

    All turn. The light has faded; the sky in consequence glows slightly.

LOUIS: I beg your pardon, Master. Beg your pardon, Mrs Dean.

MRS DEAN (*not whimsical, but with deep attention as to a piece of scientific evidence*): Now I've brought mischance upon you . . . (*Exit* MRS DEAN.)

DEAN (*fitting barrel to telescope*): Who brought the lenses? Did anybody?

SLATE: There is a leather box on the table in your room.

DEAN: Ah. (*Finishes with telescope. Looks at sky.*) The stars will be with us presently. (*Looks about.*) Where is the astronomer? Do you know, Louis?

LOUIS: No, Master.

MARY (*harshly*): She was with you a second ago.

DEAN: I'll bring the lenses. (*To* LOUIS) Tell her it's all here, will you? (*Approaching* LOUIS) . . . Er, I'm sorry I should have reprimanded you, as it were, publicly, Louis. I ask your pardon.

    LOUIS *cannot answer. Exit* DEAN.

SLATE (*looking after him*): Upon my word, a gentleman! (*Cool*) Don't you think, Mr Flax?

LOUIS: Oh, yes! Proper toff! . . . (SLATE *crosses and sits left of table.*) No, I mean that, Vice-Chancellor, he is a proper toff.

SLATE (*mildly contemptuous*): Your vocabulary is so degenerate one cannot deduce what you mean.

LOUIS (*crosses to centre stage. Starts reasonable, works up defensive temper*): I mean he's a gentleman, like you say, Vice-Chancellor. And I'm not a gentleman—like you didn't say but—

MARY: I'll say it.

LOUIS: Like Mary says—I'm not a gentleman. I'm well known for not being a gentleman. My father swung a pick on the roads.

SLATE (*more and more mild as* LOUIS *steams himself up*): I've heard you mention it before, Mr Flax; it seems to weigh very heavily on you.

LOUIS: Oh that sneer! That sneer of you people!

SLATE (*rises*): Well, I rather think it's time to be going.

MARY: I'll come with you, Sir Hugo.

LOUIS: She has a thing to tell you, Vice-Chancellor. A little thing about me, she's bursting at the seams to tell you before you get it from someone else.

SLATE: Why, what's he done?

LOUIS: Just what you'd expect, Vice-Chancellor, bearing in mind my class background.

MARY: Richard says people who explain everything by class are Communists.

LOUIS: Ooh there's a dirty word! Sorry to disappoint you, Mary! I'm not a Communist.

MARY: Richard says people can be Communists without knowing it.

LOUIS: Well tell Richard to keep his mind on his bombs and he won't make such an ass of himself.

SLATE: Mr Flax—

LOUIS: I apologise. I apologise. (*He backs about the stage bowing at the word 'apologise'.*) I apologise for wearing the wrong sort of clothes and for making it worse with the wrong sort of face; I apologise for my opinions and my table manners. (*He works himself up in self-pity*) If I smell, as I dare say I do, I apologise for that. In short I apologise for having a father who worked for the Gas Company and a mother who . . . (*voice now trembling with self-pity; this is his prize-exhibit*) My mother died of malnutrition!

MARY (*drily*): She died last year of pneumonia.

LOUIS: Of malnutrition!

MARY: Of pneumonia. Stella told me.

LOUIS (*stopped short; then coming back with defensive aggression*): People don't die of pneumonia if they've been properly fed!

SLATE: That's something different. (*Moving away, graciously.*) But I'm profoundly sorry.

LOUIS: Profoundly sorry? You don't give two hoots, Vice-Chancellor.

SLATE (*indignant*): I don't see why you should suppose that; but since you raise the issue, ought I to give two hoots?

MARY (*with relief, as one who hears the truth at last*): Hear! Hear!

LOUIS: Ha! (*Looks at her, crosses to above table.*) By Jove, that rang a bell, didn't it? You don't give one hoot, do you, Mary? And at the Air Force Staff College anyone found hooting is stripped of his buttons and drummed out of the bar! You tell Richard he can relax—it's all being arranged. Tell him just to keep his hand in on the Pacific Ocean and relax—it's all being taken care of by the hootless wonders that run this lovely community—
Enter STELLA.

STELLA (*with some authority, protective*): What's going on?

SLATE: I rather think Mr Flax is about to address us on the nuclear bomb.

LOUIS: Yes, silly Mr Flax is on about the dreary old bomb again. D'you think it makes an exception of Regius Professors? It won't. It doesn't!

STELLA: Louis, stop.

LOUIS (*looks at her, hesitates, plunges*): Why the hell should I stop? Look, Stella, don't you tell me to stop.
SLATE and MARY turn to go. He darts after them.

LOUIS: You tell Richard to keep pegging away at the old

Pacific. It's wonderful how those codfish get about—
Hiroshima to-day, Grimsby to-morrow—and we all eat
fish on Fridays up here—we're a Christian community, I
hope. If he keeps it up much longer we shall all be ticking
away like alarm clocks— D'you realise that?

STELLA: Louis, stop.

LOUIS: And it'll *start* with the Professors!

　　SLATE *and* MARY *move off.*

STELLA: Louis, stop.

LOUIS: First the Profs'll begin ticking, then the dons, then the
nice young lecturers—

STELLA: Louis, stop.

LOUIS: And their nice young wives and their nice children!

STELLA: Stop, Louis!

LOUIS: And the babies!

STELLA: Stop, Louis!

　　SLATE *and* MARY *exit.*

LOUIS (*turns to* STELLA): Do you realise that? Pretty soon
they'll be *born* ticking! (STELLA *catches him a staggering
smack across the ear. Furious*) What the hell d'you— (*He
sees her stance and expression of unbridled loathing and the
implications of what he has said fall upon him. He takes his
hand from his ear and stretching both hands nervously towards
her stomach in a gesture protective and placating, backs away
from her.*) Oh, Stella, I didn't mean that, I wasn't thinking
of that. I mean I didn't mean *that.*

STELLA (*she stops. Quite quietly, rather wonderingly, even a
shade amused*): But you know nothing . . . You don't know
anything . . . Louis, you don't know a thing, do you?
(*She goes towards him; he flinches one step and stops.*) Just
ideas. (*She holds out one hand and makes the movement of
granulating something dry and friable between thumb and
fingers. They both watch her hand. Then with cruel deliberation*)
Ideas . . . (*He ducks away and exits quickly. The stage grows
darker, the sky more luminous.*)

MRS DEAN (*off*): Lou-ee! Lou-ou-ee!

    Enter MRS DEAN *with rose.*

STELLA: He's not here. (*Sits on bench.*)

MRS DEAN: Where is he?

STELLA: He's gone home.

MRS DEAN: Home to Halifax?

STELLA (*irritated*): No, why *should* he have gone to Halifax? I mean he's gone back to Trinity, I expect. I don't know where he's gone.

MRS DEAN: Well, I imagine he'll be back to-morrow. I'll put it in water for him. (*No response.*) Have you had a quarrel? (*Slight move to* STELLA.)

STELLA: No.

MRS DEAN: You have; you've had a quarrel! Oh, that's nice . . .! (*Dreamily*) Out here . . . quarrelling.

STELLA: Oh, sure.

MRS DEAN (*admiring and envious*): Upon my word you're quite angry.

STELLA: Mother, I've got to tell you something. (*Turns to* MRS DEAN.)

MRS DEAN: As a child you had a great capacity for anger. Kick! You used to kick your little shoes off.

STELLA: All babies kick their shoes off.

MRS DEAN (*shyly*): I have a capacity for anger. (*With shy pride*) I have quarrelled, oh, really bitterly in my time—

STELLA: Well of course you have.

MRS DEAN: —with my sisters . . . No one can quarrel with your father.

STELLA: I don't find it difficult.

MRS DEAN: You are very close to him, of course. I hope you realise, Stella, what a privilege that is?

STELLA: I thought there was a quarrel about my name?

MRS DEAN (*lighting up*): Oh there was! There was! (*Rapturously*) He said Stella was a foolish name! He said it was pretentious—empty . . . we quarrelled, quite vehemently.

STELLA: Well, it is my name.

MRS DEAN (*desolate*): He gave way (*She begins destroying rose . . . Suddenly, mechanical chatter*) There are 3,000 beggars in the City of Naples, many of them without limbs. The situation in Korea is so terrible as to defy analysis. I do hope Louis will persevere with his petition. Surely if he perseveres, everyone will sign.

STELLA: Daddy won't.

MRS DEAN: He is not responsible. (*From her tone, she might be talking about Our Lord.*)

STELLA: Mother, what goes on in your head? (*Takes rose.*)

MRS DEAN: In my head? (*Sudden plunge into normality*) A great deal of nonsense— (*She sees what she has done to the flower. Her face grows very attentive. With quiet vehemence*) I really must *control* my *hands*! (*Sensibly*) Well now, you had something to tell me.

STELLA (*uneasy*): No, never mind.

MRS DEAN (*actually laughing gently at her*): Oh, my dear . . . I'm still your mother, you know. Was it serious?

STELLA: No, no.

MRS DEAN: You're going to have a child, aren't you?

STELLA (*looks at her open-mouthed*): How long have you known?

MRS DEAN: I suddenly realised just then. (*Backing away*) You had better tell your father.

STELLA: I'm going to— (*Crosses towards MRS DEAN.*)

MRS DEAN (*sharp warning*): No, don't come near me!

STELLA: Why not?

MRS DEAN: One can't be too careful.

STELLA (*as to a child or invalid*): Careful of what?

MRS DEAN: With a baby, like that . . . one can't be too careful. (STELLA *moves towards her. She dodges away.*) I think perhaps I shall not be able to take this in: you had better tell your father. Anyway I have other things to think about . . . (*She exits.*)

    The lights begin to fade.

DEAN (*calls offstage, right*): Stella . . . Stella . . . (DEAN *enters carrying small leather box, with one lens on top, and his coat over his arm.*) Oh there you are, my dear. Here are the lenses. (STELLA *crosses to him, takes the box and lenses and goes to right of table.*) This is the one you want—the long one. I can't stay, I'm dining at the Lodgings. (STELLA *wipes lens on her skirt.*) They're rather dusty, I'm afraid. No, don't do that! There's a piece of cloth in there. (*Points to leather box.*)

STELLA (*takes cloth from box*): Is Mummy going?

DEAN: To the Lodgings? No.

STELLA: Daddy, is Mummy all right?

DEAN (*looks up*): Mm?

STELLA: Daddy, I think she's in some kind of terrible mess.

DEAN: Mess?

STELLA (*having roused his attention she's not sure she can handle it*): Well, yes—haven't you noticed how unhappy she looks?

DEAN (*concerned*): Just a minute. D'you mean your mother's in some kind of trouble?

STELLA: She's not in any objective trouble, as far as I know—but she . . . she looks so terribly unhappy!

DEAN (*still concerned, partly relieved; irritated laughing protest*): Now wait! (*Serious and brisk*) Look, have you some fact to tell me about Mummy? Or are you talking— (*waves his arms*) metaphysics?

STELLA (*plunges right in, floundering*): She says such extraordinary things!

DEAN (*playing it straight back, stonily*): She's an extraordinary woman.

STELLA (*desperately*): But some of the things she says are— (*thoroughly frightened she gets it out in a flat gabble, anyhow*)

Daddy, I think Mummy's mentally unbalanced. (*A pause.*)

DEAN: You *what*?

STELLA (*wailing*): I think she needs treatment! I—

DEAN (*fury and contempt*): Stella! You had better find yourself an occupation! You inhabit a private world! Your insatiable lust for tragedy—

STELLA: It's you who inhabit a private world! Louis says—

DEAN: —Louis says! (*As one on whom the light dawns*) Ah . . . my dear girl, psychology is a specialised science—of a sort— Louis is merely a young man, with a sharp nose for decay!— I mistrust such people! You create private worlds—and fill them with suffering!

STELLA: Daddy, people do suffer! *You* suffer!

DEAN: I assure you I don't.

STELLA: Then why do you look so sad?

DEAN (*laughing it off, but interested*): I don't look sad.

STELLA: You do when you're asleep . . . When you're asleep you look as though you'd just had terrible news. I'll never forget the first time I saw you sleeping.

DEAN (*still smiling, but shaken*): Stella, this is nonsense.

STELLA: And *all* old people look like that when they're too tired to arrange their faces.

DEAN (*pacing up and down. Excitedly, but controlled*): That's a matter of mechanics—the nerves and muscles of the face after fifty, sixty years of . . . expectation . . . surprise . . . sadness yes, but alarm, amusement, irritation, disbelief, laughter—the face is more or less worn out with *all* of it—consider how wrenched about your face is when you laugh—

STELLA: Old people don't look worn out laughing! (*She starts to tell a story*) There was an old woman— (*comes to a decision; turns towards him*) on the train. (*Stops with deliberate significance.*)

DEAN: What train?

STELLA: Last time I went to London. I said I'd gone to stay
   with Jennifer.

DEAN: Yes.

STELLA: In fact, I spent the week-end with Louis.

DEAN (*after a pause, displeased*): Why do you tell me this?
   I don't want to know the degree of your intimacies.

STELLA: I'm sorry, Daddy; you're going to have to know.

DEAN (*looks at her. Quietly*): Why?

STELLA: I'm going to have a baby.

DEAN (*takes it in, goes and embraces her protectively*): Oh, my
   dear child! (*Trembling*) Oh, my baby. (STELLA *twists her
   head to look up at him. Groaning*) You're too young!

STELLA: No, I'm not; biologically I'm just right.

DEAN (*still simply distressed, unhearing, wraps her closer*):
   Hush . . . hush . . . Oh dear, dear, dear . . .

STELLA: I thought you'd be livid.

DEAN (*slowly releases her; to himself, thoughtfully*): Now what's
   to be done . . .? (*Then, uncomprehending*) Why should I be
   livid?

STELLA (*hesitant*): It's going to be a bit awkward for you,
   isn't it?

DEAN: For me?

STELLA (*gently*): Well, the election—

DEAN (*this is the first time he has thought of it*): Oh! (*Indifferently*)
   Oh, I don't think so.

STELLA: I haven't told you it all yet. You see . . . Louis
   doesn't want to marry me.

   Silence.

DEAN (*takes a step forward. Then, flatly furious*): Oh well,
   I'm afraid he must marry you.

STELLA: But I don't want to marry him.

DEAN (*agitated, rides her down*): Yes you do—

STELLA: No, I don't, Daddy.

DEAN: But you—

STELLA (*growing agitated too*): He's not in love with me—

DEAN: Does he say not—?

STELLA: Not in so many words—

DEAN (*exasperated*): 'Not in so many—' Has he *asked* you to marry him?

STELLA: In a way—not really—

DEAN: Oh give me patience—

STELLA (*shocked*): Daddy, don't put *pressure* on me!

DEAN (*distraught*): I *will* put pressure on you! (*Turns to her.*)

STELLA: Daddy, I'm sorry, but I'm not going to marry—

DEAN: Stella, you must! You must!

STELLA: I'm not going to marry a man who doesn't want me so that you can be Vice-Chancellor! (*Silence. His expression is of amazed hurt. She is galvanised a step or two towards him by remorse. He turns his back while he composes his face. She tries to walk round him but he turns again.*) No, look, that was silly . . . That was a fool thing to say.

DEAN (*cheerfully reasonable*): It must have been in your mind.

STELLA (*still behind him*): Not really.

DEAN (*the same*): Must have been.

STELLA (*pleading*): No. Only half. Less than half. I lost my temper, a bit.

DEAN (*as one unpersuaded*): Mm.

STELLA: Well, you *are* very interested in being Vice-Chancellor.

DEAN (*turning*): Yes, I am.

STELLA: And I can imagine what Sir Hugo's going to say.

DEAN (*incredulous indignation*): You equate *me* with Hugo Slate? (*Wonderingly*) Yes, you obviously do. (*Walks to table. An aural shrug*) I must have done *something* to deserve such an opinion.

STELLA (*pleading*): No-o! But you said you were going to put pressure on me—which is a thing you never do—

DEAN (*whips round*): I never before had a daughter—! (*Gesture of distress.*) What are you going to *do*, Stella? You're too young! (*Turns away quickly, blows nose. The stage has grown darker and stars are beginning to appear.*)

STELLA: I'm sorry. Top and bottom of it is I don't understand you.

DEAN (*passionately*): If only you would stop trying to understand so much and be a little practical!

STELLA: —Like Mary.

DEAN (*sits*): Yes, Stella, you may have the brains, but may I tell you, to be practical is wisdom. Oh yes, wisdom is what makes a person easy to be with, what makes Mary a support—

STELLA: Instead of a damn great responsibility like Stella! . . . Hadn't you better go? You'll be late for your dinner.

DEAN: I'll stay a moment, if I may.

STELLA: All right. Thanks. (*Goes upstage and brings the telescope down centre.*)

DEAN: Now let me see, it was the Catherine Wheel we wanted, wasn't it—well that should be fairly easy— (*Takes lens from table, and carries chair across to left of telescope, fits lens on to telescope.*) It must be up in that quarter somewhere . . . in fact I think I see it . . . get me the almanac, would you. (STELLA *hands him the book, and he finds the right place.*) Yes, that's it. See? (*Puts book and duster on floor.*)

STELLA (*brings chair to left of telescope, and sits*): Can I look now?

DEAN: In a minute. You'll see it better when it gets a bit darker. Stella, it's getting a bit chilly—here. (*Puts his coat round her shoulders.*)

STELLA: Thanks. (DEAN *sits on chair and puts his arm round her. The sky grows black gradually from now to end of act. Laughing at her own impatience*) I want to look at that damn star!

DEAN (*restrains her*): Wait . . . Doesn't Louis feel he *ought* to marry you?

STELLA: That's just about all he does feel. As far as I can make out.

DEAN: I see.

STELLA: When I've had the baby . . . I suppose I couldn't possibly go on living in the town here?

DEAN (*quietly and with absolute determination*): You'll live in this house if you want to.

STELLA: No, there's no sense in rubbing their noses in it. I still think it may lose you the election.

DEAN (*reassuring*): No. I'm not really involved. They won't hold it against me. (*Rueful smile.*) You'll be—my misfortune.

STELLA: Quite right.

DEAN (*carefully, offhand*): Have you considered the possibility of putting the child in a home?

STELLA: No, I'm not going to do that.

DEAN: They're not what they were, you know. But of course if you want the child. . . .

STELLA: I don't want it. But it's not going into a home.

DEAN: What about foster parents?

STELLA: Not that either.

DEAN (*bitterly*): No, you must have your suffering. Oh, Stella—!

STELLA: Relax, Daddy, I'm all right. (*She moves towards the telescope, and immediately he intervenes.*)

DEAN: What was that about some old woman on the train.

STELLA: Oh! She was one of those very smart old women— she must have been way past fifty, but really quite sexy; and she was wearing a pretty hat with a bird in it.

DEAN (*softly, looking down at her*): Yes?

STELLA: Only it was that awful Friday evening train and after about an hour she fell asleep. And her face began to look—like yours when you're asleep. (*He uncrosses his legs restlessly.*) No really this isn't imagination—everyone in the compartment was watching her. And by the time we got into town, this little hat looked like a crown of thorns.

DEAN: 'Crown of thorns.' (*Rises.*) Oh why will you talk gibberish!

STELLA: You asked me. (*Puts off coat.*)

 STELLA *goes to telescope and tries to line up on the star. At once her father is on edge and eager to be gone, but at the same time he hovers, fascinated. He looks from the star to the wavering end of the telescope.*

DEAN: Too high. (*He joins her and looks along the side of the telescope.*) A bit higher—to the left a little. Got it?

STELLA: Yes . . . Oh . . . Oh. (*Looks at him.*) It's lovely! (*Returns to telescope.*) It's so white! (*Looks at him.*) Do look.

DEAN: I've seen it. (*Picks up coat.*)

STELLA (*looks at him, moved*): It's rather comforting, Daddy.

DEAN: Why?

STELLA (*returns to telescope. Dreamily*): Well . . . you know . . . it's been going faithfully round the sun . . . for how long?

DEAN: A thousand million years; all the planets have.

STELLA (*comfortably*): Well that's comforting.

DEAN: Why? Is the sun going somewhere?

STELLA (*not hearing; glued to the telescope*): Dunno . . . Cor! I'd like to be up there to-night.

DEAN: You would not.

STELLA (*swinging the telescope slightly*): Isn't it dark *between* the stars?

DEAN (*looking at them, starts quietly and gradually increases speed*): So dark, that if you were up there, a candle would look like sheet lightning; so silent, that an echo would be as solid as a bank; so ignorant of human necessities, that the smell of a single privet leaf would riot through your senses like an orgy! And for all your endless gliding at a million miles an hour you would be more static than the hands of a stopped clock. Oh yes, the moons go round the planets and the planets go round the sun and the sun goes round the Milky Way, but that doesn't matter because the Milky Way is circling round itself as it goes looping from nowhere to nowhere and in twenty-four billion years the sun will be back where it started. None of it matters since happily it leaves no trace, but if all the galaxies were God's Fingers Dipped in Light d'you know what pattern they would make? Scribble! ... (*He is breathing hard. On a note of going*) So if you find them comforting (*pointing rather unsteadily at the telescope*) now's the time to stop. (*Puts on coat.*)

STELLA (*looking at him; with great interest*): Louis says you're afraid of dying.

DEAN: Louis's a fool! Don't you know that *yet*! (*Going, so that he leaves the area of light.*)

STELLA (*calling into the dark after him*): And that's why you're afraid of being involved.

DEAN (*re-entering light. Speaks calmly by dint of a great effort*): I'm not involved . . . I'm extremely distressed on your behalf, my dear. But I am not involved.

As he moves away

CURTAIN

ACT THREE

High summer again.

STELLA's *flat in a big house in large grounds on the edge of the town. A big room of good proportions; not an attic, though the tops of trees and a chimney seen through the window indicate that it is on an upper floor. The walls, dark green, and wood-work, pale yellow, are somewhat knocked about, but of sound Victorian workmanship. Doors lead left to a kitchenette, right to a bedroom—this door has a heavy curtain which can be drawn across it—and centre to the rest of the house. The furniture is a mixture of fine 'pieces' from* STELLA's *old home, and student make-do. By the window is the telescope, canted down in an attitude of disuse. There is a table, centre, covered by a cheerful red blanket, and on the blanket an old-fashioned baby cot on rockers. A smaller table has piles of clean nappies, a box of tissues, a string of celluloid toys, bottles and so on, not very tidy. A small electric fire with nappies airing on a maiden. Nobody is on stage.*

LANDLADY (*off*): Mr Flax! . . . Mr Flax! (*Enter* LOUIS, *right, plumping a pillow. He listens.*) Mr Flax! Are you there? (LOUIS *throws pillow on to chair: goes and opens door, centre. A section of landing is revealed. He leans over the bannisters.*)

LOUIS: Hello!

LANDLADY: Sir Hugo Slate is on the telephone, Mr Flax! (*She is agreeably fluttered by this.*)

LOUIS: Oh?

LANDLADY: He wants Mr Dean.

LOUIS: Mr Dean? He's not here.

LANDLADY: Then he says is *Mrs* Dean there?

LOUIS: Mrs Dean isn't here either.

LANDLADY: Oh . . . *Miss* Dean isn't back yet, is she?

LOUIS: No. (*Mildly surprised*) Does he want her?

LANDLADY: Any of them.

LOUIS: What for?

LANDLADY: Don't know, Mr Flax.

LOUIS (*on a note of termination*): Well, Miss Dean should be back any time. (*A sleepy cry from the cot. Reproachful*) Oh hell, Mrs Smith, we've woken the baby! (*Door closes downstairs; he re-enters leaving door of the room, and approaches the cot. Gently*) Hey! Hey, Fred! Nark it! (*He rocks the cot; the crying continues, but sleepy and experimental in tone.*) Hey, Spike! You in there—nark it! (*Appealing*) Ah, turn it up, mate. (*The crying ceases. Carefully continuing the rocking. He smiles.*) Wotcher, Fred. Now what have you done that for, you daft little get? (*He reaches both hands into the head of the cot, turning the baby over. Smiles.*) You know what, mate—you're backward.

Enter DEAN.

It'll be pick and shovel work for you if you don't watch it. They'll have you in a Secondary Mod.—they will. They will.

DEAN *closes door.*

Cheerful whoop from cot.

DEAN's *attitude to* LOUIS *is rigidly disapproving and becomes downright hostile.* LOUIS' *attitude to him is conciliatory.*

Oh come in, Master.

DEAN *takes off a light coat, looking coldly at* LOUIS.

LOUIS (*explaining*): I'm baby-sitting.

DEAN: I see.

LOUIS: Stella's shopping. (*Smiles.*) I'm looking after Fred so she can get round without him.

DEAN (*stiffly*): Why do you call him Fred?

LOUIS: Sorry; Nicholas. (*Sees pillow.*) Oh. (*Takes it into bedroom.*) I've been making the bed. (DEAN *hangs up coat, crosses to table, looks into the cot, gravely, then an involuntary* smile. LOUIS *emerges from bedroom.*) I can't seem to get my tongue to 'Nicholas'. (*He essays a tentative smile.*)

DEAN: I wouldn't have said you had any right to a preference in the matter. (*No answer.*) Would you?

LOUIS: No. (*Dives into kitchen, but* DEAN *is now hunting him; they are both helpless.*)

DEAN: What are you doing in there? (*Crosses upstage, looks into kitchen.*)

LOUIS (*from kitchen*): I'm putting out the bread.

DEAN: Has Stella asked you to do that?

LOUIS (*from kitchen*): No.

DEAN: Then why are you doing it?

LOUIS (*at door of kitchen*): You're having toast for tea. Stella said so.

DEAN: Are you having tea with us?

LOUIS: No.

  LOUIS *goes to the maiden, rear of table, and begins folding nappies on to table, closely watched by* DEAN; *becoming absorbed he begins to whistle 'If I were a blackbird'.*

DEAN: You seem happy at your work, Mr Flax. (LOUIS *stops whistling, works in silence.*) You do have tea here sometimes?

LOUIS: Sometimes, yes. (*Then with a hint of 'why not'*) Quite often.

DEAN: You're a curious creature. (*No answer.*) How would you describe your status here? (*No answer.*) Mr Flax?

LOUIS (*with some difficulty; he is not indifferent to* DEAN'*s contempt*): I'd describe it as lousy.

DEAN: Which being translated means . . . despicable?

LOUIS (*pause*): Something like that. (*Folds maiden.*)

DEAN: Not a bad description; not bad at all. Speaking of translation, Professor Justino tells me your thesis is a long time coming?

  LOUIS' *face expresses resentment, but no answer. He takes the cot at either end and is about to lift it.*
  (*Sharply*) What are you doing with that?

LOUIS (*tonelessly; keeping his voice steady; head bent*): I'm taking it into the bedroom.

DEAN: Why?

LOUIS (*the same*): So that I can clean in here.

DEAN: Isn't it clean in here?

LOUIS (*the same*): There are fluffs on the carpet.

DEAN (*glances at carpet*): So there are! I didn't realise you had all these domestic talents.

LOUIS (*without raising his voice*): I didn't realise you were such a bloody sadist. (*Exerts himself to lift the cot.*)

DEAN: Wait. (*He comes to table, takes an end of the cot, indicates to him to take the other. Then, more sympathetically; not looking at him.*) You like being here, Louis? You seem fond of the child. Why don't you marry her?

LOUIS: I wouldn't be marrying the child.

DEAN: You're *not* fond of Stella?

LOUIS: It wouldn't be much fun for Stella.

DEAN: She is a person who can manage on very little fun.

LOUIS: It'd be no fun at all for her.

DEAN (*angry laugh*): And you are, of course, exclusively preoccupied with what would be 'fun' for her. (*He glances significantly round the room.*)

LOUIS: Of course I'm not. *I*'d be the bad husband of a good wife—which is the worst thing that can happen to anybody.

DEAN (*raises eyebrows; mildly*): One of the worst, certainly.

DEAN *lifts his end of the cot and together they carry it into the bedroom.*

LOUIS (*off*): By the bed. Behind the screen.

DEAN (*emerging, followed by* LOUIS, *crosses to window*): I don't know what private system of ethics you are following, Louis; but I have the oddest impression that you credit yourself, in part, with motives of humility . . . In fact, you must be the most morally conceited man in these islands.

LOUIS *shuts door.*

Enter STELLA. *She has changed for the better and worse,*

is a more considerable, less immediately likeable person than she was. Her generosity is overlaid by a manner somewhat brittle and censorious. Her clothes are much better—rather consciously sober, but dignified and becoming; hair pulled back, long dark skirt, plain black jumper, brown scarf. The basis of it all is still her youthfulness.

STELLA: Hello, Daddy; sorry I wasn't here. (*She puts down handbag on table, takes shopping basket into kitchen.*)

LOUIS: I've put out the bread.

STELLA, *emerging, looks about, crosses to bedroom door.*

And Nicky's asleep, so I put him in the bedroom.

STELLA *goes to check up on this.*

And the nappies are aired, so I've folded them.

DEAN: And he was just on the point of sweeping the carpet.

They smile together at LOUIS' *expense, excluding him.*

STELLA: I'm glad you've come.

DEAN: I can't stay late, I'm afraid.

STELLA: When do you take over from Sir Hugo? (*Enters kitchen; sound of cupboards opened and shut.*)

DEAN (*crosses to kitchen door*): Ceremonially at the start of term. In practice I've already done so. I half expected to find Mummy here.

STELLA (*from kitchen*): She hasn't been since Thursday. Is she all right?

DEAN: Oh yes. We *found* a gardener by the way.

STELLA (*from kitchen*): Yes, I know.

LOUIS (*unhappily*): Well . . . I'll push off now.

STELLA (*from kitchen*): Right. (*Perfunctory*) Thanks, Louis.

LOUIS (*wanders towards door, centre*): No, that's O.K.

STELLA (*from kitchen*): Louis! (*Appearing*) Have you put the butter somewhere?

LOUIS: No? Oh! You're out. I'll get some. How much do you want?

STELLA (*indifferent*): All right. Get a pound. (*Goes to purse.*)

LOUIS (*quickly*): I'll get it.

STELLA (*mildly*): Don't be silly.

LOUIS: No, that's all right.

> *Exit* LOUIS. STELLA *closes hand-bag, looking after him, her face unnaturally composed, the eyes absent. She finds* DEAN *regarding her.*

STELLA (*brightly*): Well, how are you?

DEAN (*laughingly mimicks the social tone*): Very well, thank you; and yourself?

STELLA (*laughs*): It's a long time since I've seen you. (*Goes into kitchen.*) Properly. (*Comes out with slices of bread; sits by electric fire and begins to toast them, student fashion.*) Are you frightfully busy?

DEAN: There's a surprising amount of work attached to it.

STELLA: Isn't that rather a bore?

DEAN: No?

STELLA: No, you like administration. Sit down. (*This is rather peremptory; her father looks at her.*)

DEAN (*quietly*): Thank you. (*Sits left of table.*)

STELLA (*brisk*): How's Mary?

DEAN (*with pleasure*): Radiant. Do you know Richard is to be made a Group Captain?

STELLA: No wonder she's radiant.

DEAN: . . . A little sharp, Stella?

STELLA: No, not sharp. (*She is instructing him.*) —People fall for different things. Mary falls for success. (*Proceeds to toast.*) Nothing wrong with that—it's very healthy. And in the Air Force, you can tell exactly how successful a man is by counting the rings on his sleeve.

DEAN (*a little worried by her*): Penetrating . . . Do you still stargaze with my telescope?

STELLA: Not much. I'm reading Gamoff.

DEAN (*impressed*): Are you though?

STELLA: Yes, it's the maths I like now.

DEAN: Good.

STELLA (*a wise little smile*): I knew you'd like that.

DEAN: Why?

STELLA: Oh, I just knew.

DEAN (*places a hand on her as though to restrain her from something*): Don't be *too* penetrating, Stella.

STELLA (*upset by the contact—that being what she is starved of*): A-another piece of bread, please. (*Handing him the toast.*)

DEAN: This is only done on one side.

She takes it back.

STELLA (*a trace strident*): He'd make a good husband, wouldn't he?

DEAN: Louis?

STELLA: Mm.

DEAN: Yes, I think perhaps he would. I don't really understand why he doesn't.

STELLA (*as one who explains the self-evident*): He doesn't love me.

DEAN (*dubious*): Mmmm, that's one of those words, isn't it?

STELLA: Quite a useful abbreviation, though. *Louis* can't even *say* it.

DEAN: No?

STELLA: No. When Louis says 'love', you'd think his liver was coming up after it. As a matter of fact (*the closer she gets to her own heart, the more exaggeratedly cerebral her manner*) he does love me as much as he can; he hasn't much capacity for it. He's immature: Very immature.

DEAN: Might he not grow up?

STELLA: No, he covers up too well. There's no need for him to grow up.

DEAN (*this is hurting him, so he smiles*): What do you understand by 'growing up'?

STELLA (*looks at him*): Involving yourself.

DEAN (*pause; then chuckles. Puts hand on her head and gently rubs it to and fro.*)

STELLA: You asked me. (*Goes back to toast.*)

DEAN: Yes. I'm just thinking it's a very ungrown-up view of being grown-up.

STELLA (*shaking her head*): Don't do that.

> *Hurt, he withdraws his hand. She drops the toasting fork and seizes his hand and presses it to her face avidly.*

DEAN: Darling, don't make a parcel of yourself, yet.

> *Enter* LOUIS. *He is arrested by their intimacy, which they break off.*

LOUIS: You're wanted on the telephone, Master.

DEAN (*mildly*): I am? Who by?

LOUIS: It's your Bursar; he wants to speak to you. (DEAN *is irritated.*)

DEAN: How did he know I was here?

LOUIS: He's been ringing round—Oh . . . The VC rang earlier; sorry, I forgot to tell you.

DEAN: D'you know what it is?

LOUIS: No, Master. Something about the college—

DEAN: Well presumably. Excuse me a minute will you, Stella?

STELLA: Sure! (*Exit* DEAN.) Have you got the butter?

LOUIS: No, I answered the 'phone. Shall I get it now?

STELLA: No, leave it now.

LOUIS: Shall I push off then?

STELLA: Don't see why not.

LOUIS (*goes to door; then*): I'd rather stick around.

STELLA: Stick around then.

LOUIS: This is hopeless, Stella! (*No response.*) Don't you think it's hopeless?

STELLA: You're wearing yourself out, Louis.

LOUIS: By God, that's true!

STELLA: You're talking to yourself all the time. It's very boring.

> *Enter* DEAN. *There is nothing odd in his manner—except indeed that it might seem exaggeratedly relaxed.*

DEAN (*politely over-apologising*): Stella, my *dear*—I'm *awfully* sorry. (*Gets coat.*)

STELLA (*disappointed*): Oh have you got to go?

DEAN (*appears to consider not going; then with a tut!*): Yes, I'm afraid so. I am so sorry.

STELLA: What is it?

DEAN (*peevishly*): I can't make out—some nonsense.

STELLA (*reproachful*): Oh, Daddy . . . will you come to-morrow?

DEAN: To-morrow? I'll try. (*Pauses at doorway. Offhand*) Oh, Mr Flax, I've been meaning to ask you. What became of your petition? (LOUIS *stares.*) You surely remember your humane, your ethical, your poetic petition?

LOUIS: I lost it somewhere. Last term.

DEAN (*softly*): That's really rather typical.

> *Exit* DEAN. *Shuts door.*

STELLA (*gentle contempt*): You lost it?

LOUIS: The petition? Yep.

STELLA: You'd better take a heave at yourself.

LOUIS: All right we know; Louis Flax has gone to the dogs . . .

STELLA: They're not going to renew your Fellowship if you're not careful.

LOUIS: All *right*.

STELLA: I wish you'd go away, Louis. I wish you wouldn't come here. (*He looks at her, brooding.*) Is that hard to believe?

LOUIS: No. (*Turns to go.*)

STELLA: Well, what do you do when you do come here?

LOUIS: 'Bore' you.

STELLA: To tears, Louis, to tears.

LOUIS: All right. (*Turns to go. Baby's cry from bedroom. Turns back, eagerly*) There's Fred—

STELLA (*in bedroom doorway*): Go away, Louis. It's got nothing to do with you. Go and do some work. Go and finish your thesis. (*She shuts the door quietly in his face.*)

LOUIS (*looks at door. Half-heartedly*): Hey! (*Goes reluctantly and picks up some books in a rubber sling.*) All right, I will! (*But he looks around for something to keep him; sees the electric fire and goes and switches it off. Looks for something further. Takes bread and knife and clothes maiden into kitchen. On a note of leave-taking*) I've switched the fire off, Stella! (*No answer. He goes to door of bedroom.*) You left it on. (*No answer. He tries the handle.*) Stella, you left the fire on. (*Listens. On a note of laughing protest, as though this were all a little joke*) Hey, Stella! . . . (*No answer. Injured*) Stella! . . . (*No answer.*) Is Fred all right? (*No answer.*) I only want to see Fred! (*No answer. He puts down the books, extracts an exercise book, opens it at a certain page.*) Stella, I've got something to show you! (*No answer. He rattles the door knob. Becoming distracted and his voice rising*) Stella, please let me in! (*No answer. He suddenly pounds the door, leaning on it, almost weeping for all that is behind it.*) I want to see Fred! I want to see Fred! (*The baby, alarmed, begins to cry. He listens as the cries abruptly cease. Then, stooping, he folds up the paper and begins to push it under the door.* STELLA *opens the door quickly; she is carrying the baby. She is angry, but her anger is diminished to irritation by her surprise at seeing him on his hands and knees.*) It's a poem. (*Rises and offers it to her.*) It's a sonnet; I'm going to do a cycle. It's—I'd like to know what you think of it. (*He puts it into her free hand and she opens it.*)

STELLA (*quasi hostile*): Is it about me?

LOUIS: No, it's more about Nicholas really. (*She is looking at it.*) Let me in, Stella.

STELLA: No.

LOUIS (*calmly*): You're crying.

STELLA (*equally calmly*): I know I'm crying.

LOUIS: Let me in.

STELLA (*sincerely weary of him*): What's the good, Louis? You only want to talk to yourself. (*Softly, but determined*) No.

LOUIS (*puts hand against door*): Stella!
    Knocking at outer door.

STELLA: There's someone at the door. (*Closes bedroom door.*)
Knocking repeated.

LOUIS: All right, all right. (MARY *opens door.*)
Enter MARY *and* SLATE. MARY *crosses to kitchen.*

MARY: Is my mother here?

SLATE: Yes, is she here?

LOUIS: No—!

SLATE: Was that the Master's car we just saw?

LOUIS: Yes. (SLATE *shows vexation.*) He was called to the college.

SLATE: Oh. He's heard then.

LOUIS: Heard what?

MARY: Where's Stella? (*She goes towards the bedroom.* LOUIS *forestalls her.*)

LOUIS: Just a minute, Mary. I'll tell her you're here.

MARY: Stella!

LOUIS: Just a minute, please. (*Exit to bedroom.*)

SLATE: Well, do we wait here?

MARY: I think this is where she'll come. She's crazy about the baby.

SLATE: Very well. (*Sits in arm-chair, and looks at her with esteem.*) Mary, you are behaving admirably.

MARY: Thank you . . . I daren't think . . . (*Breaks off.*)

SLATE: What?

MARY (*moves downstage slightly, then to above table*): I daren't think how Dicky's going to react to this—outrage of my mother's.

SLATE: That has been in my mind too. I must tell you, my dear, Richard has always had a distaste for . . . irregularity.

MARY (*not shrill, quite calm*): I don't see that it's my fault if my mother is . . . (*A pause.*)

SLATE (*quietly*): Insane?

MARY: Not a very becoming thing to say about one's mother. (*This is said with some bitterness at being in the position of saying it.*)

SLATE: My dear, I agree with you. If she's not turned up by this evening I think the police should be asked to find her.

MARY: The police?

SLATE (*taking the plunge*): Mary, the action speaks for itself. She is *not responsible*. No one is responsible. What has happened to her is simply (*gestures*) the ultimate misfortune. But it must be recognised. And there can be no prevarication. It must be recognised openly. If needs must, publicly. (MARY *is startled*.) Otherwise, Mary, you are *all* going to incur the opprobrium for what she has done.

Enter STELLA *and* LOUIS.

STELLA: You want my mother, Sir Hugo? (*Sees his face.*) What is it?

SLATE: Stella, it seems I am to be the bearer of terrible news...

STELLA: What's she done?

MARY: She's slashed the Holbein. (*Rises.*) She's—slashed—the Holbein.

LOUIS *closes the bedroom door and moves to above arm-chair.*

SLATE: It's destroyed utterly.

STELLA: Daddy's Holbein?

SLATE: The college Holbein.

STELLA: But she must be mad.

SLATE (*leaves a decent pause*): I greatly fear so.

LOUIS: Just a bit—have you actually seen it, Vice-Chancellor?

SLATE: A dozen people saw her do it. She wrenched it out of its frame, dragged it into the Middle Court, and ripped it to ribbons with some kind of garden implement.

STELLA: But then what'll they do to her?

SLATE (*deprecatingly*): She is not criminal, Stella; she is sick.

LOUIS (*struggling*): Now wait a bit—

SLATE (*angry*): There is one other explanation, Mr Flax. She left it lying against the fountain. And pinned to the fabric of the picture was your petition newly signed by herself.

LOUIS: Oh no.

SLATE: Oh yes. (*Throws petition on table.* LOUIS *crosses and picks it up.*) That does afford an alternative explanation. Political publicity for your petition. Do you prefer it?

LOUIS (*steadily*): I haven't seen this since last term. I lost it somewhere.

SLATE: Pity. It's seemingly a dangerous thing to leave lying about.

LOUIS: Yes.

STELLA: Where is she, Sir Hugo?

    SLATE *spreads his hands.*

MARY: If she hasn't turned up by five o'clock, I'm going to get in touch with the police.

STELLA: No.

SLATE: I think that would be sensible.

STELLA: But—

MARY: It's probably only temporary, Titch!

LOUIS (*puts petition on table, and crosses to door*): Look, it takes two doctors to certify someone.

MARY: Well you've been saying it for years!

LOUIS (*heavily*): She's in the garden.

SLATE: What?

LOUIS (*the same*): She's in the garden; I'll fetch her.

    Exit LOUIS. *All move to window.*

SLATE: Yes.

MARY: She's picking flowers!

STELLA: Why shouldn't she pick flowers!

MARY (*crosses to* STELLA *then above her to door*): Oh for pity's sake, Titch, we know what she's done.

STELLA: But we don't know why she did it!

SLATE: That's not a question we can ask, Stella.

STELLA: She loved that picture, Mary! She loved it!

SLATE: Well there you are, my dear; it wasn't a rational action.

MARY: You said it yourself!

STELLA: What did I say?

MARY: Just now you said 'she must be mad'.

STELLA (*stubbornly*): It takes two doctors.

SLATE: Stella, it is a fact and it must be faced. You have great influence with your father. (*Both look at him, puzzled.*) I am thinking of the Master. Surely, you both must see that his whole career is in jeopardy?

MARY: Ssh! Ssh!

> *Enter* MRS DEAN *and* LOUIS, *who closes the door.*

MRS DEAN (*crosses to table, puts down secateurs and is recalled to herself by the clatter. A little dismayed*): Oh, my flowers—

LOUIS: I've got them, Mrs Dean. (*Moves to her and gives them to her then moves above table, attention focused on the secateurs.*)

MRS DEAN: Thank you, Louis.

SLATE: Good afternoon, Gwendoline.

MRS DEAN: Yes, Hugo. I know you're there.

STELLA (*crosses to* MRS DEAN): We must put them in water.

MRS DEAN: That's a good girl. (*Angrily*) No, I— (*As* STELLA *attempts to take the flowers*) I will do it. (*Exit to kitchen with flowers.*)

> *There is a moment's silence. Then* MRS DEAN *calls.*

MRS DEAN: Then how—about—a cup of tea?

SLATE (*as pleasantly as he can manage*): I'd like a cup of tea, Gwen. It's a thirsty day.

MARY: Yes, let's have a cup of tea! (*She signals to the others to join in but* LOUIS *stares at her unresponsively and* STELLA's *attention is in the kitchen.*)

> MRS DEAN *bursts out of the kitchen giggling; all flinch involuntarily, but* STELLA *keeps close to her.*

MRS DEAN: How do you like my pretty hat? (*She is wearing a tea-cosy with a bird on it.*)

SLATE (*coughing*): Very festive!

MARY (*laughing embarrassedly*): What is it, Mummy?

LOUIS (*looks at* MRS DEAN): It's a tea-cosy. (*Flatly*) It looks silly, Mrs Dean. Take it off.

STELLA: Leave her alone!

MRS DEAN: It's no good talking sensibly to me. (*Slowly removes it.*) I shall have to go away. (*Puts cosy on table.*)
      Enter DEAN. *He has been running. A pause.*

DEAN: Well? Why did you do it?

MRS DEAN (*calmly*): Don't shout at me, please.

STELLA: Don't shout!

DEAN (*barks*): Why?

MRS DEAN (*eyes flicker away from him*): I can't remember.

DEAN (*contemptuous of this prevarication*): Are you out of your mind then? (SLATE *and the others wince.*)

MRS DEAN (*quick*): Yes. (*Smugly*) I shall have to go away now.

DEAN (*a moment of fear; then thunderous*): Nonsense! (*Hangs up coat.*)

SLATE: Er, Jack—

DEAN: Don't interrupt me, please. (*Crosses to* MRS DEAN. *Calmly*) Gwendoline, I *insist* on a reasonable answer: Why did you do it?

MRS DEAN (*cries out*): I had to!

DEAN (*furiously*): You did not 'have to'. You wanted to perhaps—

MRS DEAN: Yes. I wanted to. I told myself it was for Mr Flax's petition of Peace. But in fact I wanted to! I ripped across their little faces, and it rejoiced me! . . . Oh hypocrisy, thank God I've come to the end of you!

DEAN (*his ordered manner becomes a shell in which his fear rattles audibly. Stiff faced*): 'Hyp—'? I fail to follow. What did you hope to achieve?

STELLA: For Heaven's sake—are you blind!

MRS DEAN (*smiles ruefully at* DEAN *as parents do at the youthful insensitivities of their children*): 'Blind' . . . Your father knows, Stella. Better than anyone. (*To* DEAN, *smiling, comforting*) But give up now, dear. (*Looks at him. Then the same gentle smile.*) You forget, you are tormenting *me*, too.

DEAN: Are you not well?

MRS DEAN (*smiles round at the others, shaking her head*): He will never give up. (*Then*) He is a saint.

    DEAN *crosses, sits on arm-chair.*

SLATE (*after a worried glance at* DEAN): How about that cup of tea we were to have?

MRS DEAN: Very well. (*Goes to kitchen door.*) You want to talk about me; that is natural. (*Pleading*) But don't torment him. (*Draws curtain upon herself.*)

SLATE (*advances on* DEAN *urgently*): Jack, it's inescapable. The only question we can ask is what to *do*? My dear fellow (*laying hand on* DEAN's *shoulder*) Gwen has destroyed forty thousand pounds' worth of college property. This is the action of either a criminal or . . . a madman.

DEAN: My wife is not mad.

SLATE (*impatient*): Then how are you going to explain it? A political stunt? That's what it becomes. Is that how you'll explain it? I've had the newspapers on to me already, Jack.

DEAN: So have I.

SLATE (*sharply*): What did you tell them?

DEAN: Nothing.

SLATE (*reasonable*): You'll have to make a statement sometime.

DEAN: Yes, this evening. She is not mad.

MARY (*quietly*): She is, Daddy.

    DEAN *is stopped dead by this. His gaze travels from* MARY *to* STELLA.

STELLA: I don't know— But stop riding her!

    DEAN *gives a little slow nod as though to say 'thank you' and looks at* SLATE *who sits on ottoman, below window, then looks at* LOUIS.

DEAN (*a low voice: he feels betrayed*):We haven't heard from *you*, Mr Flax. That's unusual?

LOUIS (*hesitant*): Well, if she's not, she *wants* to be pretty badly.

DEAN (*striking out*): What's that? Poetry?

    Enter from kitchen MRS DEAN. *She crosses briskly to bedroom.*

MRS DEAN: The kettle's on; I think I must lie down.

Exit to bedroom, closing door.

LOUIS: I think she's at the point of balance, Master.

There is a cry from the bedroom. LOUIS *darts into the bedroom. She comes out.*

MRS DEAN: I haven't done anything! (*To* STELLA) I didn't touch him.

STELLA (*small-voiced; horror and pitiful curiosity*): Of course not; why *should* you?

LOUIS enters, closes bedroom door.

MRS DEAN: He had to look though didn't he? (*Rib-nudging jocularity*) He knows what stuff we're made on, eh Louis?

LOUIS: You found my petition, Mrs Dean.

MRS DEAN (*surprised*): You left it with me. (LOUIS *is ashamed.*) It's curious you should mention the petition. (*To* DEAN) On his own level he really is very perceptive. (*To* LOUIS) You see, I thought I'd signed it. —Yes, I did. More than that —now this will interest you, Louis—I could have taken my oath that I'd taken it out and *looked* at it, a score of times, and seen my signature on it. How's that for the Powers of the mind? (*Sadly*) How's that for the Powers of Evil? I'll tell you: I have this document, you see, never mind what, well it's my will, as a matter of fact, that's probably significant but I can't work it out, anyway I keep this document in the extreme left-hand pigeon-hole of my bureau-bookcase. (*She makes a dreamlike movement of taking it out.*) And, of course, it has my signature. (*The only abnormality of manner so far in this speech has been the abnormal intensity of her interest: now her breathing begins to be laboured.*) Well, during the night . . . during a night of . . . when I was, dreaming, or rather when I was experiencing these . . . dreams— Only I wasn't asleep, you see; they can't be excused that way; I wasn't asleep, I was awake and walking! And you know I was dangerous then; oh yes, I was dangerous; oh, I'm not a 'funny old thing' in the night, I can tell you! (*Triumphant*) If anyone had seen me then they would have been frightened! . . . I was frightened . . . However, I would go downstairs to my bureau-bookcase and take out the petition—as I thought—and see my signature and think 'I have thrown my weight on the side of peace; goodness; mercy. My name, black and white. That's a fact.'—I am a scientist by training—I have such respect for facts—'It's only dreams', I thought. 'It's only the night. I shall harm nobody. I'm not really dangerous.' And anyway I'd sent him to sleep in the guest room—that's right at the other end of the house.

STELLA (*softly*): Mummy!

They stare at her appalled as they take in the significance of this, and her mouth quivers; faintly:

MRS DEAN: Well better safe than sorry . . .

DEAN: You sent me to the guest room because of my snoring, Gwen!

MRS DEAN (*faintly*): You don't snore . . . (*Hostile*) You know you don't snore. You sleep like an angel! (*To* LOUIS) But when your Nicky was born, Louis . . . (STELLA *looks at* LOUIS.) When Nicky was born (*she speaks quietly, but begins a rhythmic rocking back and forth in her chair*) these dreams, abominations, I had them in the daytime, too, they came *out* of the night, no question of dreams, you see! Impulses! Desires! . . . I would hold little Nicky. (*She shakes her head in incredulous horror as over the deed of someone else.*) Helpless, little, Nicky. God save us, if he's not innocent, who is? He's done no harm; he's not had time! (*Silent tears begin.*) That weighed with me no more than a tiger! I have such desires! In waking daylight I have such desires! As no one would credit! Abominable! Abominable! (*She covers her face.*)

LOUIS: But, Mrs Dean, everyone—

MRS DEAN (*passionately, composes herself*): I devised tests for myself, Louis. I kept these (*picks up secateurs*) in my room, and as soon as it began I would deliberately take them up and I would say to myself, 'Gwen, with these you could do—' oh, things you wouldn't credit. 'You could *do* it, now. And you're not (*fastens secateurs*); you're not doing anything.' Childish enough, you may say, but it was a test. But it got to be (*now her distress rises to its climax*) that I could only do my test with the light on and oh, then I needed help! I needed help! And I would go along and bump against his door; and sometimes I would go into his room! And sometimes I would knock things over! (*She is now crying noisily.*) But he never heard! He never woke! He sleeps like an angel! (*Almost shouting through her tears*) Like a pig! (*She puts her head on the table and the secateurs fall from her fingers like something dead. Everyone looks at* DEAN, *but he is staring at her sightlessly. She has set fire to his mind, and no one else dares speak. She sits up, desolated.*) As for the petition, it was under my mattress; and, of course, the *fact* was, that I hadn't signed it, at all.

LOUIS: But you— (*He breaks off, looks round, but no one else seems willing to speak.*) You've signed it now, Mrs Dean.

MRS DEAN: Yes, I've done everything necessary now.

LOUIS (*gently*): Aye, but you *wanted* to before.

MRS DEAN: Oh no, I didn't. These atomic explosions; have you noticed how beautiful they are? There's your clue. The venial sins can be very plain but the mark of out-right evil is this . . . extraordinary . . . beauty— And I didn't get that out of a book. That picture was beautiful, and often moved me by its beauty; but when I ripped it across, it was I who was beautiful—as Lucifer, Louis, for a moment I was as beautiful as Lucifer . . . (*Briskly*) I didn't sign the petition against the Bomb, because I want the Bomb to happen. That's very clear to me.

LOUIS: You did want to sign it, Mrs Dean. It was the Master
who stopped you.

*DEAN looks at him. He stops. But STELLA also has seen the
significance of this. She walks round her mother, moves to
below MRS DEAN and kneels at her feet.*

STELLA: It was Daddy, Mummy. Daddy didn't want you
to. That's why you didn't.

MRS DEAN (*fearfully*): Daddy?

STELLA: Yes. He—

MRS DEAN (*sharp*): Nonsense! . . . (*Indulgently*) Why, dear,
I remember as clearly as could be. He dipped the pen
in the ink for me— 'Come along', he said, 'Sign it. I
should like you to.' (*Smiling*) He *held* the *pen* out to
me.

STELLA: That's just his particular technique! (*She switches a
look of hatred across both DEAN and LOUIS who have drawn
together.*)

MRS DEAN: Allow me to know what I'm talking about. I
know why I didn't. *I* know where *I* belong.

STELLA: Daddy, you tell her!

DEAN: Gwen.

MRS DEAN (*quickly*): The Master has never brought any kind
of pressure to bear on me. The Master has never attempted
to influence me in any way. The Master has always left
me perfectly alone! (DEAN *puts his hand over hers convulsively.
She looks down at it, astonished. Then*) How good you are.
(*Comforting*) You don't *need* to touch me now, dear.

DEAN: But, Gwen, I want to touch you.

MRS DEAN (*to the others*): He is a saint.

STELLA: He is not a saint! And you're not mad, or wicked,
or anything else, Mummy. You're just lonely! Aren't you,
darling? You're lonely! She's just lonely! (*She crouches by
her mother, embracing her fiercely.*)

MRS DEAN (*shrinks away from her*): No, don't, Stella . . .

DEAN: I want to talk to my wife.

SLATE (*rises. Discreetly*): I've promised them a statement by six o'clock, Jack.

DEAN: If you can wait.

SLATE: Very well. If we don't get in touch with them, they'll print their own story, you know. (*Exit* SLATE.)

DEAN: Mary, you go with Sir Hugo. (*She does immediately. Exit* MARY. *Kindly*) Now, Stella.

STELLA: Leave her alone. You've left her alone for thirty years. Leave her alone now.

LOUIS *and* DEAN *look at one another.*

DEAN: Go with Louis, Stella.

STELLA: Come and live with me, Nicky and me, Mummy.

DEAN (*his control beginning to go*): Louis, will you take her!

LOUIS *approaches her.*

STELLA (*dangerous*): Don't touch me.

LOUIS (*is about to, but hesitates*): Come on, honey.

STELLA (*issues the invitation again*): Don't dare touch me.

LOUIS (*grips her by the upper arm as though she might strike him. When she remains passive, his confidence surges back and he speaks quite peremptorily*): Come on.

Exit STELLA *and* LOUIS *to bedroom.*

DEAN (*deliberately*): Gwendoline, what you are doing is very, very dangerous. (*She slips to the floor and assumes the foetal position. He registers this; forces on, crossing to upstage of her.*) There is a point at which to practise insanity becomes itself insane.

MRS DEAN: That's right, dear.

DEAN: Get up! (*Pause. She makes no response.*) If you suppose this wretched pretence carries conviction— (*Goes quickly and struggles to lift her.*) Get up—get up—get up!

MRS DEAN (*laughing*): Woo, woo, woo, woo! (*Suddenly she looks vicious and hangs her weight hard on his hands. Calmly he sustains it for a moment, a tableau. Spasm of furious dislike;*

he drops her deliberately; she cries out and resumes her former position.): Ah!

DEAN (*hotly*): Will you tell me what it is that I'm accused of?

MRS DEAN: Woo! (*She puts her hands on the top of her head as though to fend something off.*)

DEAN (*exasperated, going behind her again*): Get up, woman!

MRS DEAN (*turns and tries to kick his legs*): Get away . . . get away!

He moves to below arm-chair, horrified.

MRS DEAN (*laughs, then turns viciously to him*): Get away! Get away! (*Goes to him and hits him on the chest.*) Get away! (*Steps back, laughing.*) Look at the Master! Look at the Vice-Chancellor! (*Goes to him again, and hits him on each upper arm as hard as she can—then about to repeat the blows she changes and collapses against him.*)

He has shown no sign of having felt the blows, his face has been almost petrified with the intensity of the attention he has at last given her. As she collapses he sits on the arm-chair. He now accepts that she is if not mad, temporarily aberrant. Horror, pity and lamentation.

DEAN: Oh, what have you done to yourself?

MRS DEAN (*slumps again, like one whose last hope has gone*): Yes, you are a saint.

DEAN (*quite cool*): Is that what I'm accused of?

MRS DEAN: Why did you marry me?

DEAN (*calmly*): Because I loved you.

MRS DEAN: No.

DEAN: I loved you.

MRS DEAN: Ah, your memory's going. You're getting old.

DEAN: I'm sixty-four and my memory's perfect. I loved you.

MRS DEAN: No.

DEAN: I did, dear. I— (*He puts his hand on hers.*)

MRS DEAN (*looking at it*): How good you are.

DEAN: Stop calling me names. I did, Gwen. I—

MRS DEAN (*as to a child who has gone far enough*): Now don't be silly, Jack. How could you?

DEAN: Gwen— (*But he finds he has no words. Then, a happy inspiration*) Don't you remember how I used to row you up the river to Granting?

MRS DEAN: Twice.

DEAN: Oh, surely—

MRS DEAN: Only twice.

DEAN (*grunts, remembering*): Mm. I was still tying the ends of Agamemnon. Gwen— (*Again he finds no words. Lamely*) I was very happy! (*Conscious of his lameness*) . . . Oh, I need poetry. (*Desperately forcing on. Her face is averted.*) You were . . . fine. You were . . . lovely.

  She gasps.

MRS DEAN: Don't Jack! I know it's kindly meant, dear, but it serves no further purpose and it hurts. Why, it was *you* who showed me what I am!

DEAN (*with dawning dread*): —I—?

MRS DEAN (*twisted smile*): Mm . . . Oh, you've been very good, dear, marvellously good, but goodness isn't the same animal; no, indeed it is not . . . (*Kindly*) You can't bear the sight of me . . . Did you think I didn't know?

DEAN (*appalled*): Not true! (*He grasps her wrist.*)

MRS DEAN (*she looks at it. Then as one recording an interesting phenomenon*): When you touch me, I can *feel* the goodness in your fingers. (*He lets go; she rises and goes to the table. In the same interested tone*) Why even on our honeymoon I used to wonder, (*now the tone becomes fearful*) 'Why does he have to be so good, just to touch me?' (*Now in a tone of thrill, almost pride*) And the answer—no. I didn't know the answer then, but I felt it (*she touches herself*) get to its feet. (*Tone of interest again*) Then later when you *talked* to me I could hear the goodness in your voice and I wondered. (*Fearful again*) 'Why does he have to be good, just to talk to me?'

DEAN: Not true!

MRS DEAN: And the answer (*thrill again*) turned its head. (*Proud smile.*) . . . (*Interest*) Then I noticed even when I spoke to you, the patience in your face. (*Fear*) 'Why must he be good just to listen to me?'

DEAN: Not true!

MRS DEAN (*thrill*): And it came towards me. (*The interest intensifies to horrified fascination.*) 'Why does he never associate with me? Why have we never, never in anything been together?' (*Pride*) And the answer. (*Triumph*) Sprang! . . . (*Straightforward narrative*) Into the dreams, and when the dreams came into the day, I *was* the answer . . . (*Desolate*) 'Gracious me,' I thought, 'a man who is the very lettering of sanity; married to me who have always been evil, and am now mad. No wonder he keeps what distance he can. (*Sits by table. Idly she picks up the secateurs.*)

DEAN (*springs to her, seizes the secateurs, flings them through the window. She remains passive.*): Not true! Not true! Not true! You wrong me! (*She looks at him. With less conviction*) You wrong me! (*Falters*) You— (*And he looks away.*)

From bedroom, LOUIS *and* STELLA, *brought by the noise. They remain in the doorway. Neither* DEAN *nor* MRS DEAN *is really aware of them.*

MRS DEAN (*comforting*): It's all over now, Jack.

DEAN (*kneels by her*): For pity's sake, Gwen, it isn't you! Keeping one's distance, dissociation—it isn't you—it's my philosophy, Gwen, it's my belief. (*He is terribly distressed. This frightens her.*)

MRS DEAN: No, don't, Jack. (*Pleading*) You've been so good, so long.

DEAN: It's in my books!

MRS DEAN: Yes, you've taken endless trouble with me, endless—

DEAN: Oh, now I'm mastered. (*His head is literally bowed.*)
     Enter SLATE *and* MARY.

MRS DEAN (*anxious*): Please, dear. (*Coaxing*) See, here's Hugo
     to talk to you about college matters. (*She goes to bedroom
     door; raises a hand uncertainly to her head.*) Oh . . . I was
     forgetting . . . I can't go in there . . . (*Turns and goes
     unsteadily to kitchen.*) . . . Where shall I go? . . . (*Sees him
     overpowered. Goes to him.*) Don't, Jack, you're frightening
     me!

DEAN (*gripping her fiercely*): Gwenny! Gwenny! Gwenny! . . .
     Am *I* your evidence?

SLATE (*sympathetic murmur*): I'll deal with the Press.
     Exit SLATE. LOUIS *and* STELLA *watch him go, exchange
     uneasy glances.*

MRS DEAN: I shall be a voluntary patient, dear; it's not—

LOUIS: The VC's gone to talk to the newspapers, Master—

STELLA (*overlapping*): He's going to make a statement,
     Daddy—

DEAN: Ask him to come back, please. (*Rises.*)

STELLA (*crosses to door and calls off*): Sir Hugo! Daddy wants
     you.

MRS DEAN: Where shall I go?

DEAN: You go nowhere. Not with me for evidence.
     Enter SLATE.

SLATE: Time presses, Jack.

DEAN: Sit down, Gwen. (*He escorts her to a chair by table.
     Gently*) Sit down, sit down. (*He takes his stand beside
     her, like an old-fashioned photograph; he is grim, patriarchal,
     his intellect at the ready to cut down any opposition, very
     much the Master.*)

SLATE (*coughs*): Jack, I'm—

DEAN: Very well, Hugo; you were going to make a statement
     to the Press. What were you going to say?

SLATE: Well, er, I er— (*Frowns, glances at* MRS DEAN.)

DEAN: Don't you think I should hear?

SLATE: Of course, but— (*Again indicates* MRS DEAN.)

DEAN: Don't you think my wife should hear? You were going to say, were you not, that my wife perpetrated a meaningless outrage, being not in possession of her senses?

MARY (*shocked; looks at her mother*): Daddy!

SLATE (*the same*): My dear Jack—!

DEAN: *I* am going to say that the purpose of the action was to publicise the petition, that my wife and I had allowed the subject of, er, nuclear warfare to prey upon our minds to a possibly obsessive extent, and that we did it together!

MARY: Together!

DEAN: Together.

SLATE (*furious*): I *knew* it! (*Flat*) No, Jack, I'm sorry—

MARY: Daddy, you can't!

MRS DEAN (*pulling at his sleeve*): Jack, Jack, what are you doing, dear?

DEAN: Let it be clearly understood that I am *associated* with my wife!

SLATE: Nonsense!

DEAN: My wife's actions are my actions! (*Looks at her.*) This has always been the case, and is so now.

SLATE: I'm afraid I must persist with my statement, Jack.

DEAN: It won't be believed.

SLATE: Why not? (*Turns to* DEAN.)

DEAN: Because anyone can see that my wife is not a woman who would do such a thing . . . without good cause.

MRS DEAN: Oh, darling, you *can't*!

Baby begins to cry in bedroom. STELLA *moves to bedroom.*

DEAN: Stella, wait. Let your mother do it.

MRS DEAN: I? (*The baby's cries for assistance become momentarily strident.*)

DEAN (*mildly*): Well, Nicky seems to need your help. (*He opens door.*)

MRS DEAN (*takes a pace or two, hopefully forward and draws back*): Will you come?

DEAN (*firmly*): Yes.

MRS DEAN (*hesitates fractionally further. Then the baby's cries assume the note of infantile heartbreak. She hurries along, borne forward on a freshet of sympathy and rising hope*): It's all right, Nicky! I'm coming. It's all right!

    Exit MRS DEAN *to bedroom. The baby's cries cease.* DEAN *smiles with painful encouragement at what he can see.* LOUIS *and* STELLA, *also stationed where they can see, relax, and are moved by it.*

DEAN (*tired*): I shall make my statement this evening, Hugo. You'll do a friend's turn if you refrain from making yours.

SLATE (*preparing to go*): You realise there can be no question of your taking office as Vice-Chancellor?

DEAN: My dear fellow . . . There can be no question of my keeping the college.

STELLA (*with pity*): Oh, Daddy!

SLATE: That is so. You're going to ruin yourself.

DEAN (*still tired*): Oh, a man's not so easily ruined. (*He is about to follow his wife. He sees the petition on the table, picks it up, brings out his gold pen with a wry glance at* LOUIS.)

MARY: Daddy, you can't do it!

DEAN (*turns. A sudden blaze of arrogance*): Why can't I. Who here will stop me?

    Exit DEAN *to bedroom.*

LOUIS (*kisses* MARY): What a marvellous man! (*To* SLATE) You thought it was a tame one, didn't you? Wow! (*Goes to* STELLA.) Oh, Stella, what a bloody marvellous man!

STELLA (*as one confirming the obvious*): Well, yes.

LOUIS: Oh! (*As* SLATE *starts to go*) A gentleman, don't you think, Vice-Chancellor?

SLATE: He had a duty to the college too, Mr Flax. (*Exit.*)

    MARY *is left looking at the closed door.*

LOUIS: Well I've got good news anyway, Mary; you're going to be a legitimate aunt. Oh Jesus, why can't I say anything straight. (STELLA *crosses and sits by table.*) I proposed to your sister. (*No response.*) I proposed just now (*indicating bedroom*) to your sister. (*No response.*) We're getting wed.

MARY: Congratulations.

LOUIS: You go with the Vice-Chancellor. Yes, go on. (*Ushers her out.*) Bring 'em back alive! (*Shuts door.*) 'He had a duty to the college too, Mr Flax.' Duty? That bloke ought to be embalmed! Tell you what, duty's going to be a dirty word in our house. Any of our kids uses the word 'duty' I'll wash his mouth out with soap and water. (*Leans out of window.*) Wait a bit, will you, Vice-Chancellor, Mary's coming. (*Turns back.*) 'That's nasty soldier's talk' I'll tell 'em, 'don't use that language in front of your . . .' (*He sees* STELLA *who has followed him throughout with her eyes, her face unhappy, and breaks off. The excitement leaves his face.*) What's the matter, honey?

STELLA: I'm scared, Louis.

Turns away; mindlessly she tries on the tea-cosy.

LOUIS: Don't you think I'm scared, sweetie?

STELLA: I know you are.

LOUIS: Don't worry . . . It will be all right, Stella.

STELLA: Yes, I expect it will. You have a strong 'sense of duty'.

LOUIS: You've got it a bit wrong, honey— (*Sees that she has put the tea-cosy on her head.*) Take that off. By God, don't you—don't come that on me! (*Grabs tea-cosy and throws it on the floor.*)

STELLA (*frightened*): Louis! Louis, I didn't mean—

LOUIS: I know what you meant, my girl, even if you don't! *Enter* DEAN. *He stands in door of bedroom; his face stony. They look at him.*

DEAN: Mary?

STELLA (*gently*): She went with Sir Hugo. (DEAN *takes this in silence.*) How is Mummy?

DEAN (*flatly*): I don't know. She's very fast asleep. (*He advances on* LOUIS *holding the petition before him. His voice cracks with disgust.*) I am to give you this, Mr Flax! And there is a message to go with it. She fears her action will have 'brought discredit' on the Good Cause, but 'the idea is right' and you are to 'persevere'.

LOUIS (*takes petition*): Thank you, Master. I will.

DEAN (*savagely*): I don't doubt it. (*Going.* LOUIS *looks for help to* STELLA.)

STELLA: Daddy; we're getting married! (*He stops and turns.*) Aren't *you* pleased?

DEAN: I'm amazed. This is sensible! (*Going to* LOUIS.) Oh this is very, very *sensible*! (*Urgently*) Now get on with your thesis, there's a good fellow. Don't waste time on this. (*To* STELLA) Don't let him, will you?

STELLA (*as one who breaks bad news*): It isn't a waste of time.

DEAN: My dears, nothing will stop humanity from using that thing. Nothing *you* can do. What, a folly of those proportions within our very grasp, and you think you can turn us back with a petition? (*The last question is addressed to* LOUIS, *who again looks to* STELLA.)

STELLA: Probably not. But this is something we can do. When we've done what we can do, then's the time to worry about what we can't do. But I don't know anyone who's done even what he can!

DEAN: As your mother would say, a public duty.

LOUIS: No! Any of my kids uses the word 'duty' I'll wash his mouth out with soap and water.

DEAN: I won't pretend to understand you, Louis.

STELLA: It's quite simple, Daddy; he has a strong sense of duty, that's all.

LOUIS *looks at her. From this point they don't take their eyes off each other.* DEAN *sees the situation no longer includes him. He goes, but at the bedroom door he pauses, arrested.*

DEAN: Stella, if you really don't use this (*the telescope*) I think

I'd like it back. (*There is the germ of excitement in his voice, but they don't notice.*)

STELLA: Sure. (*She hasn't really heard him.*)

DEAN (*tries again*): I'll perhaps do a little star-gazing myself! (*No response; his smile fades, and rather sadly, he exits.*)

LOUIS: Listen, Stella, you've got it a bit wrong. I wouldn't cross the road from a sense of duty. I certainly wouldn't get married from a sense of duty.

STELLA: No?

LOUIS: No. I'd only get married if I wanted to.

STELLA: It's Fred you want though, isn't it? Fred, not me.

LOUIS: Now that's the last time you'll say that. Now get that! The very last time! Sure I love Fred, but I—

STELLA (*cups hand to ear*): You *what* Fred?

LOUIS (*takes the point but doesn't smile*): I *love* Fred. (*Smiles.*) I do too. I love you both. (*Crosses to her.*) I love you. (*Pleading*) Didn't you know?

STELLA: I wasn't sure.

LOUIS: Oh, mate, you should see in here. (*Taps himself on the chest. Then with pretended seriousness—it is merely a lover's gambit—*) The question might well be . . . Do you love me?

STELLA (*gravely*): You should see in here. (*Repeats his gesture.*)

LOUIS (*solemn and greedy, draws her to him*): Yes? What's it like?

STELLA (*leans against him, hiding her face*): It's like a forest . . . with animals . . . Oh, I can't tell it . . . But I can show you, Louis, I can show you!

CURTAIN

BUCHAN TECHNICAL COLLEGE